Evaluating Fresh Expressions

Evaluating Fresh Expressions: Explorations in Emerging Church

Responses to the Changing Face of Ecclesiology in the Church of England

Edited by
Louise Nelstrop
and
Martyn Percy

CANTERBURY
PRESS
Norwich

© Louise Nelstrop and Martyn Percy 2008

First published in 2008 by the Canterbury Press Norwich
Editorial office
13–17 Long Lane
London EC1A 9PN, UK

Canterbury Press is an imprint of Hymns Ancient and Modern
Ltd (a registered charity)
St Mary's Works, St Mary's Plain
Norwich NR3 3BH, UK

www.scm-canterburypress.co.uk

British Library Cataloguing in Publication data

A catalogue record for this book is available
from the British Library

ISBN 978-1-85311-816-6

Typeset by Regent Typesetting, London
Printed and bound by
CPI William Clowes Ltd, Beccles, NR34 7TL

Contents

Acknowledgements

The chapters in this book were first presented at a conference held at Ripon College Cuddesdon in September 2007. The conference, entitled 'Defining the Church for the 21st Century', set out to explore some of the implications of the Church of England's Fresh Expressions Initiative. The desire was to bring together senior clergy and members of the laity who are involved in 'fresh expressions of church' and/or traditional mission initiatives, alongside established academics from the fields of theology, philosophy, psychology and sociology. The aim was to consider a range of questions and issues raised by the shift in the Church of England's ecclesiology that fresh expressions of church entail.

The editors are grateful to Ripon College Cuddesdon for hosting the conference, and to all the speakers for their co-operation in making this a well-attended, stimulating and enjoyable event.

We would like to sincerely thank all the speakers who accepted the invitation to submit contributions to this volume and extend our grateful thanks our publisher, Christine Smith at SCM-Canterbury Press, for all her patient help in its production.

The contributors

Revd Dr Steven Croft is Archbishop's Missioner and Team Leader of the Fresh Expressions Initiative. He has published in the areas of evangelism and theological training and formation, and edited two collections of essays on fresh expressions and the mixed economy, *The Future of the Parish System* and *Mission-shaped Questions*.

Revd Canon Robin Gamble is Canon Evangelist of Manchester Cathedral and creator of *The Beatles Bible*. He has responsibility for mission initiatives in the Diocese of Greater Manchester.

Professor John M. Hull is Honorary Professor of Practical Theology in the Queen's Foundation for Ecumenical Theological Education, Birmingham, England; and Emeritus Professor of Religious Education at the University of Birmingham. He has been writing about religious education for nearly 40 years, and has published extensively in this area. His publications include 'Religionism and Religious Education' and 'Practical Theology and Religious Education in a Pluralist Europe'.

Dr Stephen Hunt teaches in the School of Sociology at the University of the West of England. His primary interests are in contemporary Christianity and New Religious Movements. More specifically, he has researched the areas of Pentecostalism, the Charismatic Movement, the 'New' Black Pentecostal churches, the Lesbian and Gay Christian movement, millenarianism, Alpha courses, religion and healing, and the sociology of theology. Dr Hunt has explored these themes through over 100 publications.

Recent works include, *Religion and Everyday Life* and *The Alpha Enterprise: Evangelism in a Post-Christian Era.*

Revd David Male is Tutor in Pioneer Ministry at Westcott House and Ridley Hall Theological Colleges, Cambridge, and Fresh Expressions Advisor for Ely Diocese. He is also an Associate Missioner with the Fresh Expressions Initiative and previously planted the Net Church in Huddersfield, West Yorkshire.

Mark Mason is a Ph.D. student at the University of Chichester (UK). His research focuses on the work of Jacques Derrida and John Caputo. It considers how the work of these writers, but also the (re)turn to religion in contemporary continental philosophy generally, can inform 'emerging' ecclesiology. He also helps co-ordinate an emerging church in Southsea (Portsmouth). He has previously published work on Derrida and Caputo in *Rethinking History: The Journal of Theory and Practice* 10/4 (2006), 501–22.

Revd Dr Michael Moynagh, based at Templeton College, Oxford, is Co-Director of the Tomorrow Project, an educational charity that helps organizations and individuals to understand emerging trends that will impact on people's lives over the next 20 years. He is also an Associate Missioner with the Fresh Expressions Initiative and has written widely on social issues, and has published a number of books in this area including *Changing World, Changing Church* and *Emergingchurch.Intro.*

Dr Louise Nelstrop is a Research Fellow at Ripon College, Cuddesdon, and a Fellow of the Centre for Christianity and Culture, at Regent's Park College, Oxford. She researches in the areas of practical theology, spirituality and healthcare. Her recent research focuses on the emerging church in Thailand and fresh expressions of church in the UK. She has published in the areas of mental health and Christian spirituality, and has a number of forthcoming publications, including a report on the Fresh Expressions Initiative and *An Introduction to Christian Mysticism.*

CONTRIBUTORS

Revd Canon Professor Martyn Percy is Principal of Ripon College, Cuddesdon. He is also Canon Theologian for Sheffield Cathedral. Prior to becoming Principal at Ripon, he was Director of the Lincoln Theological Institute for the Study of Religion and Society. He has also been Chaplain and Director of Studies at Christ's College, Cambridge. He teaches and researches in the areas of practical theology, modern ecclesiology, and Christianity and contemporary culture. Recent publications include, *Salt of the Earth: Religious Resilience in a Secular Age* and *Engagements: Essays on Christianity and Contemporary Culture.*

Revd Philip D. Roderick is an Anglican priest. He set up and leads Contemplative Fire <www.contemplativefire.org> – 'a network fresh expression of church'. Philip is also the founder of The Quiet Garden Movement (www.quietgarden.co.uk), – a now international movement emphasizing quiet prayer and reflection with over 300 affiliated homes and centres worldwide. Philip's publications include a book and CD package *Beloved: Henri Nouwen in Conversation, Sheer Sound,* a CD, featuring the ambient Hang Drum and *Sacred Posture,* a DVD teaching a series of body prayers from the Christian tradition. He is an Associate Missioner with the Fresh Expressions Initiative.

Dr Peter Rollins is co-ordinator of an emerging church, Ikon, in Belfast. He writes and speaks on various aspects of continental philosophy, phenomenology and emerging church theology, and the philosophical, religious and cultural situation of the emerging church movement. Publications include, *How (Not) to Speak of God* and *The Fidelity of the Betrayal: Towards a Church Beyond Belief.*

Dr Sara Savage is Senior Research Associate with the Psychology and Religion Research Group (CARTS), Faculty of Divinity, University of Cambridge, and lecturer in the Cambridge Theological Federation. Sara has published widely in the fields of psychology and Christian ministry. Recent publications include, as co-author, *Psychology for Christian Ministry* and *Making Sense of Generation Y: The World View of 15-25 Year Olds.*

Mrs Ailsa Wright was the Lay Chairman of i-church from July 2007 to June 2008. She was involved in the day-to-day running of the community, leading and co-ordinating chapel worship and running a small pastoral group.

Introduction

The last decade has seen an incredible rise in publications and weblogs discussing what is being called 'emerging' and/or 'emergent' church. This book, in some ways, belongs to this phenomenon. Yet in other ways it challenges the very idea of an emerging church. Pete Rollins (Chapter 6), in his book *How (Not) to Speak of God* (p. 5), has drawn attention to the nebulous nature of the emerging church, questioning its definability. Despite this, there is something of a tendency in much of the literature to see emerging church as an extension of alternative worship services. However, the Church of England's Fresh Expressions Initiative (as supported by the Methodist Council) cast its net more widely when seeking to define an ecclesiology for the twenty-first century. Rather than limiting itself to one church type, as Steven Croft (Chapters 1 and 4) has stated, through the Fresh Expressions Initiative the Church of England has aimed to promote a kaleidoscope of church forms. It believes that only such an approach can hope to meet the spiritual needs of today's UK society. As Steven Croft has stated in *Mission-shaped Questions* (p. 3):

> Because of the changing nature of our society, we need a range of different kinds of church, each attempting to reach out and to share in God's mission and connected to one another in the wide Body of Christ.

In some ways, this approach may seem unsurprising, given that the Church of England has always aimed to be a broad church. Yet never before has it sought to legalize a move outside the traditional parish system. Not that through the Fresh Expressions

Initiative the Church of England is seeking to move away from the parish system. It is, however, aiming to put in place what Archbishop Rowan Williams has termed in *Mission-shaped Church* (p. vii), 'a mixed economy of church', in which parish structures coexist side-by-side, as 'equal partners' with churches that exist outside of this structure – 'fresh expressions of church'. What this means in practice is still being worked out. Yet, as some of the Fresh Expressions Initiative's own literature notes, this shift presents the Church of England with one of its most significant ecclesiological challenges. It is also becoming increasingly apparent that these are challenges that involve the Initiative in the wider ecclesiological debate about what it means to be or to do 'church', which are similarly raised by the 'emerging'/'emergent' church. It is such issues that the chapters in this book set out to explore.

In order to clarify the parameters of the discussions in this book, which relate specifically to the Fresh Expressions Initiative, some background is needed. The Fresh Expressions Initiative was set up in 2004, following the publication of *Mission-shaped Church*. This report made a persuasive argument for accommodating new dimensions of church within a 'mixed economy of church', as well as within theological education and formation. It promoted a range of church types (fresh expressions of church) as churches in their own right. These included youth congregations, alternative worship services, networked groups, and groups that emphasize a return to ancient forms of spirituality. However, it stressed that the 12, later 14, 'types' described in the literature were fluid categories rather than prescriptive definitions, and that more permutations and categories were likely to exist than were named. A number of publications followed in what became a mission-shaped series. These include: Tim Sudworth et al., *Mission-shaped Youth*; Paul Bayes and Tim Sledge, *Mission-shaped Parish*; Sally Gaze, *Mission-shaped and Rural*; and most recently Steven Croft, *Mission-shaped Questions* – a publication that began itself to look at the many theological issues raised by promoting a 'mixed economy of church'.

The fact that from the start the Fresh Expressions Initiative has not shied away from the difficult questions that it raises seems commendable. However, a number of questions remain largely unexplored, not least those relating to how a 'mixed economy of church' functions in practice. Is, for example, the Church of England moving towards seeing the parish system as just one among a kaleidoscope of possible church types? Or does the parish system remain more integral to the whole than individual 'fresh expressions of church'? Questions are also raised about how and why the Church of England should want to distinguish 'fresh expressions of church' from 'traditional' mission initiatives? Or promote youth congregations as churches in their own right? It is these kinds of issues that the chapters of this book seek to address, considering issues of definition, benefit and loss, and what fresh expressions of church mean in practice. The contributors approach these issues from a number of directions: theological, sociological, philosophical and psychological, and draw together the views of senior clergy and members of the laity alongside established academics. As such they offer a lively but scholarly response to some of the complex issues facing the Church of England in the twenty-first century. The chapters are grouped together within four main sections.

Part 1   What counts as a fresh expression and who decides?

Chapters 1 and 2 address the question of 'What counts as a fresh expression and who decides?' Here Steven Croft and Robin Gamble explore some of the main taxonomical issues raised by fresh expressions of church and evaluate their place within the broader context of Anglicanism. In Chapter 1 Steven Croft approaches the notion of a fresh expression as a supporter of the Initiative; as he states, his is far from 'a neutral standpoint'. He plots the life of this terminology from its inception, along with other terms such as 'mixed economy of church', 'emerging' and 'new ways of doing church', arguing that four years after the publication of *Mission-shaped Church*, most of the Church of England and the Methodist Church are 'reasonably at ease with the language of fresh expressions of church and have a growing understanding of what the term means'. He states how, in his opinion, definitions, albeit roomy ones, are beginning to settle. In Chapter 2 Robin Gamble presents a challenge to this approach. Focusing particularly on the ecclesiological shift rendered by the idea of a 'mixed economy', he suggests that those within fresh expressions of church need to take a more gracious stance towards traditional church – recognizing their dependence and debt. In this relation he offers a revised understanding of fresh expressions of church, seeing them as an endeavour which is far more integrated into the missional activities of the whole. As such, he challenges the extent to which fresh expressions of church really constitute the ecclesiological shake-up that they seem to entail.

Part 2 Fresh expressions: possible gains and potential losses

The next section of the book offers more in-depth reflections on the questions posed by fresh expressions, focusing on what we may gain and/or lose by adopting the ecclesiology of fresh expressions of church. Part 2 begins with a critical examination of fresh expressions from a theological perspective. In Chapter 3 Martyn Percy maps out the spiritual trajectory of forerunners to fresh expressions and expresses scepticism that this latest development differs substantially from these, or constitutes that which will stem the tide of church decline. He warns against 'falling into the trap of imagining that spiritual forms of post institutionalism hold out any long-term hope for the future of the church'. He argues that fresh expressions have a tendency to promote an individualized, privatized religion that is most appealing to the middle classes, a niche religion that runs the risk of falling foul of McGavran's Homogenous Unit Principle. As such, he argues that those within fresh expressions are unlikely to appreciate that most of Christian mission is undertaken within the parish. He questions too whether fresh expressions are ecclesiologically weighty enough to really count as substantial 'church'. In Chapter 4 Steven Croft, exploring shifting patterns of ministerial training, suggests, contra Percy, that fresh expressions do in fact differ substantially from what has come before. While acknowledging that fresh expressions build on earlier evangelistic waves, for him they constitute a paradigm shift that means that models of ministerial training need to radically change. He argues that fresh expressions feels like the beginnings of 'a whole new subject area', one that entirely reshapes our existing ecclesiology and missiology. In Chapter 5 Sara Savage too, approaching fresh expressions from a psychological perspective, argues that they represent a paradigm shift that has the potential to reshape church leadership structures. Seeing them as underpinned by a postmodern turn within society, she argues that they necessarily move away from the pyramidal models of leadership that are foundational to traditional church. Although there are losses in terms of stability, Savage argues that ultimately fresh expressions allow for greater gains. The greatest of these gains lies for her in a humble cognition, in which a level of uncertainty allows for the accommodation of positions of variance. As such she suggests that fresh expressions are fundamentally underwritten by an attentive listening to the other, 'an experience quite indistinguishable from the experience of being loved'.

The final three chapters in this section explore fresh expressions from a philosophical postmodern perspective. In Chapter 6 Pete Rollins argues against fresh expressions on the grounds that it is not really possible for the church to hold within it those movements that challenge it on a fundamental level. Although not doubting the motives of those who promote fresh expressions, Rollins suggests that the very act of making space for fresh expressions undermines their potential for 'radical potentiality'. He argues that some groups, and so some fresh expressions, must always stand outside the authorized ecclesial structures if they are to present the radical call to change that is necessary for growth and vitality. As such he doubts the value of a 'mixed economy', suggesting that it ultimately cannot be much more than 'a multifarious expression of the one hegemonic economy'. Mark Mason does not share Rollins's concerns. For him fresh expressions/emerging churches have the potential of being both a community of character and a community of the question. Drawing on Hauerwas and Derrida respectively, he argues in Chapter

7 that if these groups forge a middle way by attempting to live
in the tension between these two types of community, then they
will be able to shape a new ecclesiology that is truly mission-
shaped. In Chapter 8 John M. Hull likewise asserts that Christian faith is one formed out of a tension. However, for Hull this
tension resonates between belief and action. Turning first to the
Old Testament, Hull argues that walking with God has always
incorporated a sense of justice alongside belief. He notes that
these themes, albeit less strongly, also reside within the New Testament. For Hull the challenge that fresh expressions of church
need to take up is to develop an ecclesiology that allows them to
be an embodiment of the Kingdom of God, such that their faith
is action-led and their actions are faith-driven.

Part 3 Fresh expressions: what this means in practice

The chapters in this section reflect on the practicalities of 'fresh
expressions', what it means to enculture the gospel or produce
what is often described as an 'incarnational' theology. The first
two chapters examine two fresh expressions that have been promoted within the Oxfordshire dioceses as Cutting Edge Ministries. Ailsa Wright reflects in Chapter 9 on the activities within
i-church, an internet church. Wright traces the development of
i-church and outlines its ethos. She then shares members' stories,
noting that many focus on themes of healing, welcome and acceptance, traits of community that many have found within i-church.
In Chapter 10 Philip D. Roderick likewise outlines the rationale
that underlies Contemplative Fire. He traces its development and
the importance of whole-person expression within the contemplative traditions that underpin it. He notes too the ascetic roots
from which it draws its spirituality. Roderick also emphasizes the
creativity that underwrites its use of liturgy and sacrament and
the way it strives to allow its members to be 'surprised by the
presence of God in beauty and ugliness'.

The second pair of chapters in this section address the question
of practice at a second remove. In Chapter 11 David Male explores
the question of 'Who attends and why?' He notes the dearth of

research in this area. He acknowledges that currently many fresh expressions may not be directed towards the unchurched, and cautions against using media like music, scriptures and sacraments that may be unfamiliar. While suggesting that these are important constituents of church, he argues that in order to be successful fresh expressions must first be communal and relational; only later can they become sacramental. He also warns against expecting overnight success, but suggests that while there is a long way to go, fresh expressions are moving the church in the right missional direction. Stephen Hunt is less certain. Through detailed ethnographic research, Hunt explores in Chapter 12 the Alpha course that lies at the heart of many seeker-style churches. Although some do not associate Alpha with emerging church, the Fresh Expressions Initiative includes seeker churches under this taxonomy. Hunt notes that despite acclaimed success, the number of unchurched that have been reached by Alpha seems minimal. He remains sceptical of its value, particularly in terms of the strictures that it imposes on questioning the Christian faith. Although he notes that fresh expressions allow for a greater uncertainty and doubt he, like Percy, remains unconvinced that this is what the unchurched are looking for. He thinks perhaps they are content to remain unchurched.

Part 4 Do we really want to promote a 'mixed economy'?

The concluding section consists of two short chapters that reflect on the issues raised in the book, drawing them together in relation to the idea of a 'mixed economy'. In Chapter 13 Mike Moynagh addresses some of the criticisms that have been levelled against fresh expressions by those within inherited church – with some accusing them of selling out to contemporary culture or being too fragile to have any real longevity. In response he compares fresh expressions to the early church in Antioch, exploring its relationship with the church in Jerusalem (which for him mirrors inherited church). He suggests that what is needed is a mixed economy that builds on this biblical model, one in which 'mutual support and periodic disagreement' form its overarching characteristics. As for the other criticisms, he argues that fresh expressions are too diverse to all be accused of promoting a consumerist spirituality, and that it is too early to criticize them for a lack of resilience – only time will tell. Louise Nelstrop also explores in Chapter 14 the issue of a mixed economy from the perspective of those within fresh expressions. Drawing on large-scale ethnographic studies that she has conducted, she notes that despite many negative experiences of inherited church, those within fresh expressions still value the idea of a mixed economy. She explores the underlying reasons for this and raises questions as to whether a mixed economy made up of equal partners is really desirable. She advocates an ecclesiology of reciprocity to which fresh expressions belong, but not necessarily as equivalents to parish churches. In relation to this she notes that what is meant by a mixed economy is still far from certain.

The Editors

Part 1

What counts as a fresh expression and who decides?

I

What counts as a fresh expression of church and who decides?

STEVEN CROFT

This chapter is not written from a neutral standpoint. The term 'fresh expression of church' was coined by the Church of England report *Mission-shaped Church*, which was presented to the General Synod in February 2004. I was not myself involved in the working party that produced the report. However, three months later I was invited to lead a new Archbishop's Initiative charged with encouraging these fresh expressions of church across the Church of England and the Methodist Church as part of a mixed economy of church life. For the past four years, therefore, I have spent time reflecting on the question of what counts as a fresh expression of church and how we should decide.

This chapter records the different elements that fed into the coining of the original term and the definitions and practices that have been developed over the last four years.

Mission-shaped church

The term 'fresh expression of church' was not used in print, as far as I know, before the *Mission-shaped Church* report. The working party that produced the report, chaired by Bishop Graham Cray, adopted a method of working that is, I suspect, unusual in such groups and that has proved immensely fruitful. The group set out first of all to listen to what was happening in the development and formation of new communities across England. The group only then reflected on what they had heard and how it could best be encouraged, and in the light of this produced the report.

The report pays due regard to a shifting context for mission in the UK and describes 12 kinds of new development the group had observed. These are: alternative worship congregations; base ecclesial communities; café church; cell church; churches arising out of community initiatives; multiple and midweek congregations; network focused churches; school based and school linked congregations and churches; seeker church; traditional church plants; and traditional forms of church inspiring new interest and youth congregations.

The group realized that it would be helpful to have a generic term to describe this range of enterprise and activity, and perhaps others that have yet to be discovered. They deliberately coined a new term rather than picking up one of the other generic terms in common use (such as emerging church). Their hope was that a new term would carry less baggage in terms of tradition and content and would be more flexible for the future.

It is worth quoting in full the paragraph of the report where the term is first introduced:

The phrase 'fresh expressions of church' is used in this report. The Preface to the Declaration of Assent, which Church of England ministers make at their licensing, states 'The Church of England ... professes the faith uniquely revealed in the Holy Scriptures and set forth in the catholic creeds, which faith the Church is called upon to proclaim afresh in each generation'. The term 'fresh expressions' echoes these words. It suggests something new or enlivened is happening, but also suggests connection to history and the developing story of God's work in the Church. The phrase also embraces two realities: existing churches that are seeking to renew or redirect what they already have, and others who are intentionally sending out planting groups to discover what will emerge when the gospel is immersed in the mission context. (*Mission-shaped Church*, p. 34)

It is worth noting here the attempt to use the phrase as a bridge between the new mission context and the historic tradition and also the intentional ambiguity in the two realities described. Some fresh expressions of church are about existing churches renewing or redirecting what they have. Others are about planting groups discovering what will emerge.

The working party also adopted and worked with another new phrase that has become important in what has developed since. The term 'mixed economy' was developed by Rowan Williams as Bishop of Monmouth to describe the truth that no single form of church life is adequate on its own in the development of mission to our diverse culture. We need traditional forms of church life but we will also need new forms of church to connect with different parts of our society. The phrase 'mixed economy' has proved immensely helpful in assisting people to see that the traditional and the new forms of church are not in competition but complementary. It is not either–or but both–and.

The ways in which the Church of England gives authority to new thinking is a subtle commendation of formal endorsement and popular support. The language around fresh expressions of church and the mixed economy received significant and unanimous endorsement from the General Synod in February 2004 (both in terms of the debate and the acceptance of the report) and in many subsequent diocesan synods to which it was referred. This has been accompanied by a trying on of the language in many different contexts, a testing of it in many sections of the church and a growing ease with its use.

Alternatives, antecedents and roots

Several other words and phrases were already in use at the time of *Mission-shaped Church* and remain current in what is a fluid and still developing vocabulary.

The term 'emerging church' is probably the most common but itself carries at least two meanings. The first is its use to describe a worldwide movement of churches that are seen to be 'emerging' either from our wider cultural context or from traditional church life and therefore likely to be radically different from church as we have known it. John Drane has studied this movement for many years and described the different ambiguities in the phrase used in this sense very well in his recent chapter in *Mission-shaped Questions* (pp. 90–1).

However, the term has also been in widespread use since the early 1990s in the writings of Robert Warren, who developed the contrast between the 'inherited' church of Christendom and the 'emerging church' that was rediscovering a sense of mission and adapting to its new context.[1] In this sense, 'emerging church' does not describe new congregations and communities so much as the whole church struggling to come to terms with its new context and changing accordingly.

Other parts of the church have used the term 'new ways of being church' but by 2004 this name had been adopted by a particular group, New Way, concerned to develop the insights of base ecclesial communities and collaborative ministry and mission. The Methodist Church in its official documents and resolutions has generally preferred the term 'fresh ways of being church' (see for example the Methodist conference resolution on priorities in 2004: *Book of Resolutions*).

A third stream of thinking and vocabulary has used the concept of the 'edge' of church life very fruitfully to capture both the sense of mission (these ventures are on the margins of the existing church) and the sense of creative development. The Church Army's Sheffield Centre was the first to identify and develop the significance of this new movement through its regular short studies entitled 'Encounters on the Edge' <www.encountersontheedge. org.uk>. In 2003, the Diocese of Oxford began a series of intentional investments in the creation of new communities and grouped these under the banner heading of 'Cutting Edge Ministries' (now renamed fresh expressions).

Fourthly, there is the time-honoured language of church planting that continues to play a key role in the development of the concepts around fresh expressions. *Mission-shaped Church* was originally conceived as a follow-up report to *Breaking New Ground*, which examined church planting across the Church of

England, as it was then conceived in 1994. These antecedents are recognized in the subtitle to *Mission-shaped Church*: *church planting and fresh expressions of church in a changing context*. Some of the major impetus behind both *Breaking New Ground* and *Mission-shaped Church* was the significant and ongoing work of Bob and Mary Hopkins and Anglican Church Planting Initiatives, which continues to be influential across the movement as a whole. The relationship between the terms church planting and fresh expressions is well caught in Bob and Mary's encouragement to use church planting as a verb and fresh expressions of church as a noun. The desire, motivation and activity remain the same but the emphasis is not on replicating the sending church but encouraging the right thing to emerge for the new context.

Finally, as I explore the different terms and vocabulary, I have been very struck by commonality of language between the term 'fresh expressions of church' and recent Roman Catholic vocabulary on evangelization. I have not yet established whether there is a direct line of conscious connection but at the very least I suspect indirect influence. Throughout his papacy, John Paul II called repeatedly upon the Roman Catholic Church to commit to a 'new evangelization'. This was to be understood as in contrast to but alongside the ongoing evangelization of each generation through the ministry of priests and parishes. According to John Paul II, this new evangelization was to be 'new in its ardour, new in its methods and new in its means of expression'.[2] This language is picked up in dynamic ways in the Apostolic Letter at the end of the millennium year: *Novo Millennio Inuente*. The Pope's appeal to the church is to put out into deep water (*duc in altum*), quoting Luke 5. He urges the church again towards the new evangelization and appeals to the church to 'Start afresh from Christ' (Section III).

Early definitions developed by the Fresh Expressions Initiative

The Fresh Expressions Initiative picked up the baton from the *Mission-shaped Church* working group in seeking to develop the language in ways that are helpful and supportive in encouraging what is happening without controlling or directing it. We also consciously took on board the methodology of continuing to listen and of developing partnerships with others across the churches who are encouraging similar developments.

Our earliest documents and publicity use the 12 categories in *Mission-shaped Church* and attempt short descriptions such as: 'new initiatives for people who are right outside the church as it is currently'. Simple, direct language to describe fresh expressions of church has not been easy to find.

In late 2004 we were asked to be involved in developing the special question on fresh expressions of church asked in the 2005 Parish Returns Survey (unpublished). Every parish was asked whether since the year 2000 they had developed anything that they would call a fresh expression of church. The emphasis here is therefore on parishes themselves determining where it is appropriate to use this language. However, a greater degree of definition was given in the accompanying notes as follows:

> The term fresh expression of church was coined by the working party which produced the best selling report, *Mission-shaped Church*.
>
> **A fresh expression of church is a new and/or different way of being church in and for our changing culture.**
>
> Examples include youth congregations; new initiatives in schools; midweek or additional Sunday services; midweek groups for children; network focused congregations, cells; or churches arising from community initiatives – but there are many more.
>
> A fresh expression of church is not normally seen just as an additional activity or simply a stepping stone for people to Sunday services but as something with the potential to be or become church for those who take part.

The results of this research made it clear that a very large proportion of parishes were content to use the language to describe what they were doing or planned to do in these terms. The full results have been written up by the Church of England's Director of Research and Statistics, Lynda Barley, in *Mission-shaped Questions*.

Following through the theme of listening and sharing stories, one of our earliest projects was to set up a website <www.freshexpressions.org.uk> on which people could register their fresh expression of church and tell us something about it. This enabled us to gather news and research stories quickly.

The website with the directory went live in February 2005 and now contains over 700 stories and examples <www.freshexpressions.org.uk/directory>. We used the 12 categories from *Mission-shaped Church* as a means for people who registered to self-select which best described their fresh expression. It was apparent from the beginning that most people would select two or more of these categories rather than one and that many preferred to tick 'none of the above'.

We made a critical change in these categories in that, in consultation with others in the field, we added two further groups. *Mission-shaped Church* was criticized following publication for not paying sufficient attention to work being done among children. In fact a very large proportion of fresh expressions of church involve substantial numbers of children and young people. To enable these to be included more easily within the directory, at the suggestion of Margaret Withers, then Archbishops' Officer for Evangelism among Children, we added the two categories of fresh expressions of church for children and fresh expressions of church for under-fives and their families.

Every entry to the directory is reviewed against our current definition before being added. In some cases we ask for more information. In others we deem it appropriate not to admit the fresh expression to the directory but we tend to err on the side of generosity in applying definitions. Our overall purpose as an initiative is to encourage this movement not restrict it. Admitted entries stay current for two years and are then normally updated and renewed.

It is clear from the correspondence around the directory and in a continuous process of engaging with and listening to practitioners that it is extremely helpful to most to be able to identify what they are doing with the broader movement of fresh expressions of church commended in the *Mission-shaped Church* report. Above all, this movement of naming encourages an ecclesial shift and ecclesial thinking: many different ventures that have previously been framed and conceived as activities of the church are being reframed and named now as in some senses 'church'. This reframing and naming itself enriches and extends people's understanding of what they are doing and shapes it in turn.

A more substantial working definition

After a year or so of working with the directory and listening to what was happening it became apparent that a more robust working definition of a fresh expression of church was needed. By this point the language was being widely used to describe a range of different activities. The risk of the term coming to be used for anything novel and therefore being devalued over time was very real.

We therefore set ourselves with key partner agencies[3] to develop a working definition of a fresh expression of church that could be agreed and widely disseminated, and that distilled much of what we observed happening on the ground. The definition was developed over several meetings and was originally published in May 2006 as 'Fresh Expressions Initiative':

> A fresh expression is a form of church for our changing culture established primarily for the benefit of people who are not yet members of any church.
> - It will come into being through principles of listening, service, incarnational mission and making disciples.
> - It will have the potential to become a mature expression of church shaped by the gospel and the enduring marks of the church and for its cultural context.

After much discussion, the term 'new' was dropped intentionally. It was apparent from observing what was happening that novelty was not a criterion that could helpfully be applied. The key distinctive in fresh expressions of church was a missional direction and dimension. There are parallel movements in the New Testament and in most periods of Christian history. There was much debate around the term 'primarily' in the first line. Some wanted to restrict fresh expressions of church only to those groups formed for those outside the churches. Others saw them as extending much further back, as it were, into existing congregations. In the term 'primarily' we wanted to catch the sense that the centre of this movement is going to where people are but that there are some legitimate fresh expressions of church for those who, as it were, are hanging on to the existing church by their finger tips.

With the help of the Sheffield Centre of the Church Army we had grasped by this time the key elements in the ways in which fresh expressions form and the key place of listening, service, incarnational mission and making disciples. The latter phrase is vitally important. The goal of beginning a fresh expression is not to create a permanent shallow place of faith or 'Christianity-lite'. The goal is to create a context and community where mature disciples are formed and flourish.

The definition also pays careful attention to the process by which a fresh expression of church grows to maturity. Implicit in this is the concept of a community on a journey. All the essential elements of church may not be present or observed at the start of that journey. However, there must be a deliberate intent to seek to grow in the direction of a mature expression of church. That growth will take place within a twofold dialogue between the tradition on the one hand and the particular context on the other.

As far as we can tell, the definition has been reasonably well received and has proved a useful tool for debate, teaching and training and also further reflection.[4] It has been incorporated into the three policies developed by the Church of England to take forward the agenda of *Mission-shaped Church*: the guidelines on ordained pioneer ministry (2006) <www.acpi.org.uk/downloads/ Ordained_Pioneer_Ministers_Guidelines.pdf>; on encouraging

lay pioneer ministry (2007) <www.urbanexpressions.org.uk/
Lay_Pioneer_Missionaries.pdf> and the *Code of Practice for the
Dioceses, Mission and Pastoral Measure* (2008), which can be
downloaded from the Share website at <www.sharethe_guide.
org/section5.bmo>. It is applied as a matter of course to all new
fresh expressions registering on our online directory and to stories
we feature in DVD material or publications (for details of these
see <www.freshexpressions.org.uk/sections.asp?id=3682>).

Definition through stories: DVD material and publications

These stories themselves have been a key tool in communicating
the vision for fresh expressions of church and also the heart of
what they are about. We have consciously told and retold stories
as part of this work of discerning and defining fresh expressions
of church and also as a way of rekindling the imagination of the
church for mission. Some of those stories have been told in print
media and others online. However, undoubtedly the most powerful stories have been those told through the medium of our two
Expressions DVDs: *Stories of Church in a Changing Culture* and
Changing Church in Every Place.

In every instance we have had to apply criteria to select particular stories to feature from a wide range of possibilities. For
both DVDs we tried deliberately to feature a range of different
fresh expressions and to be faithful to the diversity of the movement reflected in *Mission-shaped Church* and our observations
of what was happening across the country. We wanted to reflect
fresh expressions of church engaging with different generations,
different age groups, different social contexts and from different ecclesial traditions. In this selection we were consciously
attempting to break down a stereotype that this movement is predominantly evangelical, or predominantly about young people or
predominantly suburban.

However, we also introduced another important criterion in
selecting DVD material. We tried to include in each DVD some
stories that were inspiring and exceptional – that required considerable investment in buildings or people. These stories we hoped

would help people go 'Wow!' and inspire them to excellence and significant steps of faith. However, we also deliberately included in each DVD other stories that, while very significant, would help the viewers to say to one another: 'We could do that here!' In that too we wanted to be faithful to the movement as we observe it on the ground. There are many examples of radical, creative projects with extensive investment. But there are many examples also of modest new initiatives in parishes, benefices and circuits that don't require huge resources and that are proving remarkably fruitful.

Following publication of the first DVD in 2006, *Expressions: the dvd – 1: Stories of Church for a Changing Culture*, we received a number of requests for more resources in particular areas and attempted to meet these requests in the stories chosen for the second DVD, published in 2007, *Expressions: the dvd – 2: Changing Church in Every Place*. These are grouped around fresh expressions in places of work or leisure; fresh expressions in a sacramental or contemplative tradition; fresh expressions in a rural context and fresh expressions for children and young people.

More recently, we have developed the concept of a spectrum of fresh expressions of church embracing a range of different kinds of initiative but embodying the same principles. At one end of the spectrum are the large, well funded projects undertaken collaboratively by several parishes or by a deanery or circuit. Increasingly within the Church of England they will be recognized and encouraged through the new device of the Bishop's Mission Order. There will only normally be a handful of such projects in any diocese. At present we estimate that there are around 200 people employed in full-time equivalent posts developing fresh expressions of church across the Church of England.

However, at the other end of the spectrum are a range of smaller projects requiring much less resourcing and normally led by clergy alongside other responsibilities or by teams of lay ministers. These include new midweek all-age congregations, groups meeting in schools, cell meetings and youth congregations. Our research indicates that up to a third of Anglican and Methodist churches are involved in this kind of activity or aspire to be involved in some way. The numbers of people involved across the country are very significant.

These two ends of the spectrum are in relationship with one another. The larger projects act as a beacon and inspiration for the wider movement. Often, these are the places where the vital lessons are being learned that are then passed on to the whole church. Often they will be the places where Christians are attempting to engage with those furthest away from the traditional church.

Where are we now?

I may be wrong but I sense, four years after the publication of *Mission-shaped Church*, that most of the Church of England and the Methodist Church are reasonably at ease with the language of fresh expressions of church and have a growing understanding of what the term means. The term itself has passed through stages of people not knowing what it meant to being used very widely for a disparate range of phenomena. It is now beginning to settle around the language of the definition described above, generously interpreted. I see the term used with inverted commas less and less – a healthy sign of acceptance. There are still debates to be had and ecclesiological questions to be asked and answered, but they can happen more meaningfully if we are able to agree that we are talking about the same things.

2

Mixed economy:
nice slogan or working reality?

ROBIN GAMBLE

Ilkley Moor is in Yorkshire, the one that boasts the famous song. High up on its shoulder sit the great 'Cow and Calf' rocks. The 'Calf' is a single boulder (but a huge one) that somehow split off from the massive outcrop of Millstone grit known, affectionately, as the 'Cow'. The 'Calf' is a younger and fresher expression, and as climbing goes, although much smaller it is a bit more exciting and edgier. The two belong together, they are a pair, a cruet. Both would seem somehow smaller and less significant if they stood apart. The name says it all, they have a relationship with a binding togetherness that is far stronger than their separateness. They are mother and child, the one feeding the other with its own milk. Perhaps in some dim and distant future the 'Calf' will itself become a cow and have children of its own.

The same appears to be true for any number of ideas that we can contrast with one another within the life of the church. Without the one, the other could not exist. Without the conventional parish church, there would be nothing in relation to which to be a fresh expression. Without the traditional (trad), there could be no radical (rad). Each needs the other, and is somehow smaller and less significant, if stood apart, as the following list nicely illustrates.

- Fresh expression and conventional parish church.
- Emerging and inherited mode.
- Rad and trad.
- Ancient and modern.

Just like the 'Cow and Calf' rocks, these approaches to 'doing church' are made of the same stuff, doing the same sort of job, separate yet belonging together. They are friends, cousins, even 'mother and child'.

My first involvement with a fresh expression was about 35 years ago. I was a member of a fairly traditional 'Yorkshire Low', leaning towards evangelical, church in Bradford. A powerful conversion experience had moved me, along with a bunch of other young Christians, to set up a youth club in our church hall. The run of the mill club soon became a vibrant evangelistic coffee bar full of skinheads in one room and rock and rollers in the other.

It was all a long way from our 'matins loving' congregation. Yet it was this very traditional church that provided the building, some finance, a deep well of prayer, much encouragement and an incredibly supportive vicar to make everything possible. Though different from us young pioneers, they seemed intuitively to understand and agree with what we were about. In fact, it was within this 'bog standard' Anglican church that we who were launching our fresh expression, had actually come to faith.

Fresh and traditional modes of church belong together; we are a cruet, we are family. On a good day it is impossible to see where one finishes and the other starts, and many of us spend most of our lives and ministry floating from one to the other. Sadly, something of a crack between the two has been opening up recently.

The motherly older church and its leaders may feel a bit neglected, slightly derided and rather like yesterday's model. There is a real danger of it becoming a bit resentful, even bitter, and reacting against, instead of alongside, the younger movement. It is not always as generous and encouraging as it could be. Perhaps there ought to be a bit more parental ownership and pride in the varied and wonderful exploits of her children. For those of us who identify strongly with the parish church, there are masses of good models to learn from, good teaching to be informed by and lots of flames to become reignited by in fresh expressions.

Meanwhile it would help a lot if the younger child in the relationship stopped slagging off its parent. I know that fresh expressions people do not think they do this, but in actual fact they do, and at almost every single opportunity. They frequently describe 'traditional church' as some sort of tired, worn out and irrelevant medieval institution. A sort of a crossover between the British Rackets Association and the Grand Order of Water-Buffaloes.

For those of us who identify strongly with fresh expressions it's about time that we realized that there is still bags of mission, passion, energy and creativity left in 'mother church'. We do not own the copyright on evangelism. Parish churches are missional, incarnational and tuned in to local networks and cultures too. Furthermore, every vicar in England, even the ones that are ancient and Anglican, are also called to be 'pioneer' ministers.

A particularly problematic area here is the way in which statistics and predictions of the future are made. It is a well-established pattern for those in the evangelism and growth trade (and this is where we fresh expressions people are) to predict a forthcoming doom and then to offer themselves or their ideas as an alternative and fruitful destiny. The very tight compartmentalization of the national population as dechurched, unchurched and 'never coming near the church' is beginning to look a bit like all that post-war social planning. It is very helpful up to a point. Go beyond this point and it becomes increasingly inaccurate, restrictive and non-motivational. There has been lots of talk of the growing gap between church and people (as there needed to be). Now we need to talk about the closeness that still exists, about the 70 per cent of the population that still believe in God and the 58 per cent that believe in the resurrection of Jesus. We need to pay a bit more attention to the Church of England's own statistics. We should be exploring the doorways and windows that are there in communities, which might not attend church but still highly value it. The concepts of 'believing without belonging' and conversely 'belonging without believing' and of 'vicarious faith', all of which open up deep and promising pathways for us.

All children have a tendency to lecture their parents, who themselves have an equal inclination to write off their children. The 'shared economy' will work better when there is lots more mutual listening and the holding of the other in the highest regard.

Fresh and re-freshed expressions

In Manchester diocese we have 375 parishes. Every one is different, special and in fact unique. It is a mistake to lump this amazing variety of churches under the single title of inherited mode. They are not a uniform and institutionalized 'Starbucks' church, they are an organic rainbow of personalities, histories, social settings, theological understandings and missionary visions. Alongside and equally part of our diocesan family, we have a modest but significant number of younger and newer types of Christian communities and projects. It is impossible for us to put a precise number on this grouping; what we do know is that it is expanding and very exciting.

The basic strategy is to develop 'twenty-twenty' church alongside our re-development of 'test-match' church, in what we call 'fresh and re-freshed expressions'. Mission, evangelism, contemporary relevance, fuzzy edges and 'freshness' are common to both streams. 'Times of refreshing' come not from having a bag full of new ideas, or even as the result of a major reappraisal or make-over (although these may be part of the process) but as a result of spending time in the 'presence of the Lord' (Acts 2.20). Conversely, staleness, greyness and lack of energy, vision and colour all thrive when we spend too much time within our own churchyness.

Freshness is about mission, whether it's a fairly traditional piece of invitation being done around a harvest festival or some edgy thing late at night on the streets. Mission, especially when it includes an evangelistic faith-sharing element (and what other sort of mission is there anyway) quickens the heartbeat; brings us back to our primary values; makes people more generous with their time and money; forces us to examine our own souls and leads us to our knees in prayer. We hear much today of 'mission-shaped', but I have always felt that shape must be preceded by a missionary spirit. Our Lord who, according to the writer of Acts, is the dispenser of freshness, is a missionary Lord. He sent his own missionary Son, who in turn sent out his missionary followers empowered by the same Lord's missionary Spirit. All this sending is about the passionate, that is, 'in pain', love of God for his lost children. Missionary 'freshness', and there isn't any other sort, still flows from the heart of the Lord to the heart of his church. This applies not just to the edgy, sexy, young church, but just as much to the rather conservative one in the sports jacket.

Three categories of fresh expression

Back to Manchester diocese (simply because it's the one I know the best). Although every situation is different, I think we are seeing patterns and loose groupings emerging. Broadly speaking there seem to be three types of fresh expression. And they are all dependent on working together and a mutual appreciation society operating around the concept of a 'mixed economy'.

A fresh expression within a traditional church

As in all other parts of the country, here in Manchester the church has been running parent and toddler groups for years. It is the sort of thing we can do well. People, whether they are dechurched or unchurched, or simply ordinary people who quite like us but do not actually attend, seem to trust us. Parent and toddler groups fit beautifully into our matrix of church schools, brownie packs, and baptismal openness. There is however a new and fresh development. Many of these groups are becoming far more evangelistic, concerned to share the message as well as the practical concern of their 'Lord'. More and more I hear of such groups singing simple Jesus songs, telling Jesus stories and organizing follow-on enquirers' groups for the mums and dads. Something similar is happening with some, though certainly not all, of our drop-ins. Lots of our smaller struggling churches, often situated in the poorer areas of the city, have discovered that a very do-able way of engaging with local people is to open a drop-in. There is something wonderfully tangible in showing our love by giving people a bacon butty and a pot of tea. It is a great basis on which to build a friendship. Add in a few home-made cakes and some decent second hand clothes and there you have 'isolated local church starts meeting and serving local people'. Recently some of these churches have been taking it a bit further, however. They have been introducing a bit of prayer and listening, creating the odd little bit of worship and offering personal invitations to further events. Of course, it is very easy to knock this sort of stuff by saying 'There is nothing new here', but what has newness got to do with it. Freshness is a far deeper issue, it is about missionary fruitfulness rather than trendy newness.

Fresh expressions then within the orbit of a conventional church can develop out of a senior citizens group, a long-standing youth club, or a group of uniformed organizations. What is needed is the realization that we have a message and a deep spiritual experience to offer as well table tennis, bingo and badges.

Fresh expression as a planting out from traditional church

I am thinking of a particular church in one of the Greater Manchester textile towns. It is a large thriving church with plenty of missionary freshness. There is now however a renewed desire to go to the edge and plant a new congregation in an unchurched ex-council estate. The project is in its infancy, but is already following a fairly well-worn path. A similar project was launched by a church in central Manchester three years ago and is now thriving. The difference however is that this was more of a congregational plant at a different time in the week rather than an external venue. A recent piece of work has also seen a church in suburban North Manchester setting up a once a month youth congregation. The project is built on the back of an already existing small youth project and the entrepreneurial missional flair of a gifted leader. Here the planting out is into a new cultural group or sub-group. Our latest example of a fresh expression on the edge has been built, not on the side of a church, but in a church school. It is based in Bolton and involves assemblies, contacts and clubs that are gradually developing into church. The diocese has made this possible by providing a mission priest. It is a fresh expression established on the foundation and good reputation of local traditional church and school.

Fresh expression beyond the traditional church

Imagine a bunch of skateboarders, they could just as easily be footballers, musicians or outward-bounders. They could be elderly or middle-aged, rich or poor. They are physically close but culturally and spiritually distant from any church, be it young or old. They are one of the 'nations' that Jesus sends his disciples out to (Matt. 28.19). For how much longer are we going to leave them in their alienation and wilderness. They will never register on the radar of a church concerned with itself, only with one that is in close proximity to its missionary 'Lord'.

In Manchester our third category of fresh expression is also our smallest. The groups or projects within it are among our most vulnerable and doing some of the most difficult work. They need the most help and support. That help and support needs to be there, and on their terms, but they have got to want it and drink of it. In effect they probably need to be a bit less isolationist, that way they will be stronger and will be more able to share their experiences with the rest of the family. Meanwhile the rest of the family needs to be a bit more flexible and inclusive.

There is a small group trying to establish a presence among bikers (that is, not just those who ride motorbikes but those who turn it into a lifestyle). A group of Christian artists are trying to do something similar among other artists, a bunch of goths are doing it within their Goth world and various city-centre young adult groups are struggling valiantly to create a young adult loft-dwelling church. In deepest 'student-land' a would-be new type of student church is meeting, while a mission-minded family have started inviting friends, other family members and work colleagues to a whole range of activities in their own home, with the hope of establishing some sort of simple worship gathering. Last but certainly not least, away from the big city, hidden in a Lancashire mill valley, a group of very radically committed young leaders are building up a huge mission and evangelism initiative among local schools and disparate teenage groupings. These are all examples of local mission-minded people making it happen. In this case the 'it' is church beyond its own perimeters, even beyond its beloved 'fringe'. Church out among 'the nations'.

Growing churches

Now, if we are serious about the 'mixed economy', about seeing what the Archbishop of Canterbury terms 'received ways of
being church'[1] alongside 'new and exploratory ways', then we
will add a fourth category. Throughout the diocese we have a
constantly expanding range of parish churches that are growing.
The range stretches from evangelical to charismatic, through to
various types of catholic and on to middling-Anglican and radical liberal. They are growing qualitatively in terms of depth and
commitment and they are growing quantitatively as they reach
out to more people. In fact, the growth in traditional church is
such that over the last few years we have begun to see the whole
diocese growing.

These growing churches are reaching out in new and ever more
contemporary ways, not just to their parishes but to their human
networks too. They are building on the historical goodwill, trust
and affection that has been established over years of their 'being
there'.

As a diocese we have done three things. First, we have made
evangelism a non-churchmanship issue and established it as a
basic part of normal church life. Second, a whole range of 'do-
able' evangelistic projects have been put in place. Third, and perhaps most importantly, we have emphasized the need for training
and education. Encouraging churches to run good old-fashioned
missions (while decking them out in new up-to-date clothing).
Taking vicars and lay-leaders through a 'Leading Your Church
into Growth' course. Creating a 'Culture of Invitation' around
such luminaries as Harvest, Good Friday, Back to Church Sunday and All Souls. What could be more trad. than all of this, and
yet it works and in a funny sort of way it resonates in our still
predominantly English, and even fairly churchy, culture. None of
it is as sexy, cool or eye-catching as some of the newer stuff, but
it is all very missional and can be every bit as on, or even beyond,
the edge.

Finally

The key to these three (or is it now four) categories is not some grand diocesan plan, but the movement of the missionary God and the excitement of local Christians when they get the 'mission bug'. Suddenly new flowers, plants and trees are springing up all over the place, some have been freshly planted while others have been revived or even rediscovered in some forgotten corner. The whole thing is gradual, delicate and very vulnerable, rather like the first day of spring coming before the end of winter.

At what point did the New Testament followers of Jesus become a fresh expression? Was it when Andrew brought his brother Peter to meet Jesus? Was it when Jesus called the first fishermen? Or was it at Pentecost? And does it matter that much anyway? Sometimes we are too interested in tight demarcation and classification. I have been in café-church that was all café and no church and parish church that was all church and no parish. The essence of New Testament church, both then and now, is to go into all the world showing the loving care of Jesus and scattering his loving words. The most important issue is about mission, in whatever form we find it.

Part 2

Fresh expressions: possible gains and potential losses

3

Old tricks for new dogs? A critique of fresh expressions

MARTYN PERCY

Fresh expressions has come to prominence since the publication of *Mission-shaped Church* in 2004, a groundbreaking report from the Church of England that argued for new and complementary forms of evangelism that would work alongside parishes in their ministries. Fresh expressions abound. No self-respecting diocese is without one, and in most cases, each will have several. Resources have been poured into the movement, with many dioceses and Methodist districts having dedicated officers. In some Anglican dioceses, individual deaneries have set aside income and resources to cultivate distinctively local fresh expressions. Thus, there are fresh expressions for clubbers, goths, mums 'n' tots, silver surfers, post-evangelicals, pre- and post-Christian folk, generation X and Y, and more besides.

Indeed, the very idea of targeted or niche church seems to have captured the attention of most denominations: a 'shape' of church that reaches out to those who lack a specific 'connection' to church is the primary driver for a plethora of rhetoric that appears to respond sensitively and resourcefully to a range of neuralgic concerns about the place of faith in public life. Thus, a phrase such as 'mission-shaped church' will often accompany a theological construction of reality such as 'being church'; and 'staying fresh' will be a spiritual and missiological imperative. Cultural relevance – and by implication, something that 'ordinary' churches can no longer truly accomplish – is elevated as the primary mode of engaging with contemporary society.[1]

The self-narration of the groups though, does reveal a fascination – even obsession – with being new and alternative. That is, ironically, not an especially fresh development within the subculture of 'soft' or 'open' British evangelicalism, which has an established tradition of continually re-inventing modish associational models of the church.[2] That same tradition has been gently experimental with a variety of dense and intense forms of congregationalism in the post-war era. It has also tended to derive its ecclesiology from biblical roots (usually accessed in a hermeneutically direct rather than nuanced manner) that focus on the (alleged) pre-institutional state of the church (for example, the Book of Acts, Jesus and his disciples, and so on). Or, the configuration, organization and ethos of the model has been centred on an apparently obvious biblical grammar and theological construction of reality that assumes the New Testament church (presuming that its shape and identity could easily be agreed) was somehow its ideal and complete (or even revealed) form. Ergo, the more *like* a New Testament church a group can appear to be, the better, purer or more original it is held to be.

This, in part, accounts for why many fresh expressions resemble small church 'home groups' or early versions of house churches – but with a slightly enhanced ethos and sense of identity. The groups are trying to return to a kind of (mythic) primitive and intimate fellowship that, it is held, the New Testament primarily advocates as the 'model' for the church. Here, the size of the group will not matter especially. What binds the members of such groups together is the sense that they are participating in something that is simultaneously fresh, new, original and culturally relevant on the one hand; and on the other, securely located in the past (that is, the scriptures).

What follows from this is that 'church' – as an institution – emerges as the problem, rather in the same way that the early House Church Restorationists used to read and interpret scripture and the complex sweep of church history.[3] For it is the church, with all its trappings, miscibility, complex structures and organizational baggage, that is held to have masked or corrupted an arrangement of people and ideas that should be fairly simple, and in some ways quite virginal. For this reason, I note with interest that very few participating within the fresh expressions movement add the rider 'of church'. The second part of the phrase has been quietly, innocently and unconsciously parked by most adherents, leaving only the proponents (who need the resources and income of the church to sustain the movement) as the ones using the full phrase.

But what evidence might there be that the fresh expressions movement is a form of collusion with a contemporary cultural obsession with newness, alternatives and novelty, rather than the recovery of a lost theological, missiological or ecclesiological priority? We are on tricky ground here, to be sure. Yet a sketch of recent 'open' evangelical history in England might lend some gentle support to this hypothesis. To help us here, I wish to introduce two fictional friends, whom we shall call Geoff and Anne, and who have been leaders within English charismatic renewal and related evangelistic movements for around forty years. Geoff and Anne are 'into fresh expressions in a big way right now'. They speak for the movement, and are closely aligned with its agenda.

We first meet Geoff and Anne in the early 1970s, and are immediately aware of their interest in the Fisherfolk and other experimental Christian communities. The Fountain Trust, Michael Harper, Colin Urquhart and other pioneers of early charismatic renewal also feature in their interests and conversations during this time. During the 1970s and 1980s these foci develop apace: the church growth movement (Donald McGavran, Eddie Gibbs, and others), as well as a number of individuals who are beginning Christian healing ministries such as Jean Darnell, Jackie Pullinger, Doreen Irvine and David Pawson. The work of John Wimber then emerges as something of a breakthrough, following a close interest in David Watson's ministry and 'conversion' to charismatic renewal. First Geoff and Anne sign up for 'power evangelism'; then 'power healing'; closely followed by the third and fourth waves of the Holy Spirit, before the Kansas City prophets and the Toronto blessing.

There were other interests too: Disciple a Whole Nation (DAWN), Alpha Courses, Jesus in Me, Minus to Plus, church planting, cell churches, and many more movements and initiatives besides. As the millennium approaches, their interest with Wimber fades, and they begin to follow the revival at Pensacola, and also become more absorbed with neo-Pentecostal figures such as Benny Hinn and Reinhard Bonnke. The early years of the twenty-first century see Geoff and Anne being drawn into the new alternative of the cell church movement, and then fresh expressions.

I do not mean to offer a cynical or even critical perspective. But Geoff and Anne's spiritual trajectory prompts several questions. Is it the case that Geoff and Anne have been on the cusp of every micro and major wave of the Holy Spirit over the last forty years? Or, that they are simply part of an associational church or congregationalist culture that is almost instantly absorbed and captivated by whatever seems to be new, fresh and alternative? Or that, in the late-modern elevation of the individual in relation to God, religion and faith have become consumable commodities that constantly require updating, some discarding and regular (novel) replenishment? (In other words, the very character of believing and belonging follows the traces of all other fashions?) And what does all of this tell us about the missiological drivers that might be underneath the surface of an apparently innocent movement, such as fresh expressions? In the commentary that follows, we shall seek to flesh out some of these concerns in a little more depth, in order to try and engage in some empathetic yet critical decoding of the fresh expressions movement.

Commentary

Contemporary English church-going habits correlate with the two main religious economies that can be observed in Europe. The first is a 'market model', which assumes voluntary membership will soon become the norm. The second model is 'utility', where membership is ascribed rather than chosen. In the first model, individuals opt in to become 'members'. In the second model, all in some sense are deemed to 'belong', unless they opt out. The two models are in partial tension, and arguably depend upon each other. One may further characterize these differences as 'intensive' and 'extensive' forms of ecclesial polity. Some sociologists of religion think the extensive will not be able to survive without the intensive. Some ecclesiologists think that the intensive is fundamentally dependent upon the extensive.

If one accepts this hypothesis, one becomes immediately aware of a tension and ambiguity around the identity of the fresh expressions movement. It uses all the rhetoric of extensity, outreach and engagement. Yet it is largely composed through intensity and in-reach; apart from some notable exceptions, it would seem that many individual fresh expressions are made up of Christians who are weary of the church as an institution, but still desire fellowship and individual spiritual sustenance. This suggests that the fresh expressions movement, despite its claims to the contrary, is a form of collusion with the post-institutionalism that is so endemic in contemporary culture. Some exponents openly admit this, and point out that this is 'church' for people who no longer join bodies or associations. But this risk here is clear. Belonging together in a body with higher purposes places demands on individuals and groups, including those of duty and service; this is discipleship. Demand-led groups, in contrast, may just service people's desires for more meaning and fulfilment, while vesting this in the language of purpose, connection and even sacrifice.[4]

On a recent visit to a church that has spawned a large number of 'cell churches' and fresh expressions, a map on the wall in the foyer illustrated the problem more starkly. Maps, of course, as any anthropologist knows, are representations of reality. They require the reader to collude with scales, symbols and other codes to develop a sense of what is on the ground. But the map is not reality; the same applies to any description of anything – it must also be interpretative. This particular map placed itself at the centre of the city it was ministering to, and from the centre, ribbons flowed out far and wide to the suburbs, which were then pinned in a significant number of peripheral locations. It was a kind of web-like image, if you will. The message of the map was clear: we have the city covered.

Yet I was well aware that a number of the identified locations were far from obvious. To be sure, there could be no question that groups of Christians, who attended this church, were meeting in these neighbourhoods, week in, week out. They were praying for these localities too: 'naming and claiming' those streets in passionate and concentrated extemporary prayer meetings. But I also knew where these gatherings were held, and that, with one or two rare exceptions, the vast majority of the inhabitants of these neighbourhoods (including those that attended their own ordinary local or parish churches) were ignorant of these gatherings. In other words, for the church in the city centre, there was a map and a story that spoke of widespread engagement with all these different neighbourhoods. Yet on the ground, there was little evidence to support this. Thus, the city centre church continued to feed off and promote its rhetoric of *extensity*. Whereas the actuality – in missiological terms – was one of *dispersed intensity*. The two are not, of course, the same. Dispersed intensity lacks the complex social engagement that can really only come about through dense and reticulate institutional structures that emerge out of churches that are committed to deep local extensity.[5]

So, based on what we currently know about the fresh expressions movement, the following brief comments may be salutary for the majority of examples under consideration. First, the local church is under severe pressure from both outside and inside the church. Ironically, the proliferation of the fresh expressions movement may threaten the relationship between religious and social capital. But if the fresh expressions movement turns out to be an expression of post-associationalism, there may be serious trouble ahead.[6] The lack of 'thick' connection between a fresh expression and local commitment (duty, obligation, and so on) may diminish social capital, despite many claims to the contrary.

Second, and as Bellah notes, multiple-choice ('niche spirituality') 'suggests the possibility of million[s of] American religions – one for each of us'. So does the fresh expressions movement collude with pluralism and individualism – while cloaked in the rhetoric of 'alternative', 'new' and 'fresh' forms of church? If it does, then the survival of the 'community of memory' is at risk – replaced by 'empathetic sharing' by loosely associated individuals. Faith is privatized; it becomes the property of a sect that sees itself as engaged with but apart from society.

Third, the fresh expressions movement may lead to 'over-specialization' in the 'faith sector'. 'Quasi-therapeutic blandness' sets in, which cannot resist 'the competition [with] more vigorous forms of radical religious individualism, with their dramatic claims of self-realization, or the resurgent religious conservatism that spells out clear if simple, answers in an increasingly bewildering world' (Robert Bellah, *Habits of the Heart*, pp. 113ff). Put another way, the fresh expressions movement may represent a conservative, therapeutic and individualist *retreat* from the world, while cloaked in a rhetoric that emphasizes the very opposite of this: namely 'cutting edge', 'radical', and so forth.[7]

Fourth, it would seem that the insights of Robert Putnam concur here. In *Bowling Alone*, he notes how the [apparent] 'community building efforts of the new denominations have been directed inward[s] rather than outward[s]' (p. 123). Thus, members of the fresh expressions movement may well join important (and of the moment) politically active or campaigning groups to achieve certain ends, at local, national and international levels. But the investment in the complex relationship between spiritual and social capital will often be lacking (for example, paying church quotas that support a vast and complex ecclesial infrastructure – parish coverage, sector ministry, education, prison ministry, and so on).

Fifth, 'the primary objective of "brandscaping" is not to sell the product but to generate a fascination with the brand; to get the customer to identify with the world of the brand, creating a brand awareness and providing it with a deep emotional core' (Otto Riewoldt, *Brandscaping*, p. 10). One can conceive of the fresh expressions movement as a 'brand', but not a product – in fact, it is not clear what is actually being sold. But the brand creates the sense of 'fresh' starts, horizons and newness: just one 'expression' of something existential and grounded. It is all very postmodern. Almost anything can be a fresh expression – a Book of Common Prayer service; a drop-in centre; a toddler group with some prayer and choruses. None of these are 'church', *per se*; but they have a new 'brand' that offers hope, newness and the simulation that in-dwelling the novel will somehow take us somewhere different, and better – it is a pure but subtle form of consumerism. The websites seem to confirm this, offering an array of soft, subtle and toned spiritual choices.

Sixth, the rhetoric of 'alternative' is also problematic, because it is overly dependent on a (mostly) docile but larger 'host' body to support the implied contrast. But there are dangers here for the fresh expressions movement. After innovation and charismatic authority has waned, bureaucratization inevitably emerges as a strategy to cope with potential disenchantment. One also questions the cultural relativity of modish quasi-ecclesial rhetoric. For example, the attention to 'steps' and 'programmes' in health, wealth and prosperity movements (deeply rooted in American pragmatism, but only thinly and derivatively connected to gospel values). Or take the emphasis on 'power', 'expansion' and 'growth' in more mainstream Protestant churches in the 1980s – precisely correlating with capitalist culture, producing congregations obsessed with the latest (apparently) biblical, experiential or ecclesial steroids: how to get maximum growth with minimum effort; how to be bigger and better than your neighbour.

Seventh, the fresh expressions movement is a curiously bourgeois phenomenon. One website advertises prayer mats inspired by 'our [leaders'] visit to Tuscan', and a 'souk' that sells/exchanges home-made bags, purses, broaches, belts and other items that 'express [our] creativity'. There are meals, walks in the park, holidays, days out, art galleries, exploration and journeys. The imagery is telling – stones, rivers, sunsets, sky; children, young people and families. No old people, death, images of decay or hardship. The language is born of a middle-class thirty-forty-something age-group beholden to 'fresh' and 'organic' concepts (including nutritional advice); a God of the Gap or Habitat consumer. One idea for prayer suggests, 'it's the holiday season – and if you can, go for a swim. If that's not possible take time to enjoy the sensation of water on your body as you shower ...'[8]

Eighth, the fresh expressions movement is somewhat Janus-like in its missiological outlook. Is this movement the new highway to mission, or rather a series of new intricate cul-de-sac? For example, what is a fresh expression doing when it designates its leader 'Abbot', and key or core members as 'Guardians'? Can it really be much more than hubris that such a dense and traditioned concept as 'Abbot' is appropriated for what is still a new, thin and rather untested group? The danger is that we are all too easily immersed in a semi-detached and sacred meaning-making enclave within consumerist culture. Left to its own devices, the fresh expressions movement may actually be deeply collusive with consumerism, offering alternatives and affirmations simultaneously (but note, not critiques). As Jackson Lears notes in *Fables of Abundance*, 'under certain circumstances [the market-place holds] out a vision of transcendence, however fleeting' (p. 9).

Conclusion – ecclesiological reflections

The purpose of this short reflection has been to challenge the relationship between contemporary culture and apparently new forms of Christianity such as the fresh expressions movement. The ecclesial analysis that emerges from this brief discussion suggests that many examples of fresh expressions are symptomatic of contemporary culture, which has typically adopted the rhetoric of 'new', 'alternative' and 'fresh', which in turn is rooted in increasing individualism, and the inward turn to fulfilment and personal enhancement. This, in turn, represents an uncritical absorption of post-institutionalism within the movement that is further vested in a rhetorical cluster of tropes – 'local', 'cell', 'fresh' come to mind – which legitimize the retreat from the duties (and occasionally drudgery) of supporting and sustaining larger organizations that seek to offer something to society through utility-extensive models of service. The plethora of fresh expressions – dispersed forms of intensity – masks this, and in so doing critically undermines the very host body that sustains it. This is indeed ironic. The core body appears to be too weak to resist the onslaught of 'alternatives'; yet the alternatives can only survive if the core body is sustained.

Of course, it may be possible to counter the current momentum of the fresh expressions movement with a number of common-place observations. For example, new is not necessarily better than old; fresh is not necessarily superior to established; and effervescence is not a substitute for substance. One might also add that in theological terms, innovation should be judged by tradition. (However, this is a complex argument to mount in both Anglican and Methodist ecclesiology.) Perhaps a better way of putting this would be to underline that 'emerging church' is not likely to be superior to the emerged church; infancy is not better than maturity; that innocence (and its assumed accompanying purity) is a starting point, not a goal. Moreover, that simplicity is not better than the demanding and dense complexity of wisdom.

Defining the turn of phrase 'fresh expressions' on its own terms of reference can also be illuminating. Definitions of 'fresh', from just about any dictionary, include the following: not salted; untainted; pure; new, novel, additional; recent, newly made; not stale; lively; not faded or fatigued. 'Fresh' implies 'consume immediately' and/or 'discard after sell by date'. The question, therefore, is how long before we speak of 'traditional fresh expressions'? And then what? Similarly, the definitions of 'expression' include: the action of pressing or squeezing out; character or feeling; an act representing something in a word or symbol; an appearance; sentiment; a sign or token. The question here is, I suppose, does this have sufficient density to be church?

Part of the puzzle of the fresh expressions movement is that its newness and lack of settled identity allow it to point in several directions. There is clearly an enormous amount of energy and vision to admire and commend. The diversity of projects, encounters and ideas seems to be almost limitless, suggesting that the identity of the movement is very much caught-up in the sense of this being centred on evangelism for a post-institutional generation. (And perhaps post-ecclesial; but not post-spiritual or post-Christian?) This must partly account for why the official fresh expressions website is rather coy about ecclesiology. It acknowledges that definitions of the church are 'difficult', and that fresh expressions are therefore not easy to define.[9]

But underneath a rather playful ambivalence about what may

or may not be 'church', there lurk some potentially serious dangers. Some of these are rooted in the constituency that fresh expressions has primarily drawn upon, namely individuals who have been weaned on associational patterns of the church, but are now expressing their spirituality in a post-institutional culture. One consequence of this is that individual fresh expressions may be able to demonstrate a thick surface commitment to social and political engagement (for example, Jubilee, a variety of ecological concerns, and the like, will feature as an organization supported by individual groups). Yet this is all a matter of conscious choice – the selection of issues and projects that further galvanize the identity of the fresh expression in question. But these same groups will not usually be engaged in helping to sustain the institutional church in all its miscibility and complexity. Put more sharply, how does a fresh expression or its members *invest* in ordinary, serious, extensive ministry? Whether that is prison ministry, church schools, or simply ministry in an unremarkable place that needs sustenance and engagement? The danger for the fresh expression movement is of colluding with post-institutionalism: legitimizing support for preferred causes (with the promise of immediacy, and a clear return on a focused investment); but it does not help the organizations that sustain our social and spiritual capital.

A further question can be put here: can this new type of post-institutional associational model really Christianize and convert society? Some advocates of fresh expressions would see the movement as engaging with the 'spiritual, not religious' generation. Laudable though this may be, a potential hazard here is that the movement may collude with contemporary culture in a potentially perilous way. Is there not a danger of weaning a generation of spiritual consumers who are resistant to religious demands?[10] Where, for example, is the self-examination or deep intra-accountability of the Methodist Class system?[11] People bringing concerns and interests to a group composed through 'shared values' bears no real relation to prayer and discipleship groups of previous generations. Moreover, I have this nagging sense that the line between sacralized narcissism and some contemporary worship is wafer thin. Too much of the spirituality in fresh expressions seems to celebrate the self ('beautiful me') in a kind of spiritual aspic.

More generally on the subject of ecclesiology, there seems to be little in the fresh expressions movement that has evolved beyond the cultivation of the kind of (bourgeois?) niche groups that could potentially be advocated through Donald McGavran's homogenous unity principle (church growth) in *Understanding Church Growth*.[12] For McGavran, the most effective way to numerically grow groups of Christians was to adopt his homogenous unit principle – a section of society (or subculture) in which all members have much in common. Indeed, the lack of reference to McGavran's work in the fresh expressions movement is a puzzle, since it is clear that his missiological DNA has deeply influenced the movement.

Fresh expressions are, primarily, contemporary versions of the homogenous unit principle for church growth that was promoted over forty years ago, but was subsequently widely discredited by theologians, and also condemned by missiologists for its focus on pragmatism, and its willingness to sanction narrowly constituted groups (on the basis of age, gender, race, class, wealth, etc.) as 'church', which of course then legitimizes ageism, sexism, racism, classism and economic divisiveness.

One puzzle here is that very few advocating fresh expressions will have ever heard of Donald McGavran's work, or would know why his writings are now mostly treated with a healthy suspicion. In one sense, then, we can say that fresh expressions is a case of 'old tricks for new dogs'. Or to paraphrase and adapt G. K. Chesterton's quip, it is not that church has been weighed and found wanting by many in the fresh expressions movement. It is, rather, that it has been found too difficult and not really tried. Many fresh expressions therefore constitute a perfect fit for a post-institutional culture that does not want to invest in complex organizations and infrastructures for the common good.

That said, I do think that fresh expressions can make a modest and positive contribution to the mixed economy of church life. At worst, the movement is a distraction – another way of keeping energetic folk occupied. On one level, this is not a problem. Why not have lots of epochs that enhance energy? I can only think of one reason. And that is that many of these movements have one thing in common – they avoid the 'C' word, with a relentless appeal to another 'C' word. It is fine to talk about Christianity: but church is boring, cumbersome, institutional, messy and difficult. But I think church is also *deep*. And I am wondering – with all the emerging post-evangelical rhetoric about religion-less Christianity – when it will be realized that church is actually it. That parish ministry is still the cutting edge. And that without the institution of the church, all we'll have left is multi-choice spirituality, individualism and innovation. And that this simply won't be enough to sustain faith in future generations.

Then again, the fresh expressions movement represents a serious attempt to engage with contemporary culture, and the fact that it can be identified as an enculturated version of contemporary faith should not lead it to be judged harshly. The emerging pragmatic missiology that the movement is producing will help to shape future entrepreneurial leaders: risk-takers who may indeed help to reframe our ecclesial paradigms.

The challenge for the church will, I suspect, lie in maintaining the extensive, utility and parochial forms of mission that go on each day, and are often unsung; yet also allowing the effervescence of new movements (usually associational in outlook, market-driven, intensive, and so forth) that will continue to both challenge and feed the institution. What the church will need to avoid is falling into the trap of imagining that spiritual forms of post-institutionalism hold out any long-term hope for the future of the church. I am sure they do not. What is now deemed to be fresh cannot last, by definition. The task of the church, sometimes, is just to wait, and hope, pray and work for better times. It is, after all, one of the major themes of the Old Testament: waiting. We know that the period of exile may indeed be very long. But the answer is not to be found in turning our gaze to the new gods of a very different kind of Babylonian captivity.

4

Formation for ministry in a mixed economy church:
the impact of fresh expressions of church on patterns of training

STEVEN CROFT

It is certainly possible to see the current engagement with fresh expressions of church as one of a series of fashions and trends that come and go in the life of the Christian church in Britain (and perhaps especially among evangelicals). You will not be surprised to learn that that is not my view and represents for me a somewhat superficial reading of recent Christian history. It is indeed possible to see on the surface a number of 'movements' that appear and disappear but underneath them is a deeper trend that is now, rightly, beginning to shape the very structures of Anglican ministry and therefore ministerial training. This chapter will explore that deeper trend and look at its impact on ministry before offering reflections on ministerial training.

The evangelistic task: three stages on the journey

At the heart of this deeper trend is the dialogue between the churches' understanding of the mission of God and the society and context in which we find ourselves. The last 60 years have seen a continuous grappling with and engagement with that question: How are the churches in Britain to present Christian faith in a rapidly changing context? Different language is used by historians and sociologists to describe what is a complex phenomenon:

such as the end of Christendom or the secularization of society. There is no easy consensus and every term is shorthand for a complex reality. However, there is no disagreement that a fundamental and evolving shift is taking place around faith in British society. The church in different ways is seeking to respond responsibly and in a way that is faithful to scripture and tradition by re-engaging with what it means to be the church in mission.

God's mission, as John Hull reminds us, is about serving the whole purposes and wider horizon of the Kingdom of God and is about more than presenting the gospel to those outside the Christian faith and the nurture of believers (Hull, 2008). However, in a context where the fundamental relationship between church and society is shifting significantly, it is not, perhaps, surprising that the church has had to focus a greater degree of energy in understanding and reflecting on the way in which this faith and the claims of the gospel can be attractively and appropriately presented in a different climate. Over the last 60 years we have become, as the Church of England, much more explicit and intentional about evangelism and the baptism, teaching and the nurture of new believers.

Perhaps it is not surprising also that in making that journey, some parts of the church have embraced new approaches or methods uncritically and that some of those methods have not borne the fruit that was promised. In a similar way, I would argue, other sections of the church have responded to the changing context with a form of paralysis and denial of the change that is happening around us or else have become progressively more turned inwards in debate and discussion, focusing increasingly on church-centred issues.

However, the broader movement across the Church of England has been one of careful reflection on the mission of God in scripture on the one hand (in concert with the wider engagement with the mission of God in the worldwide church) and on our changing context on the other. That double listening to scripture and tradition on the one hand and God's world on the other has led in turn to an evolving understanding of, and engagement with, evangelism that is, I would argue, a story best told in three movements.

Presenting again a faith once learned in childhood

From 1945 to 1985 the most high-profile and effective models of evangelism in the church in the United Kingdom were in the form of presentations that summarized the gospel message either as an address or from a church pulpit or at some kind of large evangelistic meeting. This approach was typified by the high-profile campaigns led by Billy Graham but was actually widespread across the evangelical wing of the church. It depended on the ministry of a gifted preacher and was typically focused in occasional periods of activity in the life of a local church (parish missions). The focus of the work of evangelists in parachurch organizations and of many canon missioners was in this kind of event-based evangelism. Evangelism among adults was therefore seen as a separate and occasional activity of the local church and the preserve of a few gifted individuals. It was often fruitful. The evangelistic event itself was 'followed-up' with an attempt to draw those who responded to the gospel into the life of the local church.

What was happening as the summary of the gospel was presented in this way in the 1950s and 1960s? In that social context the preacher is appealing to people who already know the story of the Christian faith. They have learned it in childhood either in Sunday school or in their normal school life. An appeal and response to the gospel is essentially a spiritual moment of encounter but also a reframing of understanding: a shifting round of the pieces of a puzzle so that the picture becomes clear.

Teaching the faith to those who have not learned it as children

But what happens to this model of evangelism as culture changes and fewer and fewer people know the Christian story? As we might expect, it becomes less and less effective. By the early 1980s the evangelistic campaigns were beginning to lay more emphasis on what was initially still called 'follow-up': short courses arranged by churches after a parish mission or large-scale series of events to teach again the basics of the Christian faith. These small groups had a number of clear advantages. They gave the opportunity for real relationships and the building of a small community. There was opportunity for more sustained teaching (though typically at first they were only four or six sessions long). There was a chance for prayer and a broader Christian formation.

Little by little the more enterprising and pioneering churches began to realize that actually these small groups to teach the faith were still effective without the parish mission or evangelistic event and they could be offered at any time and as a normal part of church life. The evangelist moved from the pulpit into the church lounge or someone's home. Teaching the faith to those who knew very little became possible and this was supported by the notion of becoming part of a community that cultivates growth and development into faith. The people engaging with this kind of group and course were able, for the most part, to make the shift to membership of the local church without too much difficulty.

The effectiveness of this different model of evangelism was supported in the early 1990s by the key research of John Finney in *Finding Faith Today*. The paradigm story about conversion in the New Testament shifted from the story of the road to Damascus to the encounter on the road to Emmaus where the risen Jesus walks with the two disciples unrecognized and listens before he speaks. These models of evangelism connected in a much better way with a broader spread of traditions across the Church of England and particularly with the catholic tradition, which was attracted to the emphasis on a more incarnational mission, growing community and the explicit connections made with the early church catechumenate.

The Church of England shared in and fully owned a Decade of Evangelism in the 1990s. The major events that were planned for the decade did not bear fruit. However, the flourishing of process-evangelism courses and materials across the traditions was extremely significant and many local churches discovered a means of seeing adults come to faith, and be nurtured in faith and then incorporated into the local Christian community. The development and take-up of the Alpha course therefore needs to be seen in the context of this gradual move to a more process-based, incarnational evangelism. Evangelism is no longer seen as an occasional bolt-on to church life or the preserve of specialists. It is to be a normal and natural part of growing a Christian community.[1] The role of diocesan evangelists and others shifted to enabling the whole church to grow in its understanding and practice of evangelism.[2] Those leading the thinking of the church encouraged the concept of the missionary congregation: setting mission at the heart of our life as a continuous activity and priority.[3]

Going to those who are unable to connect with the existing church

However, even as the churches were taking on board, in significant ways, the new models and methods for teaching the faith in small groups, our wider society and mission context continued to change. Knowledge of faith among young adults and young people was lower even than in the 1980s. There was an increasing cultural distance between much of the church and society. This was matched by an increasing pluralization and diversification in our culture witnessed to and supported by (for example) the growth of the multiplex cinema; the mushrooming of television and radio stations and the internet. Whereas in the early 1990s it might have been possible to develop a single style of church worship that could engage with a broad range of the culture, this was becoming increasingly difficult by 2000.

Those observing the life of the churches in that period began to distinguish between two groups of people outside the existing congregations who together formed the mission field and context. There were those who at some point in their lives had been part of, or inducted into, church culture and could therefore, in theory, find their way back, should they wish to do so (the 'dechurched'). However, there were also those who had never been part of a church or exposed to any part of the Christian story (the 'unchurched'). Seminal research by Leslie Francis and Philip Richter published in 1998 in *Gone but not Forgotten* revealed that the unchurched at that point made up 40 per cent of the population.[4] This proportion was of course much higher among people in their

twenties and thirties and is shifting over time. Much of our existing evangelism, including the process-evangelism courses, was
proving most effective with those who already had some church
background (the dechurched) and least effective with the large
and growing section of the population (the unchurched) who simply could not cross the cultural divide.

At the same time and in response to this observation, a range
of people began to make a second shift in evangelism by seeking
to go to where people are, to listen, serve and seek to grow new
Christian communities shaped by the gospel in and for this new
cultural context. Some were inspired by stories and writers from
the world mission movement such as Roland Allen and Vincent
Donovan. Others were inspired by emerging church movements
from different parts of the world such as base ecclesial communities or the cell church movement. Others simply followed what
rapidly became the dominant methodology: prayerfully making
it up as you go along. It is this second shift into a deeper relationship between church, mission and society that has been identified and owned in the report, *Mission-shaped Church* and that
lies beneath the Church of England's intentional development of
many fresh expressions of church within a growing mixed economy of church life.

The evangelist has now moved out of the church lounge where
he or she seeks to teach faith to those who come to learn and has
gone to the young people who gather on street corners or the parents and children at the school gate or to the area of new housing
where there is no established Christian community. The model
of mission has shifted back to a much more holistic perspective.
It is no use going simply to teach or to speak. It is necessary to
sit and listen and serve. In serving new communities, networks
of relationships grow. In those networks and communities there
is opportunity, often, to witness to the gospel and to see people
come to faith. As that begins to happen, so these new communities develop a worshipping life and, in time, a sacramental life
and other marks of the church.

As with the shift to process-evangelism, the move to fresh expressions of church has offered the opportunity and encouragement

to a broader range of church traditions to engage with evangelism. Incarnational mission and a broader focus on the horizon of the Kingdom of God and God's mission to the whole of creation are not an optional extra to forming fresh expressions of church but are at the heart of the enterprise.

A key feature of developments in evangelism in the 1990s was the adopting of a franchise approach to evangelism and nurture. Rather than develop material in every local context it became easier to imitate and adopt the approach of one of the published resources. A similar approach was taken up in other spheres of church life in the 1990s as the church sought to learn from what was effective elsewhere in the world.[5] This perhaps over-franchised approach can give the impression that the church in Britain is moving through a series of phases or fashions of which fresh expressions is simply the latest. However, as I hope I have shown, something deeper is at work here. The move to fresh expressions of church is also leading, necessarily, to the abandonment of the franchise mentality: fresh expressions of church need to develop in context. They cannot adopt pre-packaged models. This adds to rather than diminishes the challenges of pioneer ministry.

The development of pioneer ministry

Mission-shaped Church makes a number of recommendations about ministry and fresh expressions of church that have now been taken forward in two sets of guidelines approved by the House of Bishops. The guidelines on ordained pioneer ministry were agreed in January 2006 and offer guidance on selection, training and deployment for what is identified as a particular focus of ordained ministry on beginning and sustaining fresh expressions of church. The guidelines on encouraging lay pioneer ministry were agreed in January 2007 and are being implemented in a range of ways by dioceses.[6]

It is important to be clear that the Church of England means by pioneer ministry the particular focus of recognized lay or ordained ministry on starting and sustaining new communities through contextual mission: fresh expressions of church.

The term 'pioneer' in common parlance can, of course, mean a number of different things, but we are thinking here specifically about how to train and prepare people to go beyond the existing church community with the specific intention of planting a new church community.

At the time of writing about 50 candidates have been recommended for training as ordained pioneer ministers. There are some 500 (mainly lay) people enrolled on the one-year course, Mission-shaped Ministry, offered by the Fresh Expressions Initiative and our partners to equip existing clergy and lay teams to begin and sustain fresh expressions of church. A number of colleges and courses have developed additional modules or routes through training to engage with this area and focus of ministry and two new church-based training providers have been recognized with a particular focus in this area.[7] There is talk of other local church-based centres emerging in the future. In addition, Church Army has, over the last decade, moved its emphasis significantly in the direction of fresh expressions of church and this is leading to a radical reappraisal and revision of its patterns of training from 2008. The Methodist Church is also exploring the ideas around pioneer ministry through a working group established by its Conference in 2007.

In 2003, as part of its regular revision of selection criteria, the Church of England included for the first time the major heading of Mission and Evangelism. *Mission-shaped Church* recommends, and the church as a whole has accepted, that the training of all candidates needs to engage with issues around planting fresh expressions of church and that, for some, this should be a major emphasis of their training to prepare them for future ministry. We now move on to explore what the content and methodology of that training should be.

Good practice in training for fresh expressions of church

I have been helping to develop good practice in training for fresh expressions of church with a range of others working in this field. Even after eight years intense engagement with theological

47

education, this has felt more than anything else like the beginnings of developing a whole new subject area in conversation.

Alongside other colleagues, my work has been focused on developing two major projects, developed by the Fresh Expressions Initiative as an agency. The first is the one-year part-time course, Mission-shaped Ministry and the second is our online guide to fresh expressions of church, which is a joint project with Church Army under the name Share <www.sharetheguide.org>.

Formational principles

Mission-shaped Ministry (MSM) was developed from a course that had already been running in Lincolnshire for five years as an ecumenical partnership between the Anglican diocese, the Methodist district and the Ground Level new church network. It was based on material developed over many years by Bob and Mary Hopkins of Anglican Church Planting Initiatives.[8] The methodology and format had been developed over time around several very key principles.

Perhaps the most important principle is that learning for this form of ministry appears to be most effective when it is in context and alongside developing practice. As each situation develops in a unique context, building habits of ongoing reflection, supervision and support is more important than advanced preparation. The course therefore is intentionally very part-time and is taught over a calendar year. It consists of one residential weekend, three Saturdays and about eight evenings. It is meant to be accessible to those in full-time work and part-time ministry, particularly complementing the latter. The gaps between the sessions are as important as the sessions themselves: they give time for ongoing development of a project and for new questions to be explored. While traditional clergy training has been on the model of high initial preparation and low ongoing support, we have tried to reverse this. For pioneer ministry there is low initial training but high ongoing support. Each project team on the course has a mentor and we encourage every course cohort to take part in an ongoing learning network once the year has come to an end.

This principle is built into the guidelines on training for ordained pioneer ministry, which envisage that it will be normal to train alongside this ministry rather than in advance of it.

Second, a vital feature of developing fresh expressions of church is that working in a team is seen as not simply desirable but essential. It bears witness in common service and allows an embryonic Christian community to grow in the love and grace of Christ. Therefore it seems vital that the project or pioneering team actually learn together rather than as individuals. MSM is therefore as accessible and affordable as possible. Our aim is to have it up and running within an hour's drive of everyone in the country. There are times and spaces for group reflection and dialogue throughout the course and plenty of material for additional reflection between sessions. We have found this group or team dimension multiplies the effect of the learning. This is not easy to replicate in ordination training though we would commend the practice of a trained pioneer minister bringing his or her core team to Mission-shaped Ministry near the start of the project.

Third, there is no rigid division in training for fresh expressions of church between theology and practice. At the heart of developing a fresh expression is being able to reflect theologically on our wider cultural context and on the emerging ecclesial community. There is therefore no division between the biblical, the theoretical or academic and the practical: all are woven together in every session and, we hope, worked through in-between the sessions. There is no formal written assessment for the course, the end product is the effective development of fresh expressions of church. At the time of writing, MSM has been validated in one local centre with optional additional assessed work for those students who wish to pursue it as part of a recognized qualification or wider ministerial training.

Subject areas

What are the areas that need to be studied and where does the training focus? We have divided the curriculum into six distinct subject areas as follows (although there are significant overlaps and an interplay between the different sessions). The first three areas normally feature in all preparation for ordained and recognized lay ministries. The second group do not. The six strands are studied concurrently throughout the one year of the course.

Personal formation

All Christian ministry is about the people we are becoming as well as the skills or learning we possess. Pioneer ministry is no different although it presents slightly different challenges. The training therefore needs to seek to develop personal qualities (such as humility), the ability to listen and a robust maturity. Time is invested in developing an understanding of leadership, team working and team roles and in growing appropriate spiritual disciplines. The practice of journalling is commended and mentoring is offered to all who take part. These habits and practices are increasingly understood and lived out in most forms of ministerial training and are unsurprisingly at the heart of preparation for pioneer ministry.

Christian formation

Pioneer ministers are seeking to form Christian community among those who are not presently connected with the church and may not know the Christian story. They therefore need a mature and well developed understanding of how people come to faith and grow in faith as adults or as children and young people. The curriculum therefore needs to pay careful and thorough attention to evangelism for individuals and communities and to questions of discipleship. Again, these elements feature in many, if not all, existing programmes of ministerial formation. One of the differences between training for conventional ordained ministry or Reader training is that if evangelism is neglected, even then there will still, normally, be a ministry to be exercised. If pioneers are not taught the skills and resources to engage in evangelism, however, there will not be a new community for them to serve.

Missiology

The two primary theological disciplines for pioneer ministry are missiology and ecclesiology and the interface between them. Missiology embraces a study and awareness of the mission of God in scripture and its outworking in Christian tradition and history, as well as its application to the present day. There are excellent resources available for teaching mission, from popular texts to magisterial syntheses, and much good writing from the history of Christian mission and the global church. Good summaries of mission, such as the five marks of the Anglican communion, are very much part of church life. Course members often arrive with a good foundational understanding. For the last 20 years the Church of England has been moving mission more and more fully to the centre of its theological agenda. So again for licensed ministers and ordinands in training this will already form part of the curriculum.

Ecclesiology

We now move on to the key areas of the curriculum that are not traditionally taught in other programmes of study and that need to be incorporated into the training of all the ordained and other recognized ministers, but that will be the particular focus of those called to pioneer ministry.

Ecclesiology (the study of the theological nature and shape of the church) has been significantly neglected in theological training. When I trained for ordination in the early 1980s the only ecclesiology one engaged with (if any) was a kind of footnote to systematic theology or doctrine. We all 'knew' what it meant to be church and Church of England (or so we thought), therefore there was no need to study this as a separate subject. In my eight years as a staff member in a theological college, the only ecclesiology students engaged with was in the context of ecumenism: a compulsory module for those in their third year of study (and only a minority of students stayed for three years). Even then (I gather) it was a dull affair and consisted only in comparing different ecumenical statements on the nature of the church.

It is manifestly impossible to form a new ecclesial community – a church – without having thought through from first principles what it means to be church and every aspect of Christian practice. Here, good resources in the recent tradition are much more scarce[9] and course members arrive with a smaller knowledge base. In a concluding chapter of *Mission-shaped Questions* I attempted a basic mapping of the subject into five areas:

1 Distilled ecclesiology: exploring the essence of what it means to be church.
2 Descriptive ecclesiology: enriching our vision of the church from scripture and the tradition.
3 Discerning or defining ecclesiology: determining what is church and what is not.
4 Derived ecclesiology: ministry, order and practice in church life.
5 Developmental ecclesiology: contrasting the actual with the ideal through the human sciences.

Some coverage of each area by every candidate is an essential part of formation whether or not they are called to be a pioneer.

Starting fresh expressions of church

Here we enter into the territory of defining and describing a significant new subject area that is still evolving. The raw material for this area of study is drawn from a combination of studies in world mission, contemporary stories and experience and the more recent church planting movement.

The material developed for MSM includes sessions on:

- The mission context and the need for fresh expressions of church
- Developing vision and values for fresh expressions
- A framework for development (listening, service, building community, etc.)
- Listening for mission

- Lessons from weakness and failure
- Questions of cross-cultural mission
- Engaging and serving your community.

Those wanting to develop their own curriculum in dialogue with this list will gain most at this point by engaging with the material on Share. This material is designed as a perpetual hypothesis, which grows and develops the practical wisdom needed to make the wisdom of pioneers widely available.

The subject remains fluid and is developing rapidly. However, this does not mean that everything is negotiable or that there is little mature wisdom. Lessons have emerged over more than a generation of observing church planting experiments that demonstrate already that certain questions or factors will make or break a new venture if not handled well. These include the careful selection of the initial team; ensuring that pioneers are well supported but not over-managed; and that the priority is kept on the mission focus rather than the needs of disaffected Christians who may seek to join the fresh expression.[10]

Sustaining fresh expressions of church

Finally a pioneer will need to give careful attention to questions of the long-term health and sustainability of a fresh expression of church even in its early stages. This is the least developed subject area of the emerging curriculum. Clearly there is a rich interface here with questions both of mission and of ecclesiology. Relevant units in MSM address:

- Developing worship and a sacramental life
- Developing community and small group life
- Engaging with the global church and mission
- Developing an emotionally healthy congregation
- Financial stability and durability
- Governance, structures and catholicity
- Developing ministry from within the community.

Again there are some good published resources emerging[11] and other material is being drawn together on Share. A key part of the dynamic here is giving the pioneers the skills and resources to refer a host of different questions back to the tradition, thus enabling them to be thought through from first principles. The Corinthian correspondence in the New Testament, the letters from Augustine to Gregory preserved in Bede's history and the correspondence between missionaries and their sending churches down the centuries all reveal the range of new questions that develop when the gospel forms community within new cultures.

Conclusion

Each stage in the development of fresh expressions of church raises new questions. We are learning as we move forward. Sharing good practice is vital. However it is clear that beginning fresh expressions of church is a fruitful and helpful way forward in engaging in God's mission; that many hundreds of people are prepared to engage in this endeavour and be equipped for this ministry; that many thousands more are forming fresh expressions of church and that we are learning little by little how to equip ministers effectively for this new challenge. Developing appropriate models of training for lay and ordained pioneer ministry needs to remain at the centre of our priorities in the coming decade.

5

Fresh expressions:
the psychological gains and risks

SARA SAVAGE

Fresh expressions of church begin with listening – listening to the voices and needs within a locale. From the outset, people are invited into a context in which they are listened to, and in which they can listen to the God who listens to them. This intersubjectivity is the first gain. How rare it is to be fully *heard* by another, to have the freedom to articulate what is good, bad and ugly in our lives. To be listened to this generously is an experience quite indistinguishable from the experience of being loved. Fresh expressions have the potential to offer an intersubjective experience that connects people with God.

Real relationship: listening to others

When people listen, real relationship becomes possible. Many fresh expressions of church understand themselves as networks of people who are there for each other, who can provide sanctuary and support for the journey of personal transformation. There is widespread longing for space to have a real relationship with God, to listen in silence before God. Authentic personal spirituality is the goal. This undoubtedly is the aim of traditional churches too. But with emerging forms of church, allowing differences, encouraging honesty and avoiding religious discourses that 'package' the right answer *in order to* foster authentic spirituality is an explicit social rule. This provides psychological permission to be honest with oneself. This honesty is the foundation of personal transformation (and is the bedrock of counselling practice and spiritual direction). It is the basis for healthy relationship with others and with God.

Close on the heels of real relationship are the gains of a 'felt' congruence with the shape of postmodern culture that takes the form of networks rather than hierarchies. Relief from traditional forms of ministry burn-out becomes possible. Healing from recent church pathologies is also a potential gain, supported by a humble, questing, open style of cognition. These gains are the focus of this chapter, with emphasis placed upon cultural congruence and humble cognition as the two bookends that hold up this stack of gains. The risks are the converse. The gains are hoped for, reached for; but without enough support, the shelf may collapse. There are no guarantees. Will people be blamed for trying? That is the real risk.

Congruence: listening to culture

In Western culture (Europe and UK particularly), people no longer experience the social world as hierarchically arranged. The pyramid-shaped worldview, with God and other authorities at the top, no longer compels belief. To enter a traditional church building is to enter a space that structures this hierarchical worldview through symbol and architecture. To the unchurched, it is to step into a foreign world that seems to demand acquiescence to a mysterious set of social norms. An exuberant welcome extended to newcomers may complicate, rather than fully dissolve, this implicit social pressure. Even charismatic church networks, despite their informal worship style, remain pyramidal (and, at times, authoritarian).

Even if newcomers become deeply enfolded into the social container of church, what remains uncomfortable is not so much the fact that leadership is expressed hierarchically (this leadership is often benevolent), but that those in leadership, particularly at senior levels, are not subject to 360-degree accountability. This is felt to be incongruent with the best practices in secular, post-industrial business and industry, even considering the forthcoming

(Anglican) clergy disciplinary measures. When newcomers finally 'twig' the social rules, they realize that they are held accountable, but that leaders may not be. This does indeed feel strange.

A number of traditional churches seek to embrace both pyramidal and egalitarian network worldviews into their fold. In his ethnographic study of a village parish church, Timothy Jenkins, in *Religion in English Everyday Life*, observed two competing interpretations of 'how things are', two commitments to different worldviews. The traditional, hierarchical interpretation of 'how things are' revolves around the parish church as a 'highly visible reminder of the old order of things' (p. 62). The parish church is seen by indigenous villagers as a system of generous patronage, supported by a (supposedly) wealthy diocese, interested in the social fabric and personal welfare of all. This contrasts with the egalitarian view of church held by newcomers to the village. Their egalitarian worldview involves intense participation ('every member ministry') in contrast to the hierarchical, patronage view of church. There is an inevitable degree of conflict and compromise to keep both these worlds revolving under one roof. Defending symbols of the 'old order of things' (such as the position of a pew) is particularly intense as it becomes more and more apparent that the church is now one of society's last bastions of the old pyramidal order that bestowed status and security for those within it.

Fresh expressions avoid this complexity. As social containers in the form of networks of relationships, they present a flatter, less threatening pathway for the unchurched to explore the Christian faith. Few younger people relate to the idea of returning to a national church fold that has been waiting for them like a kind mother. They expect to actively seek for their spirituality (online, at least). Thus, the second psychological gain is one of cultural congruence. People feel they can relate to the idea of a faith journey *as they are*.

So far so good. Yet how far is cultural congruence a good thing? The question arises whether the array of emerging or fresh expressions of church simply conform to a new set of flatter, freer cultural norms that celebrate infinite consumer choice, and thus fail to clothe the gospel in a counter-cultural way. There is a fine balance to be struck between the inevitable enculturation that is necessary for a true missionary encounter with a 'new' (arguably postmodern) culture and a slavish conformity to that culture. Listening to culture needs to be prophetic – not uncritical. Many people involved in both fresh expressions and traditional church feel an urgency to take prophetic stances, for example on poverty or the environment. These are underlying values that can lead to collaboration between them. Enculturation and prophetic stances can be intertwined. It is possible to take on cultural clothing and change it as we put it in the service of the gospel.

For other churches, there is a struggle even to comprehend the enormous cultural changes that have occurred outside their embrace. Enculturation to postmodern culture is resisted. There is a secret hope that we can massage the upcoming generations back into the church's well-beloved pyramidal social shape (whether traditional or charismatic/ Pentecostal). This is no longer possible. Even so, for many Christians, there remains a deep attachment to the pyramidal form that worked well for many generations, and brought a sense of divine order, holiness and peace. Those who long for the old pyramidal worldview are at odds with those who long for the new. They may feel that any gains for fresh expressions represent a total loss for all that traditional Christianity upholds, and vice versa.

This is a false dichotomy. A mixed economy of church, comprising both traditional and fresh expressions, is indispensable to navigate the cultural shift in which we exist. Spiritual explorers need the ratification of the settled 'experts', without which they are flying blind. Both need to listen fully to the others' perspective in order to find creative ways that integrate the best of the old and new Christian worldviews. What will vanish are the vestiges of the pyramid's monopoly. (It is assumed that it may remain a 'worldview of choice' for some.) The prospect of losing this monopoly provokes psychological reactance. Those wedded to the security and status of the pyramid are deeply rattled. Many churches hope these cultural changes will not materialize, and that adaptation on the part of traditional church to the emerging church will not be required.

But these cultural changes have already happened. That a massive shift in cultural norms has already occurred in prosperous, Western-influenced nations is demonstrated by the substantial sociological data gathered from over 80 countries by Ronald Inglehart and Christian Welzel over the past four decades and published in *Modernization, Cultural Change, and Democracy*. This huge research project provides a clear picture of the structural features underlying recent cultural shifts. Two defining cultural changes emerge clearly from the data: secularization and erosion of traditional sources of authority. Both of these are clearly linked to a particular economic base.

Countries with levels of GNP per capita of less than $15,000 show traditional values such as respect for authority, traditional family patterns, religion as important, national pride, and good and evil perceived as clearly distinct. When threats to survival such as starvation are absent, as is the case in developed countries (with more than $15,000 GNP per capita), values shift towards the goals of self-expression and personal well-being. Freedom of choice, tolerance for non-traditional lifestyles, high life satisfaction and high trust in people are the reported values in prosperous Western-influenced nations. The social flexibility brought about by the safety net of the welfare state, the internet and other communication technologies lead to relationships of almost endless choice (rather than relationships of duty) (see Inglehart and Welzel, *Modernization*). All forms of face-to-face voluntary associations show decline in wealthy countries. It is much simpler to go online.

In this sense Marx was right. A society's cultural, religious superstructure arises from a given economic base. The message for the church is: good luck trying to shift this. A decade of evangelism will not even dent it. In short, when survival needs are generally assured, traditional values (such as religion is important) change to secular and rational/scientific values (see Pippa Norris and Ronald Inglehart, *Sacred and Secular*). Survival values (such as traditional family patterns) change to self-expression values. The impact of these value changes is not just additive. A massive cultural shift occurs when these values become the norm for the majority of the population within a nation state (see Inglehart and Welzel, *Modernization*). A new 'plausibility structure' (see Peter Berger, *The Heretical Imperative*) arises; the new social shape is experienced as '*of course*'. In post-industrialized Western culture, that shape is not a pyramid, but rather a network.

Relationships of choice, and the welfare net if things go wrong, foster personal freedom. This personal autonomy precedes a widespread rejection of truths that arise from traditional and religious sources of authority. These now seem to be at odds with the individual's internal, subjective experience – now the accepted arbiter of truth. And so, modern culture has taken a 'subjective turn' and institutional religion is in steep decline.

These changes mean that traditional forms of church have almost no natural point of connection with those born since the 1980s, those young people belonging to generation Y for whom the endless possibilities of virtual communities are a birthright (see Sara Savage et al., *Making Sense of Generation Y*). Concepts of a transcendent God, of a need for salvation from sin, no longer have an existing framework to provide meaning. The symbolic cultural frameworks that enable meaningful interpretation of basic Christian concepts need to be reinvented and clothed in the new worldview's vestments. Emerging and fresh expressions of church are more congruent with the postmodern worldview, and are better placed to develop new frameworks of meaning to enable the gospel to be understood in a variety of ways appropriate to a diverse social terrain. This is a psychological gain we cannot do without.

It follows from all of this that the social shape fresh expressions take is non-hierarchical and non-authoritarian. Traditional churches too are recognizing the value of a servant style of leadership that empowers others (see Eddie Gibbs and Ryan Bolger, *Emerging Churches*). Mutual accountability, open communication and transparency are desired at all levels.

It is as if the subjective turn of Western culture has placed a lens over contemporary readings of the New Testament, selectively highlighting the values we have described so far. These values are not new. They are inherently Christian, apparent in embryo form in the early church, making brief reappearances throughout church history. It seems that the context of postmodern culture is congenial to the re-emergence of these values so expressive of Christian virtues of integrity, freedom, compassion and humility. Accepted, the very openness of postmodern culture also means that it is congenial to consumerism, selfishness, and life lived in the fast, shallow lane. Sifting and discernment is required. The new values, when sifted, can empower Christians to live and witness within the new cultural, economic conditions that require high levels of interpersonal skills, personal confidence, and flexible, transferable skills. A reinterpretation of traditional Christian virtues, such as self-denial, long-suffering, and obedience, is long overdue. These have been misrepresented for too long as requiring de-selfing, or a slavish co-dependence, rather than – more accurately – as enlightened strategies for coping with our fallen nature and life's difficulties. Life is demanding enough to require a marriage of both sets of virtues.

Relief from ministry burn-out: listening to church leaders

Burn-out is the term given to ministers who are expected to be omni-competent, and who bravely attempt the impossible for too long (for example, to care for 13 traditional parish churches and enable growth on all fronts, particularly youth ministry, even though those in the traditional services remain firmly opposed to any change).

Fresh expressions have the potential to spark a new type of leader–congregation dynamic. As the pyramidal worldview subsides and becomes a matter of choice rather than duty, faith communities may be less likely to foster the dependency and passivity that hierarchies elicit. It is highly likely that new kinds of burn-out will arise. Sheer exhaustion is the most likely candidate. But there is hope that the most pernicious aspect of traditional burn-out, the false pulpit persona that ministers feel they have to wear, will lessen, and that exhausted leaders will be able to share or pass the baton as a matter of course, rather than 'die' a shameful public death as a minister who 'couldn't cope'.

Healing from church pathologies: listening to active members

Much more is now expected of life. Self-expression in lifestyle and fulfilling relationships comprise the constellation by which people steer their way to happiness (see Savage, *Emerging*). This legacy of the 1960s has intensified in postmodern, post-industrial Western societies. Much more is expected, too, of a faith that purports to bring wholeness, peace and joy. If the Christian faith cannot make human life better in the here and now, why should it appeal? Healing and wholeness are expected qualities of church life for most Christians under the age of 55. These elevated expectations set up a 'spiritual economy' of supply and demand. People want happiness and 'victory', so this is promised – certainly a great and loving God would plan nothing less. But it does not always pan out, and many Christians express disappointment with their church experience.

It is fair to say that many traditional churches, however successful, have a big back door. This includes evangelical, charismatic and Pentecostal churches that account for the lion's share of church growth worldwide (see Alan Jamieson, *A Churchless Faith*). The leaving process usually occurs over two years, and involves different motivations and pathways for people in different phases of their personal religious development (loosely following the lines of Fowler's stages of faith). What is held in common is that church-leavers' former church life was experienced as inhospitable to authentic development. It could not deal with their agonized questioning. Those who exit church usually leave bereaved, traumatized and with a sense of shame. Yet, most have not lost their faith, and are still searching.

Often the sad fruit of disappointment results from well-meaning Christians who promise much on behalf of God but whose church context is inadequate to the task. The social container is the wrong shape. Pyramids do not liberate, nor invite honest questioning or dissent. The implicit social norms of traditional churches laud some categories of people but not others. Despite good intentions, there is rarely a universal welcome.

Fresh expressions seek to be actively inclusive. They are usually doing something, focused on a task such as concern for poverty and the planet. Many fresh expressions of church have taken root through seeking to help a particular group of stigmatized people, reaching the marginalized and oppressed. Social justice, and connecting with real life are core values. Christians want to move beyond their cosy subworlds, as evidenced by a well-known saying in churches in the USA: 'You can't get into heaven without good references from the poor.'[1]

These values, I believe, describe the 'emerging' Christian view of the 'good' in the postmodern West. They are the gains of fresh expressions. It is through these values that mission can connect with young people, the unchurched and hopefully the dechurched. Fresh expressions of church are intuitively moving towards a culturally congruent way to enable people 'from the least to the greatest ... to know the Lord' (Jer. 31.34b) through a democratization of spiritual status, spiritual resources, and the incarnating of the gospel in a variety of small groups. The unity of the body of Christ is no longer seen as a monolithic, geographic or ecclesial oneness. Like the internet, unity is dispersed. Fresh expressions seem to be both a healing response to the widespread fragmentation in society, as well as an acceptance that the social terrain is one of endless diversity. What has been psychologically maladaptive in the church now has a chance to be sifted and laundered through an array of fresh expressions.

Certainly, fresh expressions of church are not immune from recycling all the old pathologies (conformity, gossip, fear of conflict, various in-group dogmatisms, sluggish bums on pews, to name a few). Fresh expressions are an *opportunity* to shed the old social norms that prevented these pathologies from even being *named*. The old pathologies will not simply go away under new management. There is tough work ahead. Many fresh expressions are in the honeymoon period when new social norms are being hammered out. The group stages of forming and norming move on, unremittingly, to the storming stage when the leadership of the group is tested, and conflicts erupt. Depending on how fresh expressions negotiate and learn from the conflicts arising from movement between group stages (see Sara Savage et al., *The Human Face of Church*), we can expect any combination of:

(a) a resurfacing of the old pathologies in a new cultural guise, and/or
(b) new pathologies arising (an endless search for novelty, a consumerist mentality, a mysticism somewhat unrelated to the biblical narrative), or
(c) the discovery of locally contextualized ways to live out these values in ways that are faithfully Christian, with some degree of interface between traditional and emerging forms of church.

We hope for the latter.

The Holy Spirit has ever been in the business of forming and reforming church, and this must be the case here as well. There is much that both traditional and emerging churches need to learn from each other. Emerging churches need the profound theological and liturgical resources of the historic church, and the traditional churches need emerging churches to understand how to incarnate the gospel into our changed culture. The missionary theologian Lesslie Newbigin argues in *The Gospel in a Pluralist Culture* that those who are innovating in a religious tradition can only be responsibly accepted by those who are masters of the tradition. A responsible way forward therefore requires the active collaboration of both emerging and traditional church in a sustained dialogue. The traditional church needs to act generously (as always) as an 'Open University' to fresh expressions, pouring in its riches, while being open to learning at the same time. Both need to be each other's mentor and student. This interface needs to be planned and financially resourced. It won't happen of its own accord, except in a few healthy hotspots.

Humble cognition: listening to ourselves and our opponents

This chapter concludes with a vital 'bookend' to support the array of gains so far discussed: humble cognition. Lesslie Newbigin

(*The Gospel*) argues that it is God's desire to provide a space for genuine *freedom* so that people can respond to the gospel. There is a cognitive component to this freedom that has become even more vital given the 'subjective turn' of modern culture.

The cultural shift to postmodernity has brought in some ways an increased level of threat to traditional religion. Great, now we have rampant subjectivism as well as the threat of scientific rationality. Yet, it is also a wonderful ally. Postmodernity comes to the aid of fresh expressions of church in the form of humble cognition. This is an immense gain. Humble cognition may be the only way through the current conflicts over sexuality (and biblical interpretation) raging across the worldwide church, a conflict that requires both sides to perceive and respect the opponent's perspective, impossible as that may seem.

Fresh expressions (and particularly the more postmodern emerging church) are moving towards a humble cognition that allows for doubt, questioning and exploring, without succumbing to the belief-sabotaging regress of radical scepticism. Humble cognition (following the lead of Michael Polanyi in *Personal Knowledge* and *Knowing and Being*) accepts that all knowledge, religious or scientific, begins with a faith commitment, a standpoint we take as best we can towards a reality that we cannot fully comprehend. For example, as scientists, we accept that the universe is rational, and therefore open to fruitful investigation. Or as Christians we accept that God exists and acts in human history, and is worthy of our fidelity. From there, we inhabit the tools of our culturally contextualized knowledge – words, concepts, symbols, metaphors, narratives, and all means of measurement – as 'probes' through which we can explore reality.

Taking this more humble stance towards the task of knowing, Christians no longer need to be impaled upon the horns of a science-versus-religion dilemma, as if theological orientations have no choice than to wed themselves with one pole or the other. Postmodern philosophy ended the futile quest for total certainty in any field of knowledge. This has paved the way for a rich dialogue between science and religion. Through this dialogue, it becomes evident that conflicts between science and religion are in fact false dichotomies that only occur when either science or religion makes claims far beyond their particular sphere of expertise. It is popularizers of the false dichotomy such as Richard Dawkins that sustain the view that a scientific and religious worldview are mutually exclusive. Not that there is one simple harmonization between the two, but the important point to make here is that the epistemological debate has moved on. It is no longer necessary to carry on the fight as if there are only two polarized, irreconcilable ways of seeing the world. We are enabled by the likes of John Polkinghorne, Philip Clayton, Keith Ward, Alistair McGrath, and others, to see the openness of our emerging universe with new eyes, and to re-envision the material world with the presence of our God who is both transcendent and immanent.

Humble cognition is also expressed through creativity, and eclectic practice. 'Roots down, walls down' means that emerging churches sink roots deeply into a particular Christian tradition, while remaining open to nourishment from other sources. Tasting new forms of worship, and learning from different emphases in Christian teaching is part of nourishing one's own spiritual life. This supports religious knowing because more 'tools' are available with which to explore the reality of God as revealed in Jesus Christ. Emotions, bodies, narratives and the arts provide new 'probes' by which to deepen religious knowing.

Fresh expressions of church have the opportunity to reinvest Western religious knowing with a totality that is greater than the sum of its parts, a totality that is experienced psychologically when both head and heart are processing input simultaneously (see F. Watts, in *Neurology*). Many emerging churches do this through adopting an eclectic spirituality that draws from the wells of all Christian spiritual traditions: Catholic/sacramental, evangelical, holiness, social justice, Pentecostal, and contemplative, for example, blending ancient and contemporary practices – monastic with techno. Words, symbols, narratives, images, music and movement combine to create a polyvalent, cognitively freeing space to explore a relationship with God.

Conclusion

The key gain that fresh expressions provide therefore is space to try out new ways for the social container, the shared life of the faith community, to become a credible hermeneutic of the gospel. After four decades as a missionary in India, Lesslie Newbigin returned to a very changed British cultural context to carry out parish ministry in 1981. Astonished by this new 'pagan', post-modern Western culture, he asked how there could be a real missionary encounter with the changed context of postmodern Western culture. In *A Word in Season*, he writes: 'How will the new reality [of God's presence in Jesus Christ] become known? I suggest by a certain kind of shared life, by actions, and by the words that interpret those actions. The first and fundamental one is a certain kind of shared life ... This is the main hermeneutic of the gospel' (p. 152).

In order for fresh expressions of church to become a credible hermeneutic of the gospel, they first may need to act like a wash-ing machine, laundering outside existing church structures what is too difficult to launder within it. When the laundering process is well underway, and if the dialogue between traditional and fresh expressions of church is sustained, both will be changed. Perhaps the incipient emerging/traditional dichotomy may lessen. Christians may, in time, start coming back to those old buildings with the strange architecture. They may come back to traditional church simply for a rest, for respite from the labour-intensive work of sustaining fresh expressions. But they will come back transformed by the 'washing machine', and to a traditional church transformed as well.

The risks are that all the fond hopes described here will be frustrated. Learning inevitably occurs through trial and error. Thus, we need to add to our list of values *humble expectations*. We must have humble expectations because the way will not be easy. What we fear most is the pain of trying and failing. We fear that chaos will be unleashed. We are charting new pathways. We have not been here before. Or have we?

Our world is falling apart. The ramparts are built and the stones of the eternal city are dislodged. Soon our holy place will be destroyed. Those whispering ones of the Way collect like mice in the alleyways and quiet corners. They imagine they will survive when all else crumbles, when our holy place is taken away. What will happen now that the world has changed, and crushes us by its coming?

Resources for conflict transformation and change management in churches

The Conflict Transformation Course, developed by Dr Eolene Boyd-Macmillan and Dr Sara Savage of the Psychology and Religion Research Group, University of Cambridge
For information, see <www.prrg.org/prrg/research.acds?instance id=4821970&context=4821959>.

S. Savage and E. Boyd-Macmillan, 2007, *The Human Face of Church*, London: SCM Press. Chapter 10 is a manual for church consultancy/change management using a tried and tested, ethically safe process.

Conflict mediators

Alastair McKay
Director of Bridge Builders (see below)
bridgebuilders@menno.org.uk

Cecilia Clegg
c.clegg@ed.ac.uk

Olive Drane

David Williams
Conflict and Reconciliation Consultant
Coventry Cathedral
1 Hill Top
Coventry CV1 5AB
Tel. 44 (0)24 7652 1262
Email: david.williams@coventrycathedral.org.uk
<www.coventrycathedral.org.uk>

Organizational and church consultant regarding change management

Mike Clargo
<www.tesseracts.com>

Church consultancy information

Mark McMinn and Amy Dominguez
<www.markmcminn.com/contact.html>
<www.churchpsych.org>

Organizations (conflict specialists)

Acorn Christian Healing Trust (offering courses in active listening)
Whitehill Chase
Bordon
Hampshire GU35 0AP
Tel. 44 (0)1420 478121
Email: info@acornchristian.org

Bridge Builders
London Mennonite Centre
14 Shepherds Hill
Highgate
London N6 5AQ
Tel. 44 (0)845 450 0214/(0)20 8340 8775

SARA SAVAGE

Churches Mediation Network (Scotland)
Revd Dr M. A. MacLean
mmaclean@cofscotland.org.uk

The Grubb Institute
Cloudesley Street
London N1 0HU
Tel. 44 (0)20 7278 8061

6

Biting the hand that feeds:
an apology for encouraging tension between the established church and emerging collectives

PETE ROLLINS

There is no such thing as a mixed economy

The term 'fresh expressions' is employed within the Anglican and Methodist religious tradition to describe 'a form of church' that is specifically adapted to 'our changing culture'. A form that is missionary in nature insomuch as it is 'established primarily for the benefit of people who are not yet members of any church' (Fresh Expressions Initiatives 2006, p. 3). Such a definition largely arose in an attempt to describe the topological kernel of an otherwise diverse group of organic, grass-roots religious collectives that began to spring up in the late twentieth century on the fringes of more established expressions of church life.[1] These collectives were experimenting with approaches to language, liturgy and life that differed, to a greater or lesser extent, from those found in more traditional manifestations of church.

There are, of course, numerous groups that could be legitimately described in the above way, and no doubt this description has provided some fragile, fledgling groups with a much desired stamp of institutional legitimacy, and a sought-after location within the wider Anglican and Methodist structure. However, one can't help feeling that the explicit generosity of this space creation (with its desire to be welcoming to various new expressions of religious life) houses an implicit danger. For while the

explicit aim of labelling groups fresh expressions may be to encourage their continued development and provide space for their
unique voice within the church, one could say that in the very
process of doing this the radical voice of these groups is actually
suppressed.

In order to understand this let us recall how the church dealt
with St Francis of Assisi. The problem that the institution faced
concerned how to handle a man who wanted a church of weakness rather than strength, of humility rather than pride, of poverty rather than wealth. There were a number of possible solutions
(excluding, of course, the obvious one of listening to him). The
hierarchy could have labelled him a heretic and done away with
him. Or alternatively it could have called him a madman and
ignored him. But something else took place; it welcomed him into
the fold, providing a seat at the institutional table. It gave him his
own order within the church, one that could be overseen by the
authorities, one that could incarnate the radical teachings of St
Francis without infecting the rest of the church. Thus silencing
the message, not by preventing it from being heard, but by providing a space for it: a space carefully defined by and demarcated
by the institution. It does not matter whether this was done out of
good motives or bad, the point is simply that, by providing such
a space, the church did not need to seriously rethink its feudal
structures. Far from being transformed by the universal scope
of his message this new order of St Francis actually provided a
much-needed airvent for the institutional machine, one that allowed the church to continue as it had before.

Is this not what we see being played out in *The Matrix* trilogy
directed by the Wachowski brothers? What we gradually find out
as the narrative progresses is that what we took to be the very
site of resistance to the machines (the messianic figure of Neo,
his friends and the city 'Zion') was not really a threat to them but
was actually created and maintained by them. This is particularly
ironic and insightful when one remembers how so many church
youth groups saw the first film as an analogy for their own activities (as challenging the 'worldly powers'). For later we find that
the resistance force of the first film was the very thing that the

machines wanted and encouraged, the logic being that in order to create an effective oppressive system you need to allow for revolutionary voices within it. Too much oppression with no place for possible resistance and the whole system would implode.

What then if the religious message one could draw out of *The Matrix* trilogy was exactly the opposite of what was generally accepted. What if it offers us the idea that unjust worldly powers are not challenged by our prayer meetings, Bible studies and outreach programmes but actually fuelled by them? Our meetings at the weekend and on a Thursday evening would then be the very activities that refresh us so that we can work, shop and play in the unjust world for the rest of the week. We may think that these extra-curricular activities define who we 'really' are, as opposed to what we do during the week, but they simply help to solidify who we really are on a day-to-day basis.

Is this not the ultimate problem with the activities of the superhero Batman? By day he is Bruce Wayne, a wealthy industrialist, by night he is Batman, combing the streets of Gotham City for criminals to beat up and people to save. His obsession with street crime arises as a direct result of witnessing his mother and father murdered by a thief. His father was a philanthropist who attempted to help Gotham City by funding social projects and local charity work. Bruce, however, takes a different approach and uses his wealth to fund a vigilante war on terror. One could say that Bruce Wayne is fundamentally different from his father insomuch as the latter concentrated on helping victims of crime, while the former seeks to punish the perpetrators of crime. However, it would be more accurate to say that Bruce is merely continuing his father's business by different, but equally flawed, means. Both are obsessed with the subjective violent eruptions that take place on the streets of Gotham City and both seek to address them. However, in the midst of all their activities neither pays attention to his own (sublimated) violence. This violence is that which has been objectified in the very economic structures that allow corporations like Wayne Industries to make such vast sums of money in the first place. Batman is unable to see that the subjective crime he fights on a nightly basis is fuelled by the objective crime he perpetrates on a daily basis. The street crime is the explosion of violence that results from greedy, large industries obsessed with the increase of abstract capital at the expense of all else. It is not enough to hate subjective explosions of crime, one must turn one's attention to the ground that feeds these expressions.

Indeed it is the very philanthropic work of his father and the crime fighting of Wayne that actually provide the valve that allows them both to continue in their objective violence. What better way to feel good about yourself than volunteering at a local charity in the evenings (like Wayne's father) or beating up street criminals in the evenings (like Wayne). Such acts can recharge the batteries and make us feel that our true identity is pure and good, when in reality it simply takes away the guilt that would otherwise make it difficult for us to embrace our true (social) self who is expressed in the activities we engage in for the rest of the week. The philosophy here is exposed as 'do something so that nothing really changes'. While it might not guarantee an interesting franchise, he would perhaps get more done if, instead of Batman running around beating up drug dealers and pimps (an impotent project anyway as there is only one Batman for the whole city), he dissolved Wayne Industries, set up free health care in the city and campaigned for radically different socio-political structures.

In a similar way one can say that, by providing a carefully demarcated location for the revolutionary message of St Francis, the church domesticated the very voice that could have transformed it (hence the popular Catholic claim that, had the church actually listened to St Francis, the Reformation would have been unnecessary).

I am not here inferring that there is a subjective form of violence at work in the church's support of fresh expressions, one that actively seeks to silence the radical message of these new collectives via an embrace of the age-old aphorism 'keep your friends close and your enemies closer'. Rather I am speaking of an objective, systemic violence, one that is not perpetrated by any one individual or group within the church. The people involved with defining the Fresh Expressions Initiative and using it as a means of giving permission to various groups will, no doubt, have nothing but the best possible motives for what they are doing. Indeed these upstanding citizens would no doubt be hurt and rightly indignant if they were ever accused of acting disingenuously. Yet, we must not be mistaken here, for neither is this violence something that happens *in spite* of these people's good intentions, sneaking past while they aren't looking. Rather the violence being perpetrated is one that occurs most effectively *precisely because* of their good intentions. Why? Because these good intentions only eclipse the violence by making it all the more unbelievable. Yet the fact remains that the framework that the institutional church affirms is one that cannot be embraced by many of these emerging groups without them losing something substantive about their message (primarily its universal scope).

In response to this view people will no doubt point out that the Anglican Church has always been about celebrating a mixed economy, meaning that the church does not wish to extinguish difference but rather affirm and celebrate it.[2] With the embrace of a mixed economy new religious movements on the fringe of church life are integrated into the institutional edifice with the idea of providing them with space while, at the same time, reducing any possible antagonism between them and other parts of the body.

This ideal of providing a space in which we can respect each other's different expressions of faith initially sounds wonderful, yet it can only make sense if we are already unified in relation to the deeper structure in which these differences play out. For instance, in economic terms we can see a multitude of differences being played out in the West in terms of what people buy with their money. Diversity is the name of the game. People can express their 'individuality' by consuming products in a combination as unique as their desires. However, this 'difference' betrays the underlying, unselfconscious, acceptance of capitalism itself. This is not a mixed economy in any real sense, for only one economic reality is affirmed throughout. A mixed economy would involve having a single society in which a capitalist and Marxist economy operate side by side without antagonism: something that could not be imagined, because the antagonism between them exists in the very space they occupy in relation to each other. As Marx pointed out, the bourgeoisie and the proletariat can't find a way of resolving their differences via some agreed notion of justice, for the notion of justice is defined in relation to the position they inhabit. As an old Irish proverb has it, 'The well-fed does not understand the lean.'

We can easily imagine a church in which there are various different and endlessly creative ways in which one can express prayer, worship and liturgy. However, this 'difference' only masks the incommensurable, unbridgeable antagonism that must exist between the believer who lives simply, who believes in a priesthood of all believers, and who rejects the reign of dogma, compared with someone who seeks to accumulate wealth, who advocates strict religious hierarchies and who judges an individual's Christianity in terms of creedal affirmation. No liberal ideal of finding consensus between these positions is possible. The antagonism here cannot be abolished. Old wineskins may be able to accommodate an infinite variety of old wines, but the new wines will break them.

While it must be remembered that a Christian's battle is not against 'flesh and blood', and thus is never against individuals as such, we must acknowledge that our battle is against the place that certain individuals inhabit. For example, in the setting up of a republic, the aim is not to be found in the impotent desire to overthrow a particular king but rather in the endeavour to abolish the structures that make someone a king in the first place; both for the sake of the people and for the sake of the king.

So then, while many, if not the majority, of new grass-roots Christian groups are merely offering different ways of expressing the same ecclesiological structure affirmed within the Anglican and Methodist Churches (and thus can fit within the current structures), there are other 'emerging groups' that challenge these ecclesial structures at their very core, and thus cannot exist within the established structures of the Anglican and Methodist traditions without significant tension.

In order to prevent these antagonisms from degenerating into some kind of friend/enemy dialectic the answer is not to be found in the commonly proclaimed idea that we ought to draw these new groups into the institutional church, thus providing them with a place. For if the radical, critical voices are drawn into the very institution that they critique then the only place left, for those to go who are critical of the institutional church at a structural level, is in the direction of extremist fundamentalist or secularist groups. As such, some of the more radical expressions of faith in the West today (which often go under the banners of 'alternative worship', 'emergent' or 'transformation art') need to resist being drawn into the 'inherited church' so as to magnify rather than minimize the reality that many of these collectives do not merely have an important message for those outside the institutional church but also a message for the church itself. Christianity may be about peace and unity, but let us not mistake this unity for one that is without tension, antagonism and friction.

Rediscovering the potentiality in actuality

Not that the term 'fresh expressions' is without descriptive merit, for it does capture something vital about these groups insomuch as they often employ and experiment with the resources already embedded within the institutional church, expressing them in novel and interesting ways. Indeed the critique they house is one that is found within the very structure to which they stand in tension. These groups are not seeking to merely take the message of the church and present it in a culturally sensitive manner to those outside the institution, or attempting to speak a new message, rather they are showing how the radical message of Christianity speaks in a revolutionary way both to those outside the church and to the church itself. The wager is that the message of Christianity has not been spoken once, long ago to a group who now protect that message and pass it on to others. Rather the uncompromising message of *metanoia* speaks now as much as then, with a radical call to believer and unbeliever, follower of Christ and follower of capital. If such groups are missional then their mission is as much to the church as it is to those outside of it. And it is to this mission that these groups must endeavour to remain faithful.

These groups are thus concerned with uncovering the potential that is already embedded within the church and letting it speak to the church. Let us approach what this means by way of Aristotelian ontology. For Aristotle, beings are described as actualities that were once merely potentialities. In other words, what 'exists' only as potentiality can become actual in time and everything that is actual was once merely a potentiality. Existentially speaking this would mean that we experience our past as complete, finished, actualized while the future is experienced as a world of possibilities. There are so many things that we could do at any moment in our life and, exhilarating or frightening as this insight may be, it exposes the feeling we have that life is full of possibility. For Kierkegaard, Hegel's speculative philosophical system of history (as the manifestation of the Spirit's unrelenting self-realization) could not do justice to this sense of freedom because it treated potentiality as nothing more than actuality that had yet to happen (but that would come to pass by necessity). Kierkegaard thus argued that Hegel's system could not do justice to the individually existing 'I' who experiences potentiality as freedom rather than as inevitability. Regardless of whether or not we really are free agents (which interests those who debate free will and determinism, positive and negative freedom, and so on), existential thinkers want to do justice to the fact that we experience ourselves as free.

However, such thinking, which places potentiality before actuality, can eclipse a deeply important Christian insight, namely that the eschatological potentiality of the Kingdom of God is not primarily a description of some coming reality that lies ahead of us in some future time but is at work in the past and present. What this means is that the eschatological Kingdom of God is not simply some potentiality that will one day be actualized but rather is already actualized in the world (through Christ) as potentiality. The coming kingdom is already here, already among us, yet not actualized as such. The term 'eschatological' cannot therefore be used to simply refer to some future event but rather needs to be expanded in order to capture the past and the present. The Kingdom of God must be approached as a radical potentiality at work *within* the actuality of the concretely existing historical church, and yet not of it.

The result is not a view of the event of faith as some finished state devoid of potentiality, but rather of the idea that this event is infused with potentiality. The cry of Christ on the cross that 'it is finished' can be read as housing within it the very beginning; something has happened that is not closed and static but that is rather saturated with dynamic possibility. Here the eschatological movement in Christianity is not, first and foremost, one that addresses a future state that is not yet present to us, but rather it addresses a way of understanding the past as overflowing with a potentiality that has not yet been rendered actual. The incarnational logic of Christianity can thus be understood to mean that the 'to come' of the messianic event is inscribed into the past. The eschatological 'to come' is thus not related to some Kantian noumenal realm lying outside the phenomenal world but rather is inscribed deeply within it. When Jesus says, 'my hour has not yet come' at the wedding party in Cana we can say that this captures something of the eschatological reality of Christ; the Messiah who stands before us has come too early: is both now and not yet (John 2.4). A visual way of representing this eschatological idea can be seen in the following ambiguous statement: T-H-E-K-I-N-G-D-O-M-I-S-N-O-W-H-E-R-E. The fact that this statement can be read both as 'The kingdom is now here' and 'The kingdom is nowhere' captures the idea that the kingdom can be said to dwell in the 'now here', while being 'no where'. This means that the kingdom is not to be thought of as a future event of which we presently *lack an experience* but rather as an elusive presence that we *experience as lack*.

In fidelity to this eschatological logic of the incarnation it could be said that groups like Grace and Moot (who are located within fresh expressions), among others like Ikon and The Garden (who are located outside fresh expressions), house an approach to faith that is radical in both the etymological sense (of returning to the roots, of turning toward the past) and in the revolutionary sense (of offering a positively subversive act that holds out the possibility of transforming people's subjectivity). The true radical is not then merely someone who surveys the past and attempts to replay it, for what has existed in our history is all too often implicated in the current oppressive socio-political climate, but rather they find future possibilities in the past, the new in what is old. These groups do not simply offer something new, but neither do they merely present the church of the past to a new generation in some culturally sensitive way; rather they are engaging in that holy task of unearthing the potentiality that exists within the institutional church as it presently exists – a potentiality that has the power to shake the foundations of the present institution.

These groups are thus not bringing to light a new theological idea that would place them in tension with the 'inherited church', but rather find themselves in a tension with the inherited church precisely because they are taken up by the same *evangel*. So the question we must ask concerns what theological ideas within the tradition are these groups employing that allow them to develop innovative new modes of liturgical activity and ecclesial structures.

A God beyond ontological categories

It would appear that for many of these groups the apophatic tradition of Christianity has provided the soil for these explorations and a place of permission-giving. This connection with the mystical tradition can be seen in communities such as Moot, with their development of a 'rhythm of life' inspired by the idea of a rule of life, while other groups have increasingly started to use the term 'new monasticism' to express their indebtedness to the monastic tradition. However, at a deeper level, it is the apophatic idea of God as beyond being that has helped to open up and justify the liturgical innovation that one finds in groups like Sanctus1, Foundation, The Garden and Grace. This approach to God is deeply traditional and is articulated beautifully by Anselm when he addresses God in *Proslogian,* in *Monologian and Proslogian*:

Therefore, Lord, you are not merely that than which a greater cannot be thought; you are something greater than can be thought. For since it is possible to think that such a being exists, then if you are not that being, it is possible to think something greater than you. But that is impossible. (p. 109)

While Anselm is often credited with developing an ontological argument for the existence of God, it is apparent here that Anselm's description of God is not ontological in nature, for God is approached as that which dwells beyond thought, and thus beyond the realm of ontological description. This 'definition' in the *Proslogion* therefore has the structure of a non-definition, for it refuses to enter into the name game. Here we encounter the idea that God is indirectly disclosed precisely in the failure to think God. Anselm was thus not placing God in the realm of ontology, as Kant had claimed, but rather was offering a definition that did not rest upon the philosophical ideas of being.[3] For Anselm, the most majestic mode of 'existence' lay in a 'being' that could be received without being conceived, and this was none other than God.

By drawing upon such non-ontological notions of God, as a presence irreducible to metaphysical categories, emergent collectives have rediscovered a freedom to play with the language inherited by, and expressed within, the wider church body; viewing it as a provisional and iconic springboard rather than an eternal, unchanging and a-temporal set of dogmatic statements. As such this ancient tradition has given birth to innovative forms of religious expression.

Transformance art

Such an approach to the source of faith leads to an understanding of revelation that is not about providing an epistemological insight into the essence and/or mind of God that would allow for some mimetic discourse. As a result the idea of revelation is not married to some epistemological idea but rather is approached as that which overwhelms us and short-circuits any such intellectual appropriations. Instead of revelation being thought of as that which renders the source of faith manifest to the mind, revelation is approached as an event more like that found in the Eastern notion of enlightenment rather than the Western notion of scientific understanding. In the latter we grasp something while in the former we are grasped by some(no)thing.

Here revelation describes an event of (1) epistemological incomprehension, (2) experiential bedazzlement and (3) existential transformation. The first of these describes how revelation involves an overturning of our conceptual categories. We cannot intellectually grasp what is taking place because what is taking place transcends grasp. The second aspect of revelation, experiential bedazzlement, does not so much describe an experience but rather the anxiety/horror/wonder of living in the aftermath of that which cannot be reduced to experience. In the last element of revelation I am referring to a happening that ensures that the receiver of the call is never the same again. These three elements help to describe what the New Testament calls *metanoia*, a term that relates to both a change of mind and a change of heart. Here revelation is a happening rather than a mere hearing. Revelation is heard only insomuch as it is heeded, listened to only insomuch as it is lived. Is this not what we see in the conversion of Saul on the road to Damascus? For here we read that he is blinded, bewildered and born again.

In this way revelation is not understood as that which makes manifest some otherwise hidden side of God, rather revelation is that which brings the hiddeness of God into close proximity with the individual. The secret of God is not revealed in revelation but rather brought near and deepened. Is this not how we ought to approach the theological category of incarnation? Not as the demystifying of God but as the point when the mystery comes to live among us. The point whenever the mystery is felt as a mystery and envelops us in its mystery.

The result of this is nothing less than the claim that revelation is testified to in a radically subjective transformation. Not in the sense that it is somehow evoked by the subject, but in the Kierkegaardian sense of transforming the subjectivity of the individual.

The believer is one who is transformed by an event that cannot be spoken.

Again such an idea has influenced the theological texture of emergent groups. Instead of attempting to provide an understanding of faith they are more likely to engage in various rituals and reflections designed to provoke thought and encourage a receptivity to the event of faith. Instead of propositional theological discourse we find expressions of theo-poetics and transformance art (that is, modes of expression that combine a rich cocktail of poetry, prose, art, ritual, soundscapes and theatrical performance). Again this is nothing new at all. The traditional church is full of rituals and reflections designed to prepare people for the incoming of revelation. However, once again these new collectives are taking these ideas and playing with them, finding ways of making these theological insights speak in a fresh manner.

A voice that should remain in the wilderness

With the desire to approach God as that which dwells beyond ontological categories and of revelation as a transformative event, many of these emerging groups are finding ways of challenging, not just how church looks at a cosmetic level, but how the church functions in terms of ecclesial structures. As such I hope that some small groups who are experimenting with new modes of religious expression within the Anglican and Methodist structure will choose not to enter into a more well-defined relationship with the church but actually embrace a less defined, more ambiguous relationship. Attempting to find a place from which they can speak to the church as a whole rather than being embraced into one part of it. The church needs to be open to a perpetual reformation, and in each generation there will be voices that call for this in some specific, historically grounded way. These people could be called heretics in the sense that they rise up from within the tradition rather than outside of it, loving the tradition and yet reading it in a different way to the dominant hermeneutic. Their message cannot be downplayed as simply one more expression of the church universal (a missional expression designed to draw people back to the pews), but rather is a universal message to the church. It will be heeded by the church, or ignored by it, but let us pray that it is never given a demarcated space within it.

Since committing to support fresh expressions, various small collectives are eagerly lining up to receive this blessed name, to be baptized into the fold (for there is money available to the baptized, buildings to be had and titles to be gained). Such groups, however, should think twice before receiving the blessing. For the price of accepting this offer may well, for some groups, be the restriction, misrepresentation and even perversion of the very message that they offer to both those outside and those within the church. Such an offer may well end up acting as little more than a Procrustean bed upon which collectives are stretched and squeezed in order to fit a particular type of missional frame: becoming part of a 'mixed economy' that is really nothing more than a multifarious expression of the one hegemonic economy.

7

Living in the distance between a 'community of character' and a 'community of the question'

MARK MASON

Introduction

In this chapter I want to explore, in an affirmative way, one tension that I think could, and should, characterize 'emerging' and/ or 'fresh expressions' ecclesiology: the tension (borrowing from, respectively, the work of the theologian Stanley Hauerwas and philosopher Jacques Derrida[1]) of seeking to be, and living in the distance between, both a 'community of character' and a 'community of the question'. This tension is radically undecidable. Here it is important to understand undecidability as 'always a determinate oscillation between possibilities'.[2] The importance of emerging/ fresh expressions[3] living in the distance between, and oscillating between, both 'types' of community is recognized, as is the undesirability of identifying entirely with just one or the other. What I argue for here is, as Derrida puts it in an interview with Richard Kearney in *Debates in Continental Philosophy* (a collection of interviews edited by Kearney), 'a reciprocal contamination of the one by the other, from which neither can emerge intact ... One is trying to reach an additional or alternative dimension beyond [both]' (p. 153).[4] I begin to 'set up' this tension by describing the emphases of each of these types of community and then highlight some related challenges that emerging/fresh expressions need to engage with if they find the ecclesiological reading I offer useful and worthy of further reflection.[5] I conclude by stressing the urgent necessity of

living in, indeed welcoming, the undecidable tension and oscillation between both of these types of community.

My contribution here makes no spurious claims to represent cool
objective assessment, balance, or academic disinterest (as if any
of these stances were actually possible anyway!). This is a polem-
ical piece, a critical – although not unsympathetic – response to
the provocation of *Mission-shaped Church*,[6] a manifesto of sorts.
And what I want to help 'manifest' through this manifesto is the
advocacy of a particular notion of Christian discipleship leading
to the formation of disciples who are able to recognize and live
with inescapable undecidability and uncertainty in all aspects of
their faith, including how that faith is manifested in their approach to ecclesiology. Uncertainty is, of course, unavoidable in
matters of faith and my argument is that a major determining
factor as to the success of emerging/fresh expressions of church
will be the extent to which this realization is emphasized and
explored in ecclesiological and discipleship models and practices.
Although this is acknowledged to varying extents in some emerg-
ing/fresh expressions literature,[7] further attempts need to be
made to explore the challenge of this tension in a sustained and
rigorous way. Failure to carry out such explorations may result in
a full-on collision between these two indispensable community
emphases ('car crash ecclesiology'?) resulting in a derailment – or,
worse, the rendering ineffectual – of emerging/fresh expressions.

Throughout this chapter it will be obvious that I want to affirm
and embrace the idea of, as Derrida would have put it,[8] 'living in
the distance between' these two types of communities and living with the tension that this 'living in the distance between' invariably brings. Such tensions, far from being viewed negatively,
should be affirmed and regarded as opportunities to 'do' some
– or, more accurately, to 'be' a – creative ecclesiological expression. For living in this undecidable, uncertain tension between
different ecclesiological aspirations is where the exciting things
happen; it is where the ecclesiological 'action' takes place. The
tension of oscillation, of living in the distance between the perspectives of Hauerwas and Derrida, holds the possibility of gen-
erating a further measure of newness and impetus in emerging/

fresh ecclesiology that can advance the conversation initiated by *Mission-shaped Church*.

A community of character

The argument for rediscovering churches as 'communities of character' has been brilliantly advanced by Stanley Hauerwas. In *A Community of Character* he argues that the church needs to regain its social significance as a 'distinct society':

> My wish is ... [to] ... help Christians rediscover that their most important social task is nothing less than to be a community capable of hearing the story of God we find in the scripture and living in a manner that is faithful to that story. The church is too often justified by believers, and tolerated by nonbelievers, as a potential agent for justice or some other good effect. In contrast, I contend that the only good reason for being Christian (which may well have results that in a society's terms seem less than 'good') is because Christian convictions are true; and the only reason for participation in the church is that it is the community that pledges to form its life by that truth ... (p. 1)

Hauerwas places character formation at the heart of Christian community. While some will perceive this as a challenge to their 'freedom', he maintains that there is no real freedom without it:

> 'freedom' comes only by participation in a truthful polity capable of forming virtuous people. Such a people, contrary to our liberal presuppositions, are not characterized by an oppressive uniformity. (pp. 2–3)

The mark of this polity is the ability to enable diversity. Thus, Hauerwas asserts that,

> Rather the mark of a truthful community is partly seen in how it enables the diversity of gifts and virtues to flourish. Therefore the church is not only a community of character but also a community of characters, since we are convinced that God rejoices in the diversity of spirits who inhabit his church. (p. 3)

More recently, Hauerwas, together with Samuel Wells, has developed this position in *The Blackwell Compainion to Christian*

Ethics by emphasizing the necessity of the gift of the Eucharist in making the church visible:

> Because Christians need each other if they are to be able to experience the gift of the body of Christ in the food of the Eucharist, they cannot just be anywhere when they worship. Because the Eucharist is an embodied, corporate practice, God's people need to come together in one place. They become for that period, if for no other, a visible community ... By becoming something, somewhere the Church locates itself in space, and is made visible. Only thus can it begin to relate to all in God's creation who have taken the freedom of God's patience not yet to believe. (p. 20)

According to Hauerwas and Wells, the church (and so, presumably, the multitudinous visible communities that make up the church) has both a prophetic and a priestly ministry (pp. 20–4). The priestly role of the church 'is to model sustainable life before God – to show what God makes possible for those who love him' (p. 22). This life in the presence of God is described as having three features:

- the formation of disciple and community, and the ways in which the believer and the body negotiate the boundary between Church and world;
- the politics of the body, specifically the practices through which it embodies its vocation of worship, witness and service;
- the continuing conversation over the best way to follow Christ, specifically the characteristics of the disciple and the body in relation to a range of conflict resolution issues. (p. 22)

What can be said about any appropriation of this emphasis on being a community of character by emerging/fresh expressions?

First, there is the danger of excessive activism in relation to developing emerging fresh expressions at the expense of sufficient reflection and attentive passivity (not that reflection and attentiveness aren't themselves forms of action broadly understood) as regards how God might want to shape such communities and the characters within them.[9] I would suggest that there are dangers in how some Christians have understood churches – and the disciples they wish them to be composed of – solely as 'products' to be 'built', and built 'now'. Such an understanding can emphasize constant, impatient and narrowly construed forms of 'action', often at the expense of careful, time-intensive reflection (often construed by some as 'wasting our time').

A simultaneous emphasis on also being a community of the question, discussed more fully in the next section, provides a remedy to this excessive activist and action-filled mentality. To begin with, the terms of the problem I have outlined – that is, either/or, opposing 'active' to 'passive' rather than exploring the possibility of being both – would be contested by those also seeking to be a community of the question. As the theorist and literary scholar Avital Ronnell incisively points out in *Thinking Difference* (a collection of interviews with a range of intellectuals, edited by Julian Wolfreys), the very 'opposition between passive and active proffers a deluded equation', and a 'true ethics of community ... would have to locate a passivity beyond passivity, a space of repose and reflection that would let the other come'(p. 55). She goes on to argue that

> if one opened up a space of radical passivity, one might see what comes, what arrives ... From there, one might be able to hear the call; or, the call might be put out in a way that is entirely surprising, perhaps unrecognizable, and perhaps irreducible to codified meaning. Something would occur on the level of absolute and unconditional hospitality to being, to the other ... Rather than think we know in advance what community is, or what we are building, as if it were ours to build, we might *allow it to come*. To allow and allow and allow is the experiment that I would want to conduct. (pp. 55–6)

A community of the question is thus a model of 'allowing the other (e.g. a different kind of community that surprises us and is beyond what we have previously known) to come'. Thus, those involved in emerging/fresh expressions need to avoid the kinds of ecclesial (over)determinations ('It should look like this!') in their activist desire to build an expression that is new, fresh and different. A community of character that also desires to be a community of the question will develop a 'both/and' approach to character formation: reflective/passive *and* active.

Second, there is the issue of density (explored in greater detail elsewhere in this volume by Martyn Percy). Will emerging/fresh expressions be able to develop sufficient 'depth', 'density' and 'robustness' in terms of their knowledge and understanding of, as well their responsiveness to, issues of ecclesial authority and the practice of the historic Christian disciplines? In other words how seriously will those involved in emerging/fresh expressions take the challenges articulated by Hauerwas and Wells? The extent to which emerging/fresh expressions are able to establish themselves for any extended period of time will depend on their ability to successfully engage with a set of practices widely accepted across various Christian communities/denominations and time, and model a measure of authentic (borrowing from Dietrich Bonhoeffer) 'life together' (see Dietrich Bonhoeffer, *Life Together*) or, as John Howard Yoder put it in *Body Politics*, perform 'body politics' before a 'watching world'.[10] Such Christian practices cannot be isolated from the context of a community of fellow practitioners who submit themselves to one another and, together, criticize the quality of the outworking of those practices and develop and transform them over time. Are emerging/fresh expressions able to manifest sufficient maturity and commitment to sustain their corporate life together in this way?

Third, as crucial as I consider the emphasis on discipleship and character formation in the work of Hauerwas and Wells, it immediately raises a series of vital questions regarding power. Some of those involved in emerging/fresh expressions would, often due to previous oppressive and – in some cases – abusive experiences of the exercise of power in church, rather ignore or pretend such issues don't exist in this 'new thing' they are part of. In order to constitute a viable, healthy ecclesial expression I would suggest that a greater maturity towards the issues of power that exist in any ecclesial construct will be required of them.

For no church, including those emerging/fresh expressions whose participants may have been 'burnt' by authoritarian, hierarchical abuses (both perceived and concrete) in previous ecclesial models they were part of, can escape negotiating issues of power; to pretend otherwise is naïve at best and delusional at worst. Questions of power, linked as they are to concepts of truth and knowledge, are always already shaping any community whether it is one of 'character' or one of 'question'. For example, in what ways should our characters be formed and by what (and whose) methods? What are the limits on what questions I can ask? Truth is inextricably linked to the outworking of power issues in any kind of community, including church communities. As the philosopher-historian Michel Foucault argued in *Power/Knowledge*:

> The important thing here, I believe, is that truth isn't outside power, or lacking in power; contrary to a myth whose history and functions would repay further study, truth isn't the reward of free spirits, the child of protracted solitude, nor the privilege of those who have succeeded in liberating themselves. Truth is a thing of this world: it is produced only by virtue of multiple forms of constraint. And it induces regular effects of power. Each society has its regime of truth, its general politics of truth: that is, the types of discourse which it accepts and makes function as true; the mechanisms and instances which enable one to distinguish true and false statements, the means by which each is sanctioned; the techniques and procedures accorded value in the aquisition of truth; the status of those who are charged with saying what counts as true. (p. 131)

The question then is what resources emerging/fresh expressions have at their disposal to successfully recognize and respond to such a state of affairs in order to avoid replicating and repeating abuses of the past. In *Power and Passion* Samuel Wells offers hope in the form of the vision of a community of character outworking the theological resource of a specific form of power: the power of the resurrection. Wells begins by pointing out that,

> the gospel of Jesus Christ is deeply concerned with how individuals and groups use their power, how they form their

passions, and how society is going to change radically. It is not a question of getting involved in politics; everyone already is. It is more a question of becoming wiser and more conscious and more faithful in one's politics. (p. 20)

Power, according to Wells, is not necessarily a bad thing for there are many forms/types. However, no type of power can compare with God's power, 'which is the power of creation and, ultimately and definitively, of resurrection' (p. 20). Wells describes the power of resurrection available to the church, contrasting it with the power derived from property and resources:

> power based on property and control of resources presupposes a world of scarcity ... [however] the power based on resurrection is a power presupposing abundance ... Fundamentally the transformation of politics is about the transformation of the reality – and perception – of power. (pp. 20–1)

Resurrection power is characterized by forgiveness and friendship. Thus Wells argues that, when perceived afresh in terms of the resurrection, politics can itself be transformed, becoming that which is no longer bound by death, but rather is oriented towards life and 'abundance':

> Politics becomes the reorientation of life according to the freedom made possible by the power of overcoming death, and not just death but sin – through the power of forgiveness. (p. 185)

Wells provides an important theological emphasis for emerging/ fresh expressions which they would do well to employ in their attempts to negotiate power at both personal and social levels and thus develop as a community of character.[11] However, it is vital that – at the same time as doing this – those same emerging/ fresh expressions continue to seek to be a community of the question by constantly questioning (or 'interrogating') both their understanding and outworking of resurrection power. To not do so runs the risk of falling into the oppressive totalizing and exclusionary practices described by Derrida and others; it is to their contributions that we shall now turn.

A community of the question

Jacques Derrida is the philosopher most closely associated with the concept of deconstruction (a term oft cited but persistently misunderstood by countless commentators and critics). Originally developed to describe an approach to interpreting written and visual works, deconstruction has now entered everyday language (for example, in some branches of ecclesiology there has been talk of churches 'deconstructing'). Responsibly engaged with, the ramifications of deconstruction contrast with the misleading clichéd misunderstandings (sometimes deliberate) that present it as a destructive process often used to describe a practice of ripping things apart. Crucial to deconstruction properly understood is the idea that every structure – literary, psychological, social, economic, political, religious, educational or ecclesiological – is formed and maintained through acts of exclusion. In forming and shaping something, something else inevitably gets left out. Every structure is therefore to some extent exclusive and can become repressive – and with acts of repression (conscious or unconscious) come consequences. That which is repressed always returns to destabilize every structure, no matter how secure it seems. The challenge for any structure, including ecclesial structures, is to overcome patterns of exclusion that repress difference; to develop a deconstructive vision that is ethical in that it is open to, and affirming of, the call of the 'other'. As Drucilla Cornell puts it in *The Philosophy of the Limit*:

> Derrida's deconstructive exercises are unique in the way in which the limit of any system is exposed ... The Other for Derrida remains other to the system ... Derrida's project is not only to show us why and how there is always the Other to the system; it is also to indicate the ethical aspiration behind that demonstration. For Derrida, the excess to the system cannot be known positively; hence, there is no beyond to what he would call the undecidable. (p. 2)

Or, as Derrida himself states in *Debates*:

> Deconstruction certainly entails a moment of affirmation. Indeed, I cannot conceive of a radical critique which would not be ultimately motivated by some sort of affirmation, acknowledged or not. Deconstruction always presupposes affirmation ... I do not mean that the deconstructing subject or self affirms. I mean that deconstruction is, in itself, a positive response to an alterity which necessarily calls, summons, or motivates it. Deconstruction is therefore vocation – a response to a call. The other, as the other than self, the other that opposes self-identity, is not something that can be detected and disclosed within a philosophical space and with the aid of a philosophical lamp. The other precedes philosophy and necessarily invokes and provokes the subject before any genuine questioning can begin. It is in this rapport with the other that affirmation expresses itself. (p. 149)

One of Derrida's main interests is in this relationship to the other, to heeding the call of the other. This interest in the other is heavily influenced (although Derrida was also critical of certain aspects of it) by the project of the Lithuanian born philosopher Emmanuel Levinas (1906–95). Derrida's 'Violence and metaphysics: an essay on the thought of Emmanuel Levinas' has long been viewed by many as a classic in the field of contemporary continental philosophy. Here I am appropriating a well-known passage from the beginning of Derrida's essay discussing questions relating to the birth, death and future of philosophy in order to illuminate the present discussion regarding emerging/fresh expressions. The reader is encouraged to substitute 'ecclesiological/ecclesiology' for 'philosophical/philosophy' to appreciate its usefulness to, and impact for/on, the emerging/fresh expressions conversation:

> It may even be that these questions are not *philosophical*, are not *philosophy's* questions. Nevertheless, these should be the only questions today capable of founding the community,

within the world, of those who are still called philosophers; and called such in remembrance, at very least, of the fact that these questions must be examined unrelentingly, despite the diaspora of institutes and languages, despite the publications and techniques that follow on each other, procreating and accumulating by themselves, like capital or poverty. A community of the question, therefore, within that fragile moment when the question is not yet determined enough for the hypocrisy of an answer to have already initiated itself beneath the mask of the question, and not yet determined enough for its voice to have been already and fraudulently articulated within the very syntax of the question. A community of decision, of initiative, of absolute initiality, but also a threatened community, in which the question has not yet found the language it has decided to seek, is not yet sure of its own possibility within the community. A community of the question about the possibility of the question. (p. 98)

It is not my intention to explore here the vast discussion regarding the problematic of 'community' as a philosophical concept, a discussion in which Derrida and many others have been involved;[12] Derrida and those others illuminate the ways in which 'community' can do violence to difference (by absorbing it into the same), when the other is assimilated into the one. Suffice it to say that Derrida's relationship to the idea and concrete reality of community is complex and – fittingly – undecidable.[13] For our present purposes, it is enough to understand that a community of the question is one that explicitly acknowledges the undecidability of its constitution and it is this idea that is useful to and impacts upon the emerging/fresh expressions conversation.

The undecidability that lies at the heart of a community of the question is a dynamic that runs throughout Derrida's writings. In *A Derrida Dictionary* Niall Lucy helpfully unpacks the problematic of undecidability by describing its relationship to decision-making:

Every decision is the result of a process. However right and natural it might appear, and even if it seems to take only a split second, each decision undergoes a struggle before it is made. Once made, every decision could always have been otherwise. It is in this sense that decisions are always undecidable, which is not to say either that there are no grounds for making decisions (so any decision will do: thumbs up, thumbs down – same difference) or that there isn't a pressing need for decisions to be made (speak out against injustice now, or later – it's all the same). Decisions are undecidable in so far as they are structured by the law of undecidability. (p. 147)

In the chapter 'Hospitality, justice and responsibility' in *Questioning Ethics* (a collection edited by Richard Kearney and Mark Dooley), Derrida has described this 'law' of undecidability as follows:

there would be no decision, in the strong sense of the word, in ethics, in politics, no decision, and thus no responsibility, without the experience of some undecidability. If you don't experience some undecidability, then the decision would simply be the application of a programme, the consequences of a premiss or of a matrix. So a decision has to go through some impossibility in order for it to be a decision ... Ethics and politics, therefore start with undecidability. I am in front of a problem and I know that the two determined solutions are as justifiable as one another. From that point, I have to take responsibility which is heterogeneous to knowledge. If the decision is simply the final moment of a knowing process, it is not a decision. So the decision first of all has to go through a terrible process of undecidability, otherwise it would not be a decision, and it has to be heterogeneous to the space of knowledge. If there is a decision it has to go through undecidability and make a leap beyond the field of theoretical knowledge. So when I say 'I don't know what to do', this is not the negative condition of decision. It is rather the possibility of a decision. (p. 66)

Thus it is not, as Derrida says, that decisions are of themselves necessarily made in ignorance, but rather that a decision always entails a leap of faith:

Not knowing what to do does not mean that we have to rely on ignorance and to give up knowledge and consciousness. A decision, of course, must be prepared as far as possible by knowledge, by information, by infinite analysis. At some point, however, for a decision to be made you have to go beyond knowledge, to do something that you don't know, something which does not belong to, or is beyond, the sphere of knowledge. (p. 66)

On this basis a community of the question is one that never forgets the undecidable basis on which decisions about its constitution and determination (that is, structure, shape and practices) have been, and will continue to be, made. There will always be ambiguities about such a community that is defined in this way. An awareness of the undecidable and provisional (it could always be otherwise than it is) 'nature' of a community of the question will lead to a humble agnosticism regarding 'boundary' issues, for example a relinquishing – but not, perhaps, an absolute one, given the tension with being at one and the same time a community of character – of the necessity and importance of determining who's 'in' and who's 'out' in terms of this emerging/fresh expression. Also to be expected would be a greater emphasis on connecting and working out doctrine in the context of the concrete practices of the church rather than at the level of abstracted, reason driven, apodictic (that is, something that can be clearly shown to be 'true') apologetic debate. Churches that take seriously their identities as communities of the question will not rush to articulate definitive 'answers' – the curse of unreflective activism so often resulting in a superficiality that fails to engage and connect adequately with people's genuine existential dilemmas around certainty, belonging and commitment. Rather they will always recognize the provisional and arbitrary (in that they are always context dependent) character of 'answers' offered; room is made for mystery. Such a community would be aware that any attempt to offer an 'answer' will contain, because of its provisionality, an inexpungeable element of hypocrisy within it (and why not? Isn't Christianity after all, when all is said and done, a faith for those who recognize their hypocrisy, those forgiven hypocrites?). Things could always be otherwise than the way our determinate answers claim they are – and we understand this even as we offer them. We know that our claims will always fail to match the indescribable 'reality' of what is 'out there'. In this sense our answers never fully 'deliver'; they, and we who articulate them, always fall short but we continue to offer them and are cushioned by grace as we do so. And I would argue that such a distinctive based on this idea of the undecidability of our choices is a blessing for emerging/fresh expressions. It helps them to exhibit and confess a faith-fuelled 'humble agnosticism' on a range of ecclesiological, theological and ethical issues. Emerging/fresh expressions should always remain aware of the provisionality of their structures, always keeping them 'under' question. They recognize that beliefs about God and our relation to God (individual and communal) are ultimately based on faith. They know, and happily confess to others, that there are no starting points that do not involve an element of doubt. Nevertheless, and crucially so, they can live with this realization and continue to engage passionately with the God they worship.

A church that wishes to be a community of the question should be intensely concerned with the need to understand the various and complex ways that power operates to dominate and shape ecclesiological consciousness. Power is, of course, an extremely ambiguous topic that necessitates continual awareness, study and analysis in ecclesial expressions that are looking to live in the distance (or oscillate) between a 'community of character' and a 'community of the question'. Power is a basic constituent of human existence and shapes both oppressive and productive dimensions of ecclesial structures. Issues of power are inescapable in every ecclesial expression, including emerging/fresh ones. An important 'missional' strategy for such expressions should be both to demonstrate concern and vigilance towards the oppressive aspects of power as they relate to ecclesiological constructs as well as modelling a commitment to outworking the productive aspects of power: the possibility for ecclesial expressions to empower those in their orbit and to engage marginalized groups. We need to develop the kinds of communities of the question that will constantly ask themselves about the possibility that their ecclesiological constructs are being designed to provide – for those who are part of them – a legitimating ideology for colonizing and marginalizing those 'others' who do not measure up to the standards of the 'I' or 'We' who wield power from the centre of those constructs. Such communities need to be able to keep themselves under constant surveillance and remain vigilant to the dangers of developing in such undesirable ways. An emerging/fresh community of the question will remain sensitive to, and interested in, the way language, in the form(s) of theological and ecclesiological discursive practices, serves as a form of regulation and domination. Discursive practices are sets of tacit rules, active in ecclesial constructs, that regulate what can and cannot be said, who can speak with the blessings of authority and who must listen, and so on.

Obviously, there are huge issues of church governance and authority to engage with here. One area within the emerging/fresh expressions conversation where the issue of power is most clearly in evidence and urgently needs to be engaged with is that of how decisions are arrived at and which interpretations are agreed and 'authorized' vis-à-vis the direction and theological/ethical 'position' of the community. I am arguing that emerging/fresh communities of the question, while sensitive to the oppressive dimensions of power outlined above, should nevertheless be places where limits are imposed on interpretations if they also wish to be communities of character as described by Hauerwas. Thus, power/authority issues are unavoidable. While they encourage and provide a space for questions such communities do not constitute places where just anything can be said and done, given that they are also places that require a certain recognition from those who are part of them that the practices of the community constitute the condition and context for their questions. Rather, communities of the question will constantly interrogate the limits and possibilities of this context in a non-simplistic and non-naïve way. There will be a recognition that the ecclesial context can never be finally fixed or stabilized; that the context is always changing and that as finite, fallen beings we will never be able – nor should we aspire – to 'master' a given ecclesial context by believing we have fully grasped, apprehended or understood it. A context – including an emerging/fresh expression – is never 'complete' or 'saturated' although, as Derrida recognizes in *Limited Inc*, communication (and thus meaningful ecclesial action) is not possible without some measure of determination of that same context. As he puts it:

> I would not say 'that there is something politically suspect in the very project of attempting to fix the contexts of utterances.' No, not 'suspect'. But there is always something political 'in the very project of attempting to fix the contexts of utterances.' This is inevitable; one cannot do anything, least of all speak, without determining (in a manner that is not only theoretical, but practical and performative) a context. (p. 136)

James K. A. Smith, in his commentary on Derrida's work, *Jacques Derrida: Live Theory*, sums up the relationship between interpretation and community from a Derridean perspective:

> What Derrida is opposed to, then, is not the determination of communities *as such*, but rather the naïve assumption that no such determination has taken place – that these communities or rules are 'natural' or 'self-evident'. (p. 63)

Such an understanding of how determination operates within communities that are predicated on undecidability and uncertainty is both an opportunity for those involved in emerging/fresh expressions as well as a challenge. This understanding emerges as emerging/fresh expressions realize that they are not exempt from such operations in their decision-making and the development of their theological and ethical positions.

The concepts contained within Derrida's idea of the 'community of the question' have recently been articulated using a different terminology: that of 'weak thought'. Weak thought is heavily indebted to Derrida's work and has been developed in different ways and with different emphases by the philosophers Gianni

Vattimo[14] and John Caputo. In *After the Death of God* (edited by Jeffrey W. Robbins[15]), Caputo makes the following comments regarding the work of philosophy and theology that, in my view, should be embraced by emerging/fresh expressions:

> Well, on the one hand, serious philosophy and theology involve a work of ceaseless critique of our capacity to deceive ourselves. They remind us that everyone is on the same footing, that no one enjoys privileged access. This has a salutary ethical and political import because it shows us that we're all in this together and that nobody is hardwired up to the Secret. That produces a desirable ethical, political, and religious effect – an egalitarian effect. (p. 117)

Caputo goes on to argue that central to 'weak thought' is the Augustinian notion of *cor inquietem* – the restless heart. Here critique is tempered by affirmation:

> But I think that philosophical and theological thinking have to be – beyond critique and uncertainty – affirmative. If all there is to thinking is critique and delimitation, scepticism and doubt, then it will not inspire us. It will simply be disruptive and negative. So I think that philosophy is always looking for a way to articulate what we love, what we desire, what drives us. That is the Augustinian side of my work, which is emblematized by what Augustine calls at the beginning of the *Confessions* the *cor inquietum* – the restless heart. We write with both hands. Radical critique and delimitation is the left hand, but the right hand is the affirmation of something that we desire with a desire beyond desire. (pp. 117–18)

For while our objectified affirmations must always be deconstructed to prevent them from being idolized, the desire for the 'undeconstructable' remains – affirmative and hopeful:

> Something can be affirmative – we can say yes to it, for that is what we love – without being positive. That is to say we may

lack a positive formula for what we affirm. Whenever someone erects a positive content, making our affirmation into a determinate object, that can always be deconstructed. Whatever is constructed can be deconstructed, otherwise it is a menace or an idol. But the affirmation itself is irreducible. So I would say philosophy – philosophical and theological thinking, really any kind of thinking at all – has to be driven by a radically affirmative energy, by a desire for what is undeconstructible. (p. 118)

For Caputo argues vigorously that this affirmative energy, this desire for what is 'undeconstructable' will lead us to dream of the Kingdom of God, where the poor, disenfranchised and marginalized are invited to the wedding banquet:

if we are not to succumb to pessimism, we need to dream, to release the deconstructive power of the 'to come', which is the affirmative energy of deconstruction. We need to dream of a Christianity ... in which the destructive effects of the neo-Platonism that crept into the tradition will dissipate ... We can dream of a truly non-Gnostic, nondualistic form of Christianity, which has abandoned the old idea of two worlds, which is not in flight from the body and incarnation, which will make itself into another way to affirm the world, the plane of immanence. We can dream of the Kingdom of God on earth, which means including those who are out – out of power and out of luck – so that the real economic order would begin to reflect the sort of systematic reversals that define the Kingdom. Who belongs to the Kingdom? Precisely the ones who aren't invited to the banquet or to the wedding feast. The Kingdom is marked throughout by these radical reversals and privileging of the de-privileged. (p. 159)

These are some of the challenges that face the emerging/fresh expression that wishes to live in the distance (and oscillate) between a community of character and a community of the question.

Conclusion

In this chapter I have argued for a commitment from emerging/ fresh expressions to 'raise to consciousness', explore and live in the distance between being a 'community of character' and a 'community of the question'. Put another way this is a commitment to welcome and make space for 'the other' in the never-to-be-forgotten knowledge that we might be wrong; that things might always be otherwise. I hope that I have made it clear that this tension is irresolvable and inescapable and that, even if this were not the case, to actually resolve or escape such a tension would be an ecclesiological disaster resulting in a totalising approach that is profoundly exclusive, oppressive and hostile to difference. This tension should be constantly wrestled with by all emerging/ fresh expressions as one of the most important forms of 'mission' (should we still wish to use that term). Another way of describing this tension is as the challenge of discipleship/character formation in the context of any ecclesiology that is also concerned with what it means to 'be' church in a non-foundational milieu that emphasizes radical undecidability and uncertainty. We should hope and pray to always be caught in this tension – a tension that is about success not through the development of perfect structures but through relational commitment, faithfulness and willingness to 'take the strain'. This is where disciples should want to be.

How serious are we about engaging with the full implications of contemporary philosophical and theological ideas that challenge our preconceptions of what an emerging/fresh expression is and/or could be? Are we committed to working out what 'church', and Christian disciples, could be in genuine fear and trembling? Might it be that to embrace these challenges and live with the tension of them (and be seen to do so) is the most effective missional and discipleship strategy of all? Does it make sense to speak of an 'ecclesiology of undecidability'? Of an ecclesiological approach to discipleship that takes both passionate praxis and humble agnosticism as inextricably linked? Of faith-driven ecclesiological structures and disciples that can deal with doubt, ambiguity, paradox and the always unfinished provisionality of our characters and ecclesial expressions? I am arguing here for the importance of emerging/fresh church expressions engaging in sustained reflexive (that is, reflexivity as a turning back on oneself, as a form of self-awareness) praxis.[16] This praxis can be based on the resources contained within these two approaches to 'doing/being' community that I have briefly described.[17] Reflexive praxis on the basis of these resources can, I believe, yield an ecclesiological 'excess': a creative relational energy that might help to figure forth new ecclesiological expressions relatively uncontaminated by the old. Might it be that such reflexive praxis, the taking part in a journey and embracing the tensions that come with living in the distance between a 'community of character' and a 'community of the question', is what constitutes an authentic 'mission-shaped church'?

Only one way to walk with God:
Christian discipleship for new expressions of church

JOHN M. HULL

As a teenage Christian, I always felt uncomfortable when we sang the hymn by William Cowper, published in the Olney Hymn Book in 1779, which begins, 'O for a closer walk with God'. The poet had, it seemed to me, committed (or perhaps we should say that he had indulged in) some sin that, or so he thought, had caused the Holy Spirit to depart from him, leaving 'an aching void the world can never fill'. The sin was not named, but I was pretty sure it had something to do with sex. When one announced a hatred of it, the holy dove would return. But how could one hate sex? This threw me (and I am sure the same has been felt by hundreds of thousands of people) into a desperate collision course between faith in God and the attractiveness of one of life's most exciting options. This struggle culminates in the third verse, when the singer cries out:

> The dearest idol I have known,
> What e'er that idol be,
> Help me to tear it from thy throne
> and worship only thee.

I now believe that these adolescent agonies were induced by a spirituality of inwardness, in which emotional satisfaction and religious demands were opposed to one another in such a way as to make it quite impossible for one to realize what it might be to walk closely with God.

Not until my adult life, and indeed my later adulthood, did I gradually realize that I had been duped by a spirituality that had made me insensitive to the world's sufferings, and had given me the idea that my feelings were the most important thing in being Christian, which had created a psychological tension that afflicted my life for several years.

All this time, the Bible itself was telling me how to walk closely with God, but I was unable to hear it. This was not only because of the preoccupation with my inner life and my struggles of conscience, which had given me a misguided concept of purity, but a kind of inability to penetrate the veil that hung between me and the Bible. The veil was the image left on the imagination of the church by its struggle for legitimation during its first few centuries.

Walking with God

When the Old Testament speaks of walking with God in the sense of pursuing a certain way of life, the reference is usually to obediently observing the laws and commandments of God. In Deuteronomy the giving of the Decalogue concludes with the following exhortation.

> So be careful to do what the LORD your God has commanded you; do not turn aside to the right or to the left. Walk in obedience to all that the LORD your God has commanded you, so that you may live and prosper and prolong your days in the land that you will possess. (Deut. 5.32–33)[1]

Similar expressions are found in Deuteronomy 8.6; 11.22; 19.9; 26.17; 28.9 and 30.16. This ideal of the religious life is summed up in Deuteronomy 10.12–13:

> And now, Israel, what does the LORD your God ask of you but to fear the LORD your God, to walk in obedience to him, to love him, to serve the LORD your God with all your heart and with all your soul, and to observe the LORD's commands and decrees that I am giving you today for your own good?

To keep God's commandments is to walk in justice because 'The Lord loves righteousness and justice; the earth is full of his unfailing love' (Ps. 33.5), 'And the heavens proclaim his righteousness, for he is a God of justice' (Ps. 50.6). Walking with God in this way is to know God for 'The LORD is known by his acts of justice' (Ps. 9.16).

This is why those who follow the way of the Lord are said to walk in justice; 'he is a shield to those whose walk is blameless, for he guards the course of the just and protects the way of his faithful ones' (Prov. 2.7b–8). In Proverbs, wisdom calls out, 'I walk in the way of righteousness, along the paths of justice' (Prov. 8.20). And if you follow wisdom, 'Thus you will walk in the ways of the just and keep to the paths of the righteous' (Prov. 2.20). This is why those who seek an end to warfare and forge peace between the nations are described as walking in the light of the Lord (Isa. 2.4–5). The whole teaching of the Hebrew Bible on what it is to walk with God is summed up in Micah 6.8, 'He has shown all you people what is good. And what does the LORD require of you? To act justly and to love mercy and to walk humbly with your God.'

In the New Testament letters, the verb *peripateo*, which literally means 'walk', is frequently used to describe the way of life expected of Christian disciples. In many of the modern translations, however, this rather beautiful, concrete image, with its hint of making steady progress on the journey, is rendered by expressions such as living or even simply doing. So the King James Bible, the Authorized Version, translated Ephesians 4.1, 'I therefore, the prisoner of the Lord, beseech you that ye walk worthy of the vocation wherewith ye are called,' whereas Today's New International Version says, 'As a prisoner for the Lord, then, I urge you to live a life worthy of the calling you have received.' Similarly, the AV of Ephesians 2.10 reads, 'For we are his workmanship, created in Christ Jesus unto good works, which God hath before ordained that we should walk in them,' but the TNIV has, 'For we are God's handiwork, created in Christ Jesus to do good works, which God prepared in advance for us to do.'

In order to highlight the metaphor of walking we will take further illustrations from the AV. To walk with God through Christ is to live the ethical life, characterized by honesty, sincerity, acts of mercy, and above all by love. 'Let us walk honestly, as in the day; not in rioting and drunkenness, not in chambering and wantonness, not in strife and envying' (Rom. 13.13). Christians 'have renounced the hidden things of dishonesty, not walking in craftiness, nor handling the word of God deceitfully; but by manifestation of the truth commending ourselves to every man's conscience in the sight of God' (2 Cor. 4.2). This walking is an imitation of Christ: 'As ye have therefore received Christ Jesus the Lord, so walk ye in him' (Col. 2.6), and its climax is love: 'And walk in love, as Christ also hath loved us' (Eph. 5.2). This love continues and enriches the Old Testament walking in obedience to the Lord, so that 'Love worketh no ill to his neighbour: therefore love is the fulfilling of the law' (Rom. 13.10), and 'And this is love: that we walk in obedience to his commands. As you have heard from the beginning, his command is that you walk in love' (2 John 1.6).

It is clear that to walk with God, to be in a state of steady fellowship with God through Jesus Christ according to the Bible, is essentially a horizontal relationship.[2] God is loved through the neighbour, and obedience to God is shown through seeking after justice for others. Any personal or direct relation with God must be on the far side of that walking, not on this side. It is not a matter of loving God first and then as an outcome loving our neighbour but rather the biblical model is that as we love the neighbour and seek justice for him and her, our love of God finds concrete expression, is enriched, and finds a closeness with God who has commanded us so to walk. This is to be in Christ, to walk the way of Jesus Christ, to seek to live as he did, the man for others. But if someone believes that he or she is walking with God and neglects the ethical, interpersonal character of this walking, such a person has a faith that is dead.

We must ask how it came about that the plain teaching of the Bible appears to have been lost, to some extent, and the interpersonal relationship was turned into an introspective one, as we saw in the famous hymn.

The Old Testament and the struggle for Christian legitimacy

Nearly all the authors of the New Testament were Jews, and they were caught up in a dispute about their legitimacy as inheritors of the traditions of Israel, and about their claim that the crucified Jesus was the promised Messiah (Barrett, 1963, p. 2). Early Christian faith was a form of Judaism,[3] at a time when there were many groups claiming the right to be true Jews, and the issue hung on an interpretation of the Jewish scriptures.[4] Christians tried to prove that their faith, although new, was not a novelty. That mattered a great deal in a society in which antiquity was a mark of authenticity. The classical world valued antiquity highly, as can be illustrated by the disputes about the relative chronology of Greek and Hebrew culture and law.[5]

One of the things the Jews, gathered in Jerusalem for the feast of Pentecost, found impressive about the speech of Peter was his claim that 'This is what was promised by the prophets' (Acts 2.16). The criterion of quality was prediction, and every aspect of the birth, life, death and resurrection of Jesus Christ was soon found to have been predicted. So the use of parables by Jesus had been foretold (Matt. 13.14, 35); his miracles were anticipated (Matt. 8.17), even the soldiers throwing dice for his clothes were fulfilling scripture (John 19.24). This element of foretelling gave an air of normality, of expectation, to what otherwise must have seemed claims of enormous originality. To those who knew their Bibles, the message proclaimed, even the resurrection of Christ, need come as no surprise (Acts 2.27). These things had to be, and to recognize this necessity was to be converted to Christian faith (Luke 24.25–34; Acts 8.30–38).[6]

In spite of the urgency of the demand for legitimation, significant traces of the character of the God of Israel do remain in the Gospels, and perhaps particularly in the Gospel of Luke. The concern of Luke for the marginalized and the outcast seems to have made him more ready to hear the message of the Bible (Luke 1.52–53), as it then was, or maybe it was the other way round: Luke's deep knowledge and love for the Bible made him more open to the cry of the outcast (Luke 4.18; 19.10–20). Perhaps this might have been expected of Matthew's Gospel as well, and we do find many examples of it in Matthew, but on the whole the concern of Matthew to give a theological rationale for the emergence of the Gentile church, in which strong Jewish elements remained, proved the stronger motive.[7]

There is some evidence that at least some elements within the later first-century church were well aware of the way that fore-telling was taking the place of forth-telling in the understanding of the Bible. One example of this may be found in the story of the rich man and Lazarus (Luke 16.19–31). This passage is often read under the influence of John 5.46, 'If you believe Moses, you would believe me, for he wrote about me,' but there is no Christo-logical element in the Lukan story. The rich man had completely ignored the presence of Lazarus although the destitute man was sitting at his very gate.[8] Perhaps he had never even noticed Lazarus was there. He was punished in the next life because he had not listened to the voice of the poor. He now wants to warn his family about the dangers of the fiery torment, but Abraham's reply is, 'They have Moses and the prophets, let them listen to them' (v. 29). They were to listen to the judgement of God upon those who failed to hear the cry of the destitute.[9] The one who returns from the dead is the poor man Lazarus, but even when the poor rise up against them, the rich cannot perceive the justice of God (Job 20.19–27). The Christian readers of Luke's Gospel might have seen this as a reference to the resurrection of Jesus. The idea, however, is not that the resurrection of Christ was fore-told in Moses and the prophets but that if you ignore the claims of justice, you will still do so even as a Christian believing in the resurrection. Christ's resurrection inaugurated the Kingdom of God, and the great reversal spoken by Jesus was now in full force, but to those who do not pay attention to the God of justice the resurrection becomes just a sensational nature miracle.

The need to establish worthy credentials did not cease when Christian faith was clearly distinguishable from Judaism, but continued with even greater vigour, because it had become an important aspect of a struggle between what had, by the middle of the second century, become two religions. This can be seen very clearly in the works of Justin Martyr in the middle of the second century, where the details of the life of Jesus are proven by prophecy.[10]

The result of this long drawn out situation of rivalry was that the meaning of the Old Testament, as it came to be known, for the New Testament was that of promise and fulfilment. The two covenants were related as type and antitype, as looking forward and as realizing that vision of the future (see Beryl Smalley, *The Bible in the Middle Ages*, p. 71). What was concealed in the old is revealed in the new, covert in the first, overt in the second.[11] The Old Testament became preliminary, and so the foundations of a theology of supercession were laid. The message of the law and the prophets could no longer be heard in its own integrity but only as a foreshadowing of Christian faith.

This way of approaching the Old Testament continued throughout the Middle Ages, and became even more prominent during the Reformation. Martin Luther's Christ-centred interpretation of the Old Testament led to him dismissing everything that was not clearly to do with Jesus Christ.[12] He rejected the apostolic authority of James because 'he names Christ several times; however he teaches nothing about Him, but only speaks of general faith in God' (Luther, 'Preface to the Epistle of St. James', p. 396).

This approach to the first covenant is still inculcated into every Christmas, when traditional services such as the nine lessons and carols teach congregations and the general public that the Hebrew Bible is basically a series of adumbrations of the coming of Jesus,[13] and such influential music as Handel's Messiah adds to this impression. There is a messianic strand running through parts of the Old Testament, but this is by no means its major theme. Not until the twentieth-century theologies of the Old Testament by Eichrodt, von Rad, and above all Walter Brueggemann was the message of the Hebrew scriptures heard in its own characteristic voice.[14]

We must ask, then, about the nature and purposes of the God of Israel. What makes Yahweh god-like is the fact that God 'loves justice' (Ps. 99.4), not that justice is a quality outside Yahweh to which Yahweh conforms, but justice is the very nature of Yahweh, 'For I, the LORD, love Justice' (Isa. 61.8). In ancient Israel justice was not so much an abstract ideal, to which the legal code should adhere, as the principal characteristic in the personal life of God, a characteristic that must be shared by those who desire to walk in covenant with God (Gerhard von Rad, *Old Testament Theology*, pp. 94–5, 370–83). The main concern of God is to establish a community of inclusion, where the aliens and strangers will be welcomed, and where unprotected sectors of society will be guaranteed security and welfare. Because God loves justice, God is known in the works of justice, since in performing such actions, the likeness of God is appropriated. 'The God with whom the people of Israel make a covenant is regarded as the source and foundation of justice and that is his first form of action' (Leon Epsztein, *Social Justice in the Ancient Near East and the People of the Bible*, p. 139). Moreover, it is only possible to walk closely with God by means of following justice in the community. Referring to the philosophy of Emmanuel Levinas, Epsztein says, 'Relations with the divine ... pass through relations among human beings and coincide with social justice: that is the whole spirit of the Jewish Bible' (p. 140).

Although interpersonal, the justice demanded by God in the Bible does not relate mainly to individuals. 'The tradition of justice concerns the political-economic life of the community and urges drastic transformative and rehabilitative activity' (Walter Brueggemann, *Theology of the Old Testament*, p. 193). God 'defends the cause of the fatherless and the widow, and loves the foreigners residing among you, giving them food and clothing' (Deut. 10.18).

In the ministry of Jesus Christ we see a similar proclamation of inclusion of the marginalized, liberation of the oppressed, and announcement of the coming of the reign of God. In that kingdom, ethnic and social barriers will be broken down, and religion will be fulfilled in mercy and love.

The early Christian community could not continue the same embodiment of social justice as the prophets of Israel proclaimed, and we may suggest several reasons for this. In the first place, as a small and threatened community, the Christians of the first century, and indeed, of the first three centuries, were in no position to create the social conditions leading to justice. Israel had been a state, but Christian faith was not embodied in a state until it became the official religion of the Roman Empire in the fifth century. By then, the state was as resistant to Christian faith as the Hebrew kingdoms had been resistant to the message of the prophets.

The second reason why the church did not sustain the same interest in social justice as the ideals of the Old Testament was that the return of Christ and the end of the age was anticipated. Hence the advice of Paul that slaves should not seek their freedom, nor married partners separate from their partners, for the end was at hand (1 Cor. 7.5, 17–31). So not only did the early church have no power to abolish slavery; they had no real motivation either. Jesus would look after all that when he came, which would be soon. The mission policy of the early church has been described by Stephen Spencer as 'filling the ark' (*SCM Study Guide to Christian Mission*, p. 46). The whole effort was devoted to snatching at least some from the wreck of society.

The third reason was that the early church was naturally preoccupied by its own struggle for survival, not so much in the presence of a hostile state, as in relation to the Jewish tradition out of which it was only slowly emerging. The Old Testament, as we have seen, was called into the service of this ideological crisis, and it never emerged. It was in the interests of a church that had entered into the power of the state to collaborate with that state in creating empire. So the demand for justice became the desire to extend the Christian empire.

Biblical theology of mission

When the church of today considers the meaning of its biblical roots for its contemporary mission, its view is still clouded by its interpretation of the Old Testament as predictive or at least preliminary. An example of this influence may be found in the various books that deal with the biblical theology of mission. These mostly interpret the mission theology of the Old Testament as consisting in the self-understanding of ancient Israel toward the gentile world. We find discussions about the universal blessing that Abraham's faith would bring to the nations, and about the degree to which the ethnocentricity of ancient Israel was qualified by some readiness to see the God of Israel at work beyond the borders of Palestine. So the books of Jonah and Ruth are often regarded as indicating an openness to foreign mission, but the book of Ezra is an example of exclusive identity. Such descriptions often conclude with an account of the missionary work of the Jewish diaspora throughout the Graeco-Roman world, which became one of the opportunities of the Christian mission that succeeded it.

Even David Bosch, perhaps the most influential scholar of mission in the twentieth century, makes no direct reference to the mission of the Old Testament but concentrates upon mission *in* the Old Testament, that is, the degree to which ancient Israel engaged in mission. In spite of this, Bosch in *Transforming Mission* is confident that 'the Old Testament is fundamental to the understanding of mission in the New' (p. 17), but he seems to see this mainly in the revelation of God as the One who acts, and whose actions offer a promise for the future. He refers to the essential character of the covenant between Israel and God as meaning that 'Israel is to serve the marginal in its midst: the orphan, the widow, the poor, and the stranger' (p. 18), but he does not appear to recognize this as the fundamental implication of the Old Testament for the historic mission of Christian faith. Perhaps this is why in the 519 pages of his book, fewer than four are immediately concerned with mission in the Old Testament.

To take another example, the work of the Dutch missiologist Johannes Blauw, when preparing his survey for the World Council of Churches, was mainly concerned with the extent to which the Old Testament offered a universal picture of the grace of God. In *The Missionary Nature of the Church*, he deals with the call of God to all nations according to Genesis 1–11 and shows how this gave a universalizing direction to Israel's self-understanding.

One of the authors that deals with the ethics of the Old Testament as a basis for Christian mission is Carroll Stuhlmueller. Oddly enough, what she derives from the Old Testament is not justice but violence. In *Biblical Foundations for Mission*, having decided that,

> We cannot deny inspiration to the 'violent passages' and still uphold the overall inspiration of the Old Testament. Nor can we relegate the statements about war and struggle to a few isolated and minimally inspired passages,

she concludes,

> Violence ought to be considered a charism or gift put to the service of God's people and God's providential plan, just as truly as any other quality, like pacifism or prayer. (pp. 42–3)

Such treatments of the mission of Israel and how it prepared the way for Christian mission may be surprising in some cases and convincing in others, but they miss the vital question as to what the mission of the Old Testament, as the word of God, is for the contemporary world.

Social justice or a personal relationship with Christ?

How far much contemporary Christian discipleship has wandered from the biblical model of walking with God may be seen in a comment made by a minister of a church in the West Midlands during his Good Friday sermon in 2007. He said, 'I have nothing against social justice but the heart of the Christian faith is a personal relationship with Jesus Christ.' This remarkable comment could be reversed, and would still be just as true and just as false. 'I have nothing against a personal relationship with Jesus Christ but the heart of the Christian faith is social justice.' Although this inversion has the advantage of highlighting the choice that the preacher presented to his congregation, it is no nearer to describing Christian discipleship. Whether we preserve the original or invert it, the error remains. It resides in the little word 'but'.

This contrasts features of Christian living that should be brought together, not as alternatives but as part and parcel of new life in the Spirit of Christ. The truth is that if we have a personal relationship with Jesus Christ it should, to be consistent, result in a commitment to neighbourly love, in short to social justice. This consistency or mutual implication is so complete that it does not matter which way round the emphasis is placed. The works of justice and love lead us to Jesus Christ, and faith in Jesus Christ leads us to the works of justice and love, where 'leads' means 'implies' and 'is equivalent to'. That this conclusion follows from the very nature of justification by faith is set out clearly by Karl Barth in *Church Dogmatics*.

Here is what he says about the righteousness of God:

> In this connexion it is important to notice that the people to whom God in His righteousness turns as helper and Saviour is everywhere in the Old Testament the harassed and oppressed people of Israel, which, powerless in itself, has no rights, and is delivered over to the superior force of its enemies; and in Israel it is especially the poor, the widows and orphans, the weak and defenceless. (Vol II, p. 386)

Thus Barth argues that God as the Saviour of those who cannot save themselves has a preferential option for the poor. He continues:

> For this reason, the human righteousness required by God and established in obedience – the righteousness which according to Amos should pour down as a mighty stream – has necessarily the character of a vindication of right in favour of the threatened innocent, the oppressed poor, widows, orphans and aliens. (p. 386)

The righteousness of God is shown by the pouring out of God's justice in favour of those who are denied it.

> For this reason, in the relations and events in the life of His people, God always takes His stand unconditionally and passionately on this side and on this side alone: against the lofty

ONLY ONE WAY TO WALK WITH GOD

and on behalf of the lowly, against those who already enjoy right and privilege and on behalf of those who are denied it and are deprived of it. (p. 386)

It is in the very nature of God to justify those who are oppressed by the powerful.

> God's righteousness, the faithfulness in which He is true to Himself, is disclosed as help and salvation, as a saving divine intervention for man, directed only to the poor, the wretched and the helpless as such, while with the rich and the full and the secure as such, according to His very nature He can have nothing to do. (p. 387)

Barth then applies this to the condition of all people before God, and so to the doctrine of salvation, which relies on faith in the justice of God before whom we have nothing to offer and no ground of goodness of our own upon which to stand. However, Barth does not forget the literal and political implications of the doctrine:

> there follows from this character of faith a political attitude, decisively determined by the fact that man is made responsible to all those who are poor and wretched in His eyes, that he is summoned on his part to espouse the cause of those who suffer wrong. Why? Because in them it is manifested to him what he himself is in the sight of God. (p. 387)

In this remarkable manner, Barth draws out the political implications of salvation by faith alone. The Protestant principle is also a political principle of justice for the excluded. Barth specifically refers to both James and Luke in this connection, contrary to Martin Luther, who did not seem to draw out of the doctrine of justification by faith this kind of social implication. Barth concludes this part of the discussion as follows:

> The man who lives by the faith that this is true stands under a political responsibility. He knows that the right, that every real

claim which one man has against another or others, enjoys the special protection of the God of grace. As surely as he himself lives by the grace of God ... he cannot evade this claim. He cannot avoid the question of human rights. He can only will and affirm a state which is based on justice. By any other political attitude he rejects the divine justification. (p. 387)

Thus the righteousness and the mercy of God are united. In fidelity to his own nature as a God of justice, God helps those who cannot help themselves. In his justice, he supports the poor with mercy and grace. Only by extending grace to those who have nothing to offer can God be true to his own nature as a righteous God. Thus it is that, in Jesus Christ, God offers that which is worthy of God, God's own grace poured out upon the lost and the excluded, and accepts them all in God's own justice, a justice that rejoices in accepting those who are lost. Jesus is true to the nature of God. And so becomes the righteousness of God for us.

Alternatives to walking with God

Much of the life and practice of the contemporary church has, as remarked above, wandered far from the biblical model. Some of the alternatives that take its place may be mentioned here.

Words of faith without faithful actions

Some Christians are so divorced from the real world into which they are invited to walk with God that they attach an almost magical quality to the mere words that announce the salvation of God through Christ. People are invited to give credence to these words, and this is described as conversion. One may, in faith, have a personal relation with Jesus, but there is only one way to be sure in faith that this is not the product of self-deception. This is how we know that we love God, because we love others. This is the fruit that indicates the nature of the tree; this is the walking with God that is true to the God and Father of our Lord Jesus

Christ. Any other claim to personal relation with Jesus fails in both the love of God and the love of the neighbour to which Jesus gave commandments, for faith without action is dead. Walking with God through Christ describes a steady, consistent way of life lived in obedience to the life and death of the incarnate Lord, and not an isolated sitting before his imagined presence. Such an escape too easily leads to a Christian life more or less entirely preoccupied by feelings of blessedness. However blessed, it is not, taken in itself, to be described as walking with God because it lacks obedience.

Kingdom of God words without Kingdom of God actions

This tendency is certainly getting closer to walking with God, but it falls short because it also stops short at words. The words are the words of Christian justice and peace, but they are only words. I give two examples of this. First, when churches pass resolutions urging certain reforms or policies, if the state or the other authorities addressed ignore them, it often seems that nothing further takes place. The brave resolution remains only words; words that seem to express a will, but the will disappears when the words are ignored. Second, in church services, when prayers are offered in support of the suffering people of the world, but nothing else happens, it is to be feared that the prayers are not so much the inspiration of action but the alternative. Surely such prayers, in which we ask God to do this and that, but take no actions in the Spirit of God to bring about the desired outcome, are almost blasphemous in their emptiness.

Uninterpreted actions

If apparently Kingdom of God activities are performed but remain uninterpreted by Kingdom of God words and gospel words, once again, actions and words have become divorced. We are to pray to be one so that the world may know, to let our light shine before people that they may give glory to God (John 17.21; Matt. 5.16). Actions without words are certainly to be preferred to no actions at all, but they are not examples of walking with God unless God through Christ is acknowledged. Otherwise, what we have may be a good works ethic but not a gospel ethic.

Here then we have a criterion for assessing those new expressions that claim to be, or hope that they might be, fresh expressions of Christian faith, ecclesial structure or mission. Do the Christians involved in the fresh expression make a habit of walking with God? Do the structures make the mission of God visible? And if not, how is this to be brought about? There are many religions and many varieties of religious experience, some of which may have as their content the Christian symbols, but if we want to walk with God, the God of the Bible, there is only one way.

Part 3

Fresh expressions: what this means in practice

9

i-church:
the unfolding story of a fresh expression of church <www.i-church.org>

AILSA WRIGHT

History

'Cutting Edge Ministries' was set up by the Diocese of Oxford in 2002 as an initiative designed to encourage and support new kinds of church. It was hoped that eight such churches would be in existence by 2010 and would then be self-supporting. Funding was received from the Church Commissioners for mission and this allowed financial support in the early years for these new churches. Five churches had come into being by the end of 2004, and i-church is one of the five. Ideally, what is learnt from these new ventures will encourage others to think of new ways to do church in their own situation.

By January 2003 there was a holding webpage that announced that i-church was 'building God's family on the web'. The purpose of i-church was 'to give people an alternative way to engage with the life of the church, to learn more about the Christian faith and to express their Christian commitment'. The holding page gave people a chance to sign up, requesting information about i-church when it came online, or to volunteer to help with the project from the beginning.

A little over a year later, in March 2004, there was a website offering the option to join the mailing list or apply for membership. The search for a web pastor to lead i-church was announced.

This search led to the appointment of Alyson Leslie, amid a media fanfare with a feature on CBS and an interview on the BBC World Service broadcast on 18 May. In the second half of June members of i-church were interviewed by Voice of America. A trial pastoral group was running and lessons were being learnt ready to apply to a larger membership.

i-church was dedicated at a service on Friday 30 July 2004 in the University Church of St Mary the Virgin, Oxford, attended by about 85 people. The service was led by the Bishop of Dorchester and was filmed and made available as a webcast. In his homily, Richard Thomas told of the overwhelming numbers who had applied to be community members of i-church, around 700 people. According to the web pastor's letter in June this was 20 times more than expected and there were an additional 1,000 people showing interest. Richard also talked about how appropriate a Benedictine spirituality would be to an internet-based community. In particular he highlighted the commitment to stability that would be needed to learn to love those with whom we disagree or who irritate us, without leaving the community. The other Benedictine principle, conversion of life, he said would be achieved by members committing to prayer, study and social action.

Purpose

On the webpage of March 2004, the purpose of i-church was defined in terms of three groups of people who were likely to benefit from membership. The purpose is still expressed in the same terms, although i-church has developed over the years of its existence.

i-church provides:

- *a Christian community for people who want to explore Christian discipleship but are not able to belong to a local congregation.* This would include those who are not yet ready to join a local church, for whatever reason, and those prevented from doing so due to illness, transport difficulties, work commitments, home responsibilities or the lack of availability of a local Anglican church.

- *an additional means of support to those who do not find all that they need within their own worshipping community.* It could be that these people feel alienated in some way or need more teaching than their church can supply.
- *a supportive spiritual community for people who travel, and who are not able to maintain relationships with a geographical Christian community.*

Structure

i-church is a charitable company with a Board of Trustees appointed by the Bishop of Oxford. The Trustees guide, support and encourage the leaders of i-church. They ensure that the activities of the community are consistent with the objectives of the Diocese of Oxford and the beliefs of the Church of England. They also monitor financial propriety. Episcopal care comes from the Bishop of Dorchester, who is on the Board of Trustees.

The web pastor supports key volunteers and provides pastoral support for individuals. S/he looks after the vision of i-church and holds the whole church together by offering an overview. S/he reports to the Trustees.

The web pastor is helped by assistant pastors who can provide additional support to members. In future this role is likely to be developed into a pastoral team that will allow for sufficient support for growing numbers of members. Small groups of a pastoral nature are led by members approved by the Trustees and they are the first person a member of their group should turn to for pastoral help.

Where possible, i-church follows the patterns of a bricks-and-mortar (B&M) church, and so has a Council in a similar way. There are nine elected members, each serving for three years. There are also ex-officio members – Assistant Pastor, Treasurer, Technical Manager – and co-opted members when needed. Currently the only co-opted member is the PR officer. A Lay Chairman and Deputy Lay Chairman are elected from the nine elected members, as is the Secretary. The Lay Chairman supports the work of the web pastor, chairs the 24/7 Council meetings and is responsible for the implementation of the grievance procedure. Council meetings take place continuously because they are conducted using forums, with the discussion being added to at all hours of the day and night as different members log on and read what others have written.

Among the key volunteers is the Lead Moderator, who heads a team of moderators. Their job is to make sure that the forum rules are followed by all members. They all deal with the complaints procedure, although the final say is that of the Lead Moderator.

There are also several teams of members working on specific tasks such as website development, *The NET* newspaper, worship, finance and welcoming. There are also Special Interest Groups such as Amateur Radio and i-church History.

Facts and figures

Of i-church members, 58 per cent are UK-based and 19 per cent are in the USA. Others are spread across the world in Australia, New Zealand, Canada, several European countries, Sudan, China, Thailand, Singapore and many other countries. The Mission to Seafarers is in partnership with i-church, and their members can be anywhere in the world.

Members join for various reasons: 43.5 per cent want something additional to their B&Mchurch; 15.7 per cent anticipate i-church being their main church; 13.1 per cent are exploring the Christian faith; 16.2 per cent are just curious and 11.5 per cent are unsure why they joined.

Membership has grown to nearly 300, with just under half visiting the site each month. Nearly 10 per cent of members are aged under 28 and 16 per cent are 58 or older. Over 60 per cent of members are male, which is not the case in B&M churches, where the majority of members is female.

The fact that i-church is part of the Church of England is valued by many members, although members come from a variety of denominations and none: 64.6 per cent are Anglican; 17.7 per cent describe themselves as Protestant; 2.7 per cent are Roman Catholic. The churchmanship of members is 39.8 per cent liberal; 23.9 per cent central; 12.4 per cent conservative and 20.4 per cent other than these three.

Nearly 50 per cent of members attend a B&M church regularly and about 35 per cent never attend one; 93 per cent have regularly attended church in the past. Several reasons have been given for no longer attending – lack of spiritual nourishment, poor welcome, shyness, health issues, family or work commitments, too much asked of the member in terms of jobs, sexual orientation caused a problem, moving regularly prevented attachment to a church. One-fifth of members have mobility problems and 30 per cent have health problems including depression, anxiety, agoraphobia, arthritis, deafness, partial sight, ME, serious illnesses or chronic pain. i-church is reaching people who would not otherwise have contact with a church, even if many of them did in the past. There is more potential to exploit here in the future.

The public website

Many churches choose to have websites, but as an internet church the website is an essential part of what i-church is. At first the website took the form of a simple holding page. Gradually it grew and developed. Looking back through the archives it is possible to see four distinct designs. All of them have in common the fact that they only show part of the picture. They are like the shop window but those looking cannot see what's inside.

The current site is divided into several sections. The 'About us' section shares the thoughts of some of the members regarding what i-church means to them as individuals. The purpose of i-church is explained and an attempt is made to show what goes on behind the public website – the chatroom and the forums.

There are many articles available to read – news, sermons, experiences, all written by i-church members. There are copies of *The NET* (our own online newspaper) to download. There is a link to the videos that members have created for Lent and posted on YouTube. That has been a very successful outreach initiative, with requests to use the material being received regularly. The total number of 'hits' on the videos is more than 12,000. Some i-church members have joined as a result of seeing the videos. Others have joined having posted a prayer request on our public prayer board.

The problem with the website is that what is available for the public is not representative of what happens in the members' area. The new website is being developed with the intention of making it closer to what members experience. There will be at least one discussion forum and chat facilities, including online worship, at least some of the time. This is an exciting development and one that will better enable i-church to reach out to those who use the internet and are looking for a church there. It will also be a challenge as the members develop strategies to help those who come to i-church.

Within the members' area there are various forums for discussion such as theology, Bible study, social action, ethics and fresh expressions of church. There is also an area for prayer requests to which there have been many wonderful answers. Virtual votive candles can also be lit. In the spirituality area members share items that have helped their walk with God and share ideas on worship and on a personal rule of life. There is also a relaxing area where new members are greeted, birthdays celebrated and jokes and games are shared. As not all members are familiar with all the technology, there is a technical helpdesk where questions can be asked. All these forums are seen by all members.

There are also forums that are only seen by those who choose to be members. These include pastoral groups and special interest groups such as Amateur Radio, Bible Study, Spiritual Direction, Worship Leaders and Vocations. New groups are being formed on a regular basis according to need and interest.

Live Chat gives i-church a place to meet for worship daily. There are four or five services every day. Some are more suitable to the UK but one is now aimed at those in the USA. The worldwide nature of i-church makes the timing of worship a challenge but allows for the meeting of a congregation from many countries. There are 17 worship leaders, some of whom lead at a regular time every week and some who help now and again. Special services are held at Christmas, New Year, Lent, Holy Week and Easter, Pentecost and Harvest. The issue of online sacraments is one that is discussed regularly. There are plans to have an online retreat. A weekly Open House takes place where discussions on the Bible or current affairs are held. There are also occasional visits from special guests.

Not all chat is formal. There is a café where members meet to chat and build up friendships. This is a very good way of learning about other members and developing a knowledge of other cultures. Chat is not something that many participate in but it is valued by those who do.

Ethos

i-church is a church for all people wherever they live, whatever their denomination or churchmanship. It holds together the very liberal and the very conservative; gay people and those who are not comfortable with homosexuality and so on. Members need to work at acceptance and moving towards each other rather than tearing apart from one another. In order to achieve this it is necessary to develop the discipline of mutual listening as much as possible; being open about feelings and apologizing for actions that cause hurt to others. All members make mistakes at times, jump to conclusions or take offence. Respect helps to grow integrity, allowing a community to develop, though we may differ in our views.

i-church provides a sanctuary, a safe place, a place for refugees from other churches. It may give an opportunity for a new start in church or a rebuilding of faith. The membership has a large proportion of vulnerable people. A model of reaching out to one another has developed almost like passing the baton of care from member to member. A lot of informal mentoring takes place, often between members of very different traditions, ages or backgrounds.

i-church is also a place of refreshment. Here it is possible to find other people who think that the questions you want to ask are important enough to address together. In prayer, members address both God and neighbour. In the uncluttered environment of the chatroom chapel, the words take on their own power and work to bring new insights and hope to those worshipping.

Members' stories

In the end church means people, not statistics or structures. It is their stories that make sense of what i-church is. I want to conclude by sharing a few stories gathered from members which reiterate what i-church means to them. I asked a cross-section of members to share what i-church has contributed to their lives in their particular circumstances. Each story probably represents a similar one that several others could have told.

For many of the members of i-church, mentors have helped them to rebuild and/or strengthen their faith.

I joined i-church as a last chance to rebuild my faith, it having been badly affected in my B&M church. I felt I was hanging on by a thread to Christian belief. In i-church I was listened to with patience as I went over and over my experience, trying to make sense of it. So many people mentored me and helped me to belong. Soon my faith was more alive than it had ever been.

I found one particular mentor and we prayed and chatted together, finding so much in common though we live thousands of miles apart. He encouraged me as I prepared to walk the last 100 miles to Santiago de Compostella to raise money for charity. I was sure I could not do it and he was equally determined that I could. Seventeen people attended a service to wish me bon voyage. It was an incredibly moving occasion. On the walk itself I developed really bad blisters but could walk as fast as most of those in the same group. I knew that I was being prayed for, and it made such a difference.

One member felt that it had allowed them to grow into who they were intended to be.

i-church has helped me to become totally new. I am now the person I was meant to be and I am able to exercise my God given talents to the full. I'm learning and growing every day, which can be uncomfortable and challenging but is certainly not boring.

It has also provided a spiritual haven for those whose jobs take them away for extended periods.

During 2005 I started working on a freelance contract which involved being away from home in South Africa and Holland. In particular, the trips to Johannesburg would be for periods of 3–5 weeks at a time, and I was not going to be able to 'do church' in my normal way! i-church proved to be the perfect answer.

For the business traveller, i-church does provide a link with fellow Christians back home and around the world. Once I came back home I found that although I was able to re-kindle B&M church participation, the contacts I'd made whilst I was away remained firm. Highly recommended!

One member was surprised by the spiritual intimacy that online worship generated.

The most surprising aspect of i-church worship is the intimacy that can be generated over a computer link – you might think that personal contact is required but I found the conversations I held in the café and worship in the chapel to be every bit as 'real' as those in a bricks and mortar church.

Another was surprised that it was possible to worship online.

I will never forget the day I first went into the i-church chapel online. I was sceptical. How could I worship God with people I had never met before? Quietly but dramatically that evening during Compline, my messy lounge was tranformed into a sanctuary. I experience Emmanuel: God with us, sitting in front of my laptop!

Members also found it a great support in times of illness.

About two weeks after I started attending these services, I was diagnosed with cancer. I posted in the forums and asked for prayers. Many miracles were associated with my healing and I believe that some of them were due to the prayers I received from i-church members.

People sometimes made comments of support in the forums along with their prayer. On days when I was feeling particularly tired or sick, I would read (and re-read) these posts. It was a great comfort to know that people cared about me.

The experience of praying and being prayed for through i-church was said to be transformational.

This experience has really changed my understanding of prayer. One part of my current devotional life is to pray with all the people who ask for prayers in the forums, responding in words, lighting a virtual candle or praying silently. I know that God is hearing me and helping the situation.

Members also described i-church as an extremely welcoming place.

A friend of mine mentioned i-church to me. She had become a member and always talked about it with such enthusiasm that it was easy to see that this was a church worth trying. My personal problems made change hard to cope with but eventually I decided to join; it was one of the best decisions I could have made.

Right from the start I was warmly welcomed by many of the existing members. Several of these have since become very good friends.

At the moment I can't even begin to imagine life without i-church!

There are two things from my infant membership of i-church that I will never forget, one is the astonishing warmth of the other members and the other is being in the chapel one morning when a member from across the world joined. We led each other in prayer and then stayed a while and chatted about our day ... like it was perfectly normal to speak to someone thousands and thousands of miles away about the daffs out in Spring !!!

Even younger members said that they felt their views were valued.

From the moment I introduced myself, I was (and still am) made to feel extremely welcome by everyone, and I feel that my opinions are respected and my questions valued. I only mention this because, as a teenager, this is not something that I experience every day.

That's another great thing about i-church ... on the forums and in Live Chat – there is a 'level playing field', so to speak. We experience someone's personality before we learn their vital statistics – which is a brilliant and almost unique thing for a church.

For those who are housebound i-church also provides a lifeline to Christian communities.

For the past four years I have had ME. I went from being an active missionary working overseas, to someone who needs quiet and can't get to church. The worship aspect of my life was deeply lacking. Since that first compline, I've made chapel visits a regular part of my week. The sense of connection with i-c friends has come to mean a lot. Even when I am not well enough to go online, I feel connected, knowing services are going on. It has helped me at more desperate times, to know I can post a prayer request and receive love and support back again. I now lead compline once a week. It isn't much but it means a lot to me to be able to do something – even if I'm wearing my pyjamas and lying on my sofa.

Others found it a place of healing.

I came to i-church bruised and wounded, and i-church as a church, as well as a Christian community, is among many wonders of God's grace for me.

While not suggesting it should replace bricks-and-mortar church, for some members, i-church is church in a form to which they feel they can belong, including those as far away as China.

In China where I currently live, there is no existing local Anglican congregation with which I can share worship and prayer, as far as I know. I attended a few Protestant church services, but felt confused and not at home. I began Bible study in English although it is a second language for me, and wish to continue in the same language. There is nothing wrong with studying and worshipping in Chinese – it is just I feel I understand God's Word better in English.

I am not saying Internet churches like this one can or should take over from traditional churches. The local Catholic Cathedral is still a physical sanctuary for me on some Sundays when I feel the need of good comfort, but I do not feel it possible to belong to a local congregation. For me i-church is special. It is my way of connecting to the Anglican and the wider Christian world. I value what i-church gives to and asks of me: members and leaders all full of goodwill and love, [I value its] stance in Christendom and missions to the world, individual commitment to the community and brethren.

Conclusion

i-church is not perfect. Members and leaders are listening, learning and adapting. For some the pace of change is too fast, for some too slow, but this is inevitable as members learn how to be church and community on the internet.

10

Dynamic tradition:
fuelling the fire

PHILIP D. RODERICK

A year spent in a Russian Orthodox hermitage in the early seventies proved to be a powerful shaper both of my spiritual practice and of my appreciation of the interplay between discipline and freedom, hiddenness and hospitality. The DNA coding of Contemplative Fire – <www.contemplativefire.org> the subject of this chapter – as post-monastic community and fresh expression of church, has its roots in the learning journey of my own interior seeking and finding and so I risk a touch of autobiography! As the hermitage, with its three monks, moved to mid-Wales, I came to understand the extraordinary role of spiritual influence, of seeds of truth blown in the wind and nurtured in the dark earth of lived faith. Participating in the daily monastic immersion in scripture, sacrament, mystical theology and 'liturgy after the liturgy' or service after the service, I became aware of the compelling authenticity of a mission that flows from holiness. Radical outreach requires profound in-reach.

In my attempt to do full justice to the rigorous simplicity of the eremitical lifestyle in a landscape of hills and harmonics, I was fuelled by Celtic Christianity's and the Orthodox Church's celebration of the world as sacrament. Stretched into fuller consciousness by these traditions' embodied understanding of the awesomeness, beauty and beckoning of God, I knew even then that this encounter would be instructive for my own contemplative discipleship. In essence and in energy, in word and in simplicity, in interiority and in the created order, Christian life was manifested in a way that I had not experienced before.

Though I was not to know it then, instructive for my future pioneer ministry was the evidence archaeology had discovered for the extraordinary ways in which gospel roots, wisdom teachings, and even the particular design of book satchels and beehive-shaped monastic cells, found their way to British shores. This, it transpired, was via third- and fourth-century desert and Gallic saints by means of coastal settlements and seaways. I came to appreciate for the first time the significance of communication systems and trade routes in the distribution not only of secular but also of spiritual wealth. A combination of pragmatic and spiritual acuity guided generations of merchants and sailors to tell their stories of transformation in the coastal outposts of Britain and Ireland.

What had inspired such zeal? These inveterate travellers had been introduced, either directly or by hearsay, to the followers of Christ, laymen and women, who flooded into the desert to find God and wrestle with their lives, their 'demons'. So evocative were the tales of these earliest hermits and cenobites from the sketes and monasteries of Palestine and North Africa, that the seafarers felt impelled to pass on their legacy. The twin themes of the contemplative and the apostolic that were to influence and shape Contemplative Fire in the twenty-first century had presented themselves in an earlier timeframe. The urgency not simply to authenticate but also to proclaim 'the mystery made known' (Eph. 3.3) was underlined.

The vocational quest of this young spiritual pilgrim revealed, through his studies, an interconnectedness between three elements: first, the mystical theology of the patristic period and of the catechetical schools of Alexandria and Antioch; second, the ascetical practices, earthy solidarity and idiorhythmic (in one's own rhythm) lifestyle of Egyptian and Syrian saints; third, the bold, artistic and missional response of the Celtic Christian communities to the call of Christ in the first millennium. Whether the consecrated life was to be positioned in the majesty and barrenness of sand dunes and scrub, in urban desert, or at the interface between land, sea and sky, the transmission of truth by means of a lifestyle at the edge was potent. This early Christian patterning of prayer, study and action came to undergird not only my own faith but also the eventual provision of 'sweet water wells' for those attracted to the reflective praxis of Contemplative Fire and its sister project, The Quiet Garden Movement.

In one of the formative conversations of my early twenties' quest, Bishop, now Metropolitan, Kallistos Ware, Oxford don and idiorhythmic monk of Patmos, articulated one of the key principles of the Eastern Christian perception. In the course of what was perhaps the first and only symposium of British and European hermits, taking place in St Davids, Pembrokeshire in 1973, Bishop Kallistos said: 'In Orthodoxy, tradition can never be static, it needs always to be dynamic.' That norm continues to leaven much of Contemplative Fire's commitment to re-imagine the faith and its outworking in our culture.

In not dissimilar vein, Jean Leclercq's article entitled 'Contemporary monasticism' describes Christian tradition as the manifestation of the Holy Spirit: 'the stream of life ... coming to us through the Church from the crucified and glorified Christ' (Leclercq, 1979, p. 7). Commenting upon this, Ellen F. Davis, in her *Wondrous Depth: Preaching the Old Testament*, highlights how

> Tradition in that sense can exist only in the stable yet dynamic environment established by active ministry and mission, worship, study, and interactive conversation about the things of God – all that ongoing from generation to generation. In such an environment, we may trust that the work of the Holy Spirit will indeed manifest itself in the periodic emergence of the radically new, which can be accepted and valued because it stands in discernible continuity with what the church has already recognized as God's work. (p. 83)

The phrase 'the periodic emergence of the radically new' could be taken as a descriptor of what is happening in and through the best of the fresh expressions and emerging church networks. We are called to become skilled in a tightrope theology. For those with adequate understanding and support from their dioceses or

districts there is a safety net. For others, that safety net is notice-
able by its absence and a 'balance or break', or 'sink or swim'
mentality has to be the survival strategy. As pioneer ministers,
together with our core teams, we are on the high wire. Whether
here or, deliciously mixing metaphors, we are swimming with the
flow, surfing the wave, the challenge is clear. The Holy Spirit is,
with quiet insistence, inviting each of us to be alert to, to dance
with the dynamism of tradition. The Holy Spirit is, I believe,
match-making between tradition and what needs now to be post-
postmodernity. The radically new is breaking through with what
might be described as a 'mystical realism'.

When disciples of Christ, all of whom are called to be 'participants in the divine nature' (2 Peter 1.4) inhabit the 'abundant
life' of Jesus' teaching, the inheritance of the saints will be alive
in us. No longer will 'the way we do things here' be governed
by traditionalism. Contemplative Fire's premise is that every
Christian has, by virtue of our baptism, elected to live in the
paradox of wisdom – in wild structure, released containment,
elected vulnerability. Rowan Williams, in a 1995 interview with
Todd Breyfogle, published in *Cross Currents*, said: 'Theology is a
language used by a specific group of people to make sense of their
world – not so much to explain it as to find words that will hold
or reflect what ... is sensed to be solid, authoritative, and creative
of where we stand. Thus theology is always involved with doing
new or odd things with speech'.[1]

'Theology is ... doing new things with speech.' Contemplative
Fire has, from the outset, felt an imperative to work with the deconstruction and reconstruction of language, liturgy, metaphor
and symbol. The deep structure of language has the power to
create and transform reality and relationship. This was heralded
in the first seven centuries AD by the Logos theology of patristic
theologians. Today's work in neuro-linguistics extends this exploration as it enquires into the efficacy of parable, proverb and
metaphor as catalysts for personal and organizational change.
Contemplative Fire's leadership training seeks to harness the
power of such insights. We believe that the exercise of reconstruction is costly but vital. As the word becomes flesh in our euchar-

istic liturgies and our theological equipping, in our experiential workshops, pilgrimages and small group processes, leaders and participants regularly comment upon the often poignant admixture of liveliness and depth, on the interplay of symbols and the refashioning of meaning.

'Behold, I make all things new' (Rev. 21.5). Such a focus, where centuries-old wisdom both retains and regains a vibrancy and currency, is received as 'pure air', 'new wine' by those of all ages who have felt stifled and alienated by what they perceive as the institutional compacting of liberational grace. Instead of what they have often experienced as jaded formulae, fixtures and fittings, such contemporary searchers are hungry to enjoy the freedom to create, respond and celebrate within a Christian milieu. Then, the momentum of faith that has found its fuel will carry the person into 'random acts of kindness'. Contemplative Fire seeks, in its work with small and large groups, to be in alignment with the theological premise that each person is made in the image of God. As God is the creative source of all life, so the intention and structure of the different group processes that we offer seek to foster spaciousness and the attendant creative imagination within each participant.

In affirming silence and solitude as precursors to service, it has become clear that insight that arises in aloneness needs to be tested in community. Contemplative Fire's small groups of Threes, Sevens and Twelves (or Open Circles) are designed to complement the individual's keeping of the community's rhythm of life, 'Travelling Light, Dwelling Deep'. Whether it involves awakening to the present moment through meditation and movement, following a programme of theological study or 'engaging with wisdom on the boundaries' through compassionate action, the keeping of this rhythm is critical and instructive. As the *Guide* to the community puts it: 'We ask prospective Companions on the Way who are considering making their commitment to the journey, to engage with the Contemplative Fire vision at different levels: the personal, the small local group, and the regional and national expression of this body of Christ.' The *Guide* goes on to talk of 'the willingness to be set alight by the fire of God' and quotes Luke 24.31–32: 'Then their eyes were opened and they recognized him ... They said to each other, "Were not our hearts burning within us while he was talking to us on the road, while he was opening the scriptures to us?"'

Contemplative Fire, authorized as an emergent, fresh and network expression of church, maintains that the 'newness' in which it rejoices is not in contradistinction to 'the faith as it has been received'. Rather, that the treasury of engaged belief, gleaned and garnered over the centuries, is the spiritual lineage upon which we draw, explicitly and implicitly. The semantics of sign and sound, gesture and posture, creed and catalyst, articulated in earlier Christian centuries, is honoured and re-imagined. For example, the liturgy planning groups in every Contemplative Fire community expect and enjoy a real generativity. The promise is clear: 'Where two or three are gathered together in my name ...' (Matt. 18.20). Despite the demands of diaries, these regular meetings of three to six people to build worship and witness are foundational. They are beginning to inform not only larger Gatherings but also house or mini-Gatherings. The resultant graced and creative zest draws upon the gifting of the Holy Spirit and upon the liveliness and depth of the lectionary readings. Also grist to the mill are the shape and poetry of early and medieval liturgies as well as contemporary insights from the arts, literature, science and psychotherapy.

Whether planning for worship in a barn or an abbey, in a school hall or a cathedral, the teams organizing Contemplative Fire liturgy are conscious of what has been called 'psychoactive space'. This concept names the potential of what lies around us, to be a container for and a transmitter of the sacred. Whether it is through the ordering of furniture or the use of textile screens, whether through a simply choreographed penitential movement or prostration, space and place, architecture and body become once again sacramental and are put to the service of gospel and life.

Essential to the 'call, equip and send' of those attracted to our dispersed community of faith is the convergence of the ancient and the future, of the profound and the playful, of mystery and the mundane. This juxtaposition of apparent opposites is inspired by generations of anchorites and Anglicans, hesychasts and activists, charismatics and contemplatives. Here we meet the inherent discipline of creation, the intricacy and subtlety of flow. It is with this dynamic that the church has wrestled over the centuries. How does the organism, the body of Christ, live this necessary paradox of faith and freedom, of content and process? Paul Lacey, in his book *The Inner War*, points to a not dissimilar aspiration in the Jewish Hasidic tradition: 'One puts off the habitual but does not repudiate it; when the habitual is seen afresh, it testifies to the holy' (p. 114).

Stanley Hauerwas could be penning a section of the manifesto for Contemplative Fire when describing the activity, the 'performance' of life in Christ and the necessary presence of a latticework of order that undergirds and nurtures all genuine creativity. After drawing the attention of his readers to fellow scholars who have also addressed this dimension, such as Nicholas Lash, Frances Young and Walter Brueggemann,[2] Hauerwas explores the relationship between performance and improvisation. In *Performing the Faith*, he writes:

If Christian faith is from start to finish a performance, it is so only because Christians worship a God who is pure act, an eternally performing God ... to be made part of God's speech lies at the heart of the Christian understanding of God. In short, our God is a performing God who has invited us to join in the performance that is God's life. (p. 77)

A point then follows in Hauerwas's thesis in *The State of the University* that is particularly pertinent for each and every fresh expression of church:

It is particularly important to our case that improvisation not be thought equivalent to 'spontaneity,' if the latter means 'undisciplined' action. Improvising, after all, is only possible within a disciplinary set of skills. A 'disciplinary set of skills' is another way of describing what we mean by tradition. (p. 78, n. 5)

'To some extent every improvisation rests upon a series of conventions or implicit rules' (*Performing the Faith*, p. 79, n. 9).

What Contemplative Fire has discovered in its recruiting, training and supporting of facilitators is the counter-cultural nature of our equipping process. In a hyperactive world, to privilege centredness and serenity in the midst of activity, to insist upon pacing and pausing, this is demanding. Our educational processes highlight the value of step-aside time, of time spent in 'the cave of the heart'. Hauerwas resonates:

> If improvisation is a kind of activity or movement, it is equally a kind of suffering, a pause in or cessation of movement, an undergoing, a receptivity. In other words, performance that is truly improvisatory requires the kind of attentiveness, attunement and alertness traditionally associated with contemplative prayer. All of which is to say that the virtuoso is played even as he or she plays. For music plays the performer as much as if not more than the performer plays the work; likewise language speaks the speaker as much as if not more than the speaker speaks the language. (*Performing the Faith*, p. 81)

One of the challenges in this militantly secular and yet superstitious age is that the wisdom of holiness enshrined in the Judaeo-Christian faith tradition tends to be neither known nor validated. Spiritual searchers invariably have only the sketchiest understanding of our sacred text and tradition. How can we transfer some of the skills and nuances of earlier modes of transmission? In this context, Hauerwas was clearly inspired by a delightful story of how the very pragmatic technology and wisdom of stone masonry was inculcated in a new generation. In *The Stone Carvers: Master Craftsmen of the Washington National Cathedral*, Marjorie Hunt tells the story of Vincent Palumbo and Roger Morigi, who had spent a lifetime carving the stone for the National Cathedral in Washington DC. Vincent and Roger were both brought up in the 'trade'. Vincent describes it this way:

> When you come from a traditional family you learn from the talking. What happened to me, we was in that trade. We was

talking about work anytime; at breakfast, dinner, supper, most of the subject was work. Think about this stone, how we gonna do this, who was gonna do that, we gotta use this trick. So you're growing, and you listen, and your mind, it gets drunk with all those things, and then when it comes time, you remember. (pp. 20–1)

Highlighting the significance of the family in equipping and training, Hunt observes,

Like a child learning language, he [Vincent] began to acquire a grammar of stone carving; he began to piece together knowledge of the various elements of the craft and the underlying principles that governed them. Sitting around the dinner table listening to his father and grandfather tell stories and discuss work, he became familiar with the names of the tools and the different types of stone. Little by little, he became familiar with the names of the work processes and specialized terminology of the trade. (p. 21)[3]

Every family and every spiritual path, to ensure its continuing savour, needs to develop sources and resources of sustenance. In addition to the medieval integrity of prayer, study and action, a further hallmark of Anglicanism and Methodism is the tripod of scripture, reason and tradition. This tripod provides the momentum for Contemplative Fire's open programmes such as 'Living the Mystery: the Way of Christ the Contemplative', and 'Pioneer of Consciousness: Jesus Christ'. Here, as well as in the bi-monthly 'Wisdom on the Way' days near Oxford, Contemplative Fire is wrestling with and reflecting upon the considered and delicate balance between biblical text, the teachings of the tradition and the renewal of the mind and of the whole person.

Martin Atkins, General Secretary of the Methodist Church and one of the speakers at the 2007 Fresh Expressions 'Hard Questions' tour, said there that fresh expressions of church challenge the 'gatekeepers' of mainstream denominations to be open to change, and to recognize that a mixed economy of historic and new ways of being church is both 'inevitable and welcome'. The identification of church leaders as gatekeepers is instructive in our context. Guarding 'the edge' is one of the prophetic elements in spiritual leadership as highlighted in the scriptures. In recognition that this prophetic role of gatekeeper is part of Contemplative Fire's calling, our strapline, intended to be a descriptor of this cutting edge ministry, is 'creating a community of Christ at the edge'.[4]

The efficacy of the mixed economy model will be measured in large part by the extent to which gatekeepers of both mainstream and fresh expressions facilitate storytelling and theological cross-referencing between the two cultures. Consequently, Contemplative Fire has now initiated 'Reaching In, Reaching Out: Formation for Mission'. This emerges directly from our own facilitator training and has been designed as a modular programme to enable local churches, deaneries, districts and dioceses to build strategic partnerships with Contemplative Fire. Lindsay Urwin, the then Bishop of Horsham, also a speaker at the Fresh Expressions 'Hard Questions' tour, rightly challenges church leaders to 'both rediscover the possibility of an encounter with Jesus in sacramental terms and to enable the experience in new ways for the sake not only of those who do not yet believe but to rekindle the desire in existing believers'.[5] In its commitment to further both the sacramental and the contemplative/apostolic dimensions of Christian ministry, Contemplative Fire draws upon the graced directness of *lectio divina*, the ancient monastic process. This prayerful engagement with scripture not only informs personal faith and discernment but also provides an exquisite methodology for the design of sacramental worship and teaching through the Christian year.

One of the primary contexts through which Contemplative Fire 'enables the sacramental experience in new ways' is the natural environment. This focus and context is pivotal, for example, on the 'Land, Sea, Sky' programme and also on the Contemplative Fire leaders' and the Companions' annual retreats, both taking place in the Pembrokeshire Coast National Park. The intricacy of nature will provide the setting for body prayer and a beach

Eucharist in Bosham or for a 'Pilgrimage to Now/here with the Christian Mystics' along the seashore walk in Emsworth or in the beauty of rural Oxfordshire. In more urban vein, Christ in 'the within' of the outdoors may be sensed and celebrated in both the vibrancy and quietude of an awareness walk in London from St Andrew, Holborn Circus and St Paul's Cathedral to All Hallows by the Tower via the Tate Modern, the Globe Theatre, the Golden Hind and the River Thames. As John Muir put it in *John Muir, John of the Mountains*, 'I went out for a walk, and finally concluded to stay out till sundown, for going out, I found, was really going in.'

Terry Pratchett, the hugely popular and prolific author, puts this fruitful centre/edge, exterior/interior charism in compelling vein. Towards the very end of his novel *The Wee Free Men*, Pratchett's young protagonist, Tiffany, says:

> 'There's always been someone watching the borders. They didn't decide to; it was decided for them. Someone has to care. Sometimes they have to fight. Someone has to speak for that which has no voice ... protect them, save them, bring them into the sheepfold, walk the gale for them, keep away the wolf.' Mistress Weatherwax confirms: 'We look to the edges ... there are a lot of edges, more than people know, between life and death, this world and the next. We watch them. We guard the sum of things. And we never ask for any reward. That's important.' (p. 357)

'Looking to the edges' is one way to describe the particular orientation of Contemplative Fire. Lay and ordained are invited and challenged, through small and large group activities and events, as travelling companions with the risen Christ, sometimes to be hidden on the margins, sometimes to be bold at the heart of things. Companions on the Way, the members of the Contemplative Fire Community, are centred on the mystery of God as Trinity. They are deeply committed to pattern their lives on Christ, yet open to learn from those who are examining different routes and pathways. They are researching and utilizing new and proven methods of communication yet conscious of the need to identify space and time to 'go silent and slow' in a fast-paced world. Members and attenders are encouraged to incorporate in their own lifestyles the twinning characteristics of the apostolic and the apophatic, of the priestly and the poetic, of the contemplative and the cataphatic.

Within the priesthood of all believers, each member of this dispersed community of Christ at the edge, as a Companion on the Way, is furnished with opportunities to step into his or her authority. Educational outreach and provision has, in fact, been one of the guiding principles and realities for Contemplative Fire since its inception. This is evidenced, for example, in the 'Way beyond Religion' series for small groups of about seven participants. The provision is of simple but evocative liturgies and resources that address the festivals and seasons of the church's year. In the context of an agape meal in someone's home, participants share responses to textual and visual catalysts from early, medieval and contemporary sources and then discern and respond to invitations and insights that have arisen as a result of the immersion in the theme.

The subsequent task is to do justice to points of intersection and integration between conscious and unconscious, heart and head, male and female, black and white, clerical and lay, privileged and underprivileged. We have found that core to the successful implementation of such goals is a willingness to embrace and evolve a rhythm of life that is congruent with the Way of Christ. The pure and applied dynamic and 'felt texture' of such a trellis or rule, both for the individual and for the wider Contemplative Fire community, will flow from the quality of attentiveness to the interior vocation to love God, self and neighbour.

It is evident, of course, that no 'fresh expression of church' is in a position to see itself as 'the only way' of coming to and continuing in the faith. There has to be a humility of intention as well as of definition. Contemplative Fire is one among many articulations and embodiments of life in Christ. For some, its particular style and ethos will be both challenging and congenial, stretching and nurturing. Each emerging Christian community needs to discern its place within the body of Christ, within 'the great church'.

It has to find ways to remain aligned with the living tradition that began with Christ and the apostles, and with its own God-given character and charism as that unfolds and becomes manifest.

As it touches the hearts and lives of people within and without the mainstream churches, Contemplative Fire recognizes both a real eagerness for and a caution in being welcomed into a community of belonging. The requirement for those involved is to offer openness and sanctuary. Like all Christian communities across the globe, we need to nurture our capacity to be awed and surprised by the presence of God in beauty and in ugliness, at the centre and at the edges of life. As a young organization we wrestle with the nature of authority and decentralization, power and sacrifice, responsibility and autonomy. In this encounter, we have come to know that authenticity is marked by self-emptying, by kenotic lifestyle and leadership. The community is learning by experience that 'life in all its fullness' is witnessed to by an inner joy at the fabric of creation, by the gentle allure of the risen Christ and by the nudges of the Holy Spirit towards a discipleship that proves to be both discipline and delight.

II

Who are fresh expressions really for?
Do they really reach the unchurched?

DAVID MALE

A leader in fresh expressions commented to me recently concerning newly started churches that, 'There are too many safety nets and not enough fishing nets.' Is this true? Are too many of these newly started churches that come under the fresh expressions banner really safe havens for those who are bored, frustrated or constrained by their present experience of church rather than connecting with those outside our walls?

Does it really matter whether fresh expressions of church are safety nets or fishing nets? The Fresh Expressions Initiative (of the Church of England and the Methodist Church) defines fresh expressions as churches 'established primarily for the benefit of people who are not yet members of any church'.[1] This suggests it does matter greatly what kind of nets they offer. To use the rhetoric of the advertisers do fresh expressions of church really do 'what it says on the tin'? The fresh expression movement has defined itself in terms of connecting with those outside the church and so the question has to be asked as to whether it is achieving this aim.

This issue of who fresh expressions of church are really trying to reach needs some clarification before we can proceed further. In terms of statistical analysis researchers have based much of their evidence upon the work of Leslie Francis and Philip Richter, published in *Gone but not Forgotten*. Their research was based on 27 in-depth interviews and over 800 questionnaires and was focused on answering the question of why people were leaving church. This research reappeared in the *Mission-shaped Church* report with some new definitions not used by the original authors (pp. 36–40). Those who had previously attended church but had subsequently left were rebranded the 'dechurched' and made up 40 per cent of the adult population. Those who had no attendance at church except perhaps for the very occasional funeral or wedding were now termed the 'unchurched' and also made up 40 per cent of the adult population. The *Mission-shaped Church* report makes a key point that there are important differences between these two groups of people, although they are often lumped together as those outside the church. The dechurched have some concept of church from their previous experiences, but the vast majority of the unchurched have no real sense of what church is all about. The report goes on to state,

> Thus it must be accepted that any approach at evangelism or community involvement that assumes we can 'bring people back to church' can only – at best – be effective for a diminishing proportion of the population. (p. 39)

For the Church of England the report concluded,

> The social and mission reality is that the majority of English society is not 'our people' – they haven't been in living memory, nor do they want to be. The reality is that for most people across England the Church as it is is peripheral, obscure, confusing or irrelevant. (pp. 39–40)

More recent research has been undertaken in 2007 by Tearfund (Jacinta Ashworth, *Churchgoing in the UK*). Their research is based on a representative poll of 7,000 adults. Although this was conducted 11 years after Francis and Richter's research the results are very similar. They concluded that 66 per cent of adults or 32.2 million people have no connection with any church (nor with any other religion). This group is evenly divided between the unchurched and the dechurched. The report concludes that, 'This majority presents a major challenge to churches. Most of them

– 29.3 million – are unreceptive and closed to attending church; churchgoing is simply not on their agenda.' Lynda Barley, Head of Research and Statistics for the Church of England, commented on these figures in *Time to Listen*. As the report notes,

> Mission opportunities are very different when to step over the church threshold is an unknown experience compared with attitudes when there is a known church to which they can return. The Tearfund research helps us to understand that the further people are from church (in terms of churchgoing), the less likely they are to attend in the future. (*Churchgoing*, p. 1)

Both these research projects help in clarifying the differences between the safety net and the fishing net. There is presently a large pool of people with previous or even present church experience who are looking for a reworking of church, or even faith, that is more appealing or satisfying to them. This group has recently been well documented by writers like Alan Jamieson in his book *A Churchless Faith*, but is this the constituency that fresh expressions of church have been created for? Is this the group fresh expressions of church should be trying to connect with? I would suggest that the main priority must be for those within this unchurched group. Surely this is where the definition of fresh expressions leads us. But this is the group that according to any statistics we are struggling most to connect with in any meaningful way. The reason for this is partly that we do not share a common language of church with them and there is no golden age that we can help them return to. Vincent Donovan, in *Christianity Rediscovered*, sets out the challenge before us when he says,

> do not try to call them back to where they were, and do not try to call them to where you are, beautiful as that place may seem to you. You must have the courage to go with them to a place that neither you nor they have been before. (p. vii)

We must be prepared to move to unchurched people and with them in creating churches that both faithfully reflect our tradition but in ways that make that tradition accessible and possible for the majority in our nation.

My experience of planting one of the first Church of England fresh expressions called The Net in Huddersfield is that our inspiration was discovering a local survey that suggested 53 per cent of people in Huddersfield had no contact with any religious institution.[2] A small group of us then felt called and compelled to try and create something that could connect with this group. When we started, the fear of local clergy was summed up by one Methodist minister who asked me if we were going to be 'a predatory church'. Another church leader asked me if our intention was to cream off the best people from his church. Yet we were quickly able to assuage such fears with a promise that we did not want to attract attendees from existing churches but connect with this 53 per cent. We made it clear in our publicity and on our website that we would not allow people from other churches to join us (as far as it was possible) and on a number of occasions sent people back to their churches. I am sure that this helped us to stay focused on connecting with the unchurched majority in Huddersfield.

When I knew I would be writing this chapter I rang up a leading researcher on fresh expressions and asked him if he could direct me to research on this issue of whether fresh expressions were really reaching unchurched people. To my surprise he replied that he could not. He added that a national leader from the Methodist Church had asked him the same question two days before. It does seem imperative that research is undertaken to help us know what is really happening in terms of fresh expressions of church truly connecting with unchurched people. It will be very difficult to conclude with any certainty the impact of fresh expressions without good qualitative data. This issue is not only related to fresh expressions of church, though. We also need to discover whether traditional churches are connecting with the unchurched through their missionary and evangelistic endeavours. It would be fascinating to see more research, for example, on how some larger churches are doing in this whole area. I wonder how much of their growth is based on transfer of membership or attracting those who have stopped going to church and how much through unchurched people becoming disciples of Jesus.

The unadorned figures for fresh expressions are very encouraging. This has been achieved in a remarkably rapid timescale since the advent of the *Mission-shaped Church* report in 2004. The Fresh Expressions website has over 650 fresh expressions registered while recent national statistics suggest that over half the parishes in the Church of England either have a fresh expression or are planning something in the next two years.[3]

Unfortunately there has been little research into these base figures so that we cannot ask the more complex questions about what is happening behind these headline figures. Eleanor Williams in research for her MA thesis, published as *Fresh Expressions in an Urban Context*, examined the statistics for mission in Ely Diocese Parish Returns 2006. The statistics returned by the churchwardens were initially very encouraging. Thirty-three per cent of multi-parish benefices were involved with a fresh expression and 27 per cent of single parishes. Williams then contacted these parishes to ask them some supplementary questions. One of them asked for whom these fresh expressions were intended. Their replies were very revealing: 17 per cent said they were aimed at frequent attendees, 44 per cent at occasional attendees, 10 per cent were aimed at anyone who might come and 29 per cent were aimed at non-attendees of church.

What Williams discovered was that one-third of churches in the diocese saw themselves involved in developing a fresh expression but only one-third of these were aimed at people outside the church! The first figure of total churches involved is very encouraging but the second figure does reveal issues about who these activities are really for.

We do need to ask if fresh expressions of church are being created, or if what is really happening the development of fresh expressions of *worship*? Under the banner of fresh expressions of church are we seeing the repackaging of our services to make them more accessible and culturally relevant? It leads to important questions about what are the differences between fresh expressions of church and good and effective mission and evangelism in a traditional context. The good news is that we are seeing churches who want to be more mission-shaped, who are considering how they may reconnect with people who have stopped coming or only come to the occasional service at Christmas, Harvest or Easter. I meet many church leaders who want to design something more appropriate for parents who bring their children to be baptized or for young people who stopped coming to Sunday school when they started attending secondary school or who joined a local sports club that plays on a Sunday morning.

I often meet people who say to me, that having looked at the Fresh Expressions website, churches that are registering as fresh expressions are not fresh but simply display good missionary practice. It can be too easy to criticize the many fresh expressions that don't seem to be doing anything vastly different from what churches have done for years. They might be starting something for young children or a less traditional or non-Eucharistic service. But for some of these churches a simple change to a regular all-age service, for example, is a very radical step in their context. We should not diminish their actions or their courage in wanting to change and develop their church's mission. But we also must not stop there. We must be thinking not only how we can reconnect with those on the fringe of the church and the dechurched but how we can also connect for the first time with the unchurched of Britain. This group is continually growing and includes the youngest sector of society. They have nothing to return to and not much concept of what church is or should be. We will need to take risks to develop Christian community that can flourish among such people. Let us celebrate the developments so far but do not let us think we are far along the journey. There is much further to go and some deep thinking and radical practices to develop.

George Lings, Director of the Sheffield Centre, has done some research with students at St John's College, Nottingham, working in a mixed-mode context. They are both studying at the college and also involved in a fresh expression of church. By questionnaire they are discovering whether people joining their placement church have any previous church experience. This is small-scale research, but initial results suggest the numbers of unchurched people joining has been small but has started increasing after three years. Ironically this is often the point at which some fresh expressions decide to close. It may suggest that we need to be looking at much longer-term missionary work to truly connect with unchurched people. Lichfield diocese has recently appointed pioneer ministers for seven years to create a church for the unchurched. We may be discovering that our mission to connect again with the majority of people outside the church is more complex and takes longer than we ever expected.

Anecdotal evidence I have gathered from fresh expression leaders also suggests the missionary endeavour of fresh expressions will take time. The danger is that we want to shorten this process for the glamour of instant results either for ourselves or for ecclesiastical authorities. Quick results can be achieved with those who have prior church experience, but this then gives a misleading picture of what is really happening in terms of connecting with unchurched people. We do need to be honest about what is happening, which is why further research is of paramount importance. Recently I read this comment on a blog site about emerging church: 'Being missional is one of the big objects of this movement but many of the churches I have come into contact with have not been able to reach the unchurched.' We must not abandon this opportunity to create churches that engage with people far outside the normal orbit of the church. For example, we need more fresh expressions of church that go beyond our normal cultural frameworks of race, class, education and interests. We need more radical models that are willing to inhabit the radical gospel of Jesus Christ.

Loren Mead summed up the challenges we face in *The Once and Future Church*:

In the Christendom paradigm the church understood its mission one way ... We have awakened to find out that the mission moved on us. To keep focusing on mission, we have to turn the furniture around and face a different direction. We may have to move into another room. For many of us it is going to feel very different, as if the world were turned upside down, but the function and direction of our calling demands that we turn around. (p. 58)

There are no 'flat pack models' of church that can solve overnight the complexities of connecting with unchurched people. I have been involved in church planting and fresh expressions of church for the last ten years, but I believe our certainties presently are more related to the questions we should ask rather than the answers we have found. I do think, though, we have discovered some initial indicators of what churches need to be like for the future, which at least might send us off in the right direction.

Church worship probably isn't the best starting place

Across our ecclesiastical traditions we tend to have default positions for our primary starting point of the practice of church. Our starting place may be the Eucharist, the liturgy, a charismatic 'knees up' or a preaching series through Mark's Gospel. The danger of starting with church worship, in this way, is that it works well for those looking to reconnect with church culture but does not hold much attraction for those with no previous experience of church. I would even suggest that the recent phenomenon of increasing cathedral attendances is often made up both of those escaping the pressures and demands of their local church and dechurched people wanting to make some reconnection.

I am not suggesting that worship is not important for the beginnings of a fresh expression of church. I believe corporate worship is vital for nourishing the mission but it may not be the place to make the first connections. If the *Mission-shaped Church* report is correct in claiming that 'mainstream culture no longer brings people to the church door' we cannot rely on attractional methods of connection that in the past have been so fruitful. Our previous proven method of putting on services and expecting people from outside the church to attend is generally meeting with diminishing returns these days.

I was fascinated recently to read an article by Sally Morgenthaler,[4] an important worship leader for both mainstream evangelical and emerging churches in America. Two years ago she stopped teaching on worship and last year she pulled the plug on her worship resources website. Part of her statement on the website said,

> But as culture has become incessantly more spiritual and adamantly less religious, we have become convinced that the primary meeting place with our unchurched friends is now outside the church building. Worship must finally become, as Paul reminds us, more life than event (Romans 12:1–2). To this end, we will be focusing on the radically different kind of leadership practices necessary to transform our congregations from destinations to conversations, from services to service, and from organizations to organisms.

The catalyst for the massive changes she has been making was the survey of a large church she had been working with. They had estimated that of the people they were connecting with 50 per cent were unchurched. They discovered the reality was 3 per cent!

We are discovering that those fresh expressions that are most effective at reaching the unchurched are often starting at a different place as they seek to establish outposts of the kingdom in unfamiliar territory. The places of connection seem to be more around service and community than worship services at the initial stages of the church's life. One of the best-known stories is that of the Methodist minister Barbara Glasson in *I am Somewhere Else*, and the development of Somewhere Else. She began this community in city centre Liverpool from people who gathered to make bread together. It was four years of developing this community before there was what we might term 'public worship'. Again it is important to say that this does not mean worship played no part in the life of this fledgling community, but it was not determinative in the initial stages of the emergence of a church. This pattern is repeated in places like Hirst Wood, Shipley, West Yorkshire, and The Lighthouse on the Hartcliffe Estate in Bristol.

There does seem to be an emerging pattern in which connecting with unchurched people through service leads to the creation of community, which generates its own mission, evangelism and discipleship, and this in turn creates a worshipping community as they express corporately their new life together in Christ.

The centrality of relationships and community

Many people in our society today are not only asking 'Who am I?' but also 'Whose am I?' There is a strong desire to belong to a community in an increasingly fragmented society. What people today are looking for is not meetings but relationships. Recently I was looking at the website for Crowded House in Sheffield, a rare fresh expression from conservative evangelicalism. Their emphasis may surprise many people, but their first two values were stated as 'mission through community and community in mission'.[5] I think that both those values are vital if we are to connect with unchurched people. The danger in church life is that we become isolated from each other and from our local context outside the church walls. It is vital that we are thinking about where there are places of connection with people, not only through church but outside it. We need to renew a vision for Christian community which is both deeply attractive and yet also profoundly incarnational. There need to be pulses of both inward and outward movements for any new fledgling Christian community. There must be an inward movement that draws people into creating authentic Christ-like community. By this I do not mean some kind of pietistic, quasi-perfectionistic enclave but the kind of community Jean Vanier describes when he writes in *Community and Growth*,

> There is no ideal community. Community is made up of people with all their richness, but also with their weakness and poverty, of people who accept and forgive each other, who are vulnerable with each other. Humility and trust are more at the foundation of community than perfection. (p. 47)

But there must also be a movement that takes this newly forming community in an outward direction that is seeking to serve its context and to share Christ by action and word.

We need a renewed confidence in evangelism or evangelization

The 'E' word has become a word of embarrassment for many churches and Christians today right across the ecclesiastical spectrums and divides. I was in America recently consulting with leaders in the emerging church world. I found them very happy to talk about mission. I even discovered you could attach the term missional to almost any concept. The problem came when you asked them about evangelism. The negative connotations associated with the word made any further discussion very problematical.

Some of this negative reaction is correct and many of our models of evangelism are very tired but this does not mean we should abandon this word. If we are facing the need for a new missionary initiative in our country as we strive to connect with unchurched people then we cannot ignore evangelism. The missiologist David Bosch comments in his article on evangelism in *International Bulletin of Missionary Research*:

> evangelism is the core, heart or centre of mission; it consists in the proclamation of salvation in Christ to nonbelievers in announcing forgiveness of sins, in calling people to repentance and faith in Christ, inviting them to become living members of Christ's earthly community and to begin a life in the power of the Holy Spirit. (p. 100)

We do need to rethink our practice of evangelism in the new reality we face. There is much hard work to do in working out what the role of evangelists might look like in the future. Here we may find much help from traditional organizations such as the Church Army, the Church Missionary Society (CMS) or the Salvation Army who are having to rethink their approach to evangelism for a new era.

We need to move from a church focus to a mission focus to enable people to live as local missionaries

Often the organization of church can be like a whirlpool of activity that over time mysteriously sucks us into it so that eventually our lives revolve around it. Church leaders can often doubt members' commitment when they do not attend services and meetings regularly. We need to be introducing a much more centrifugal dynamic that sends people out to live their daily lives as salt and light outside church. I was talking to someone today about their church, which is always encouraging people's vocation to the church. She has been involved in local radio for the last 15 years, but that has never been seen as a valid ministry that the church should be encouraging, supporting and praying for. Church leaders must be enabling, encouraging and equipping people to live transforming lives.

We need a ministry of steadiness in the present times

I already hear the critics lining up to write off fresh expressions of church as a passing fad or the next latest idea while they wait for the next idea to be unveiled. The danger is that the church becomes like the education system where teachers continually wrestle with ever-changing policies, ideas, schemes and systems. If these fresh expressions are really going to reach the unchurched we need to give them time. They will not be overnight successes that will immediately transform the church's present predicament in the UK. We are in a very different missionary situation where the majority of people are outside and they are not looking towards us in any meaningful way. It will take time and proximity to unchurched people as the church moves outside of its walls to discover new places of connection. I do believe that this movement of fresh expressions of church is prophetic. It is leading us on to what and where God is calling us. It may not be the ultimate answer but a further destination on the journey. Whatever its precise place in the future we must have the courage to stick with it. It would be too easy to say it's not really doing its job now in reaching the unchurched, but I believe it is leading us in the right direction and is providing pointers and milestones on the way to wherever we are going. As Loren Mead commented in his book *The Once and Future Church*, written nearly 20 years ago, in which he predicted many of the changes we now face,

DAVID MALE

'Without steadiness at the core, a steadiness that supports and studies the changes and innovations and then transmits the good to the next generation, the structures merely fibrillate anxiously and aimlessly' (p. 77).

The precise nature of the fresh expressions of church that will evolve to reach the unchurched is presently clouded in uncertainty. This does not mean that our present attempts and experiences are wasteful as we seek our missionary identity for the rest of the twenty-first century. Early signs suggest that the emerging communities of faith both locally and nationally will become far simpler in their organization, more relational in their life and both incarnational and transformational in their outcomes.

'Packing them in the aisles'?
Some observations on the Alpha course

STEPHEN HUNT

Questions about God have fascinated human beings since time began. Many men and women today experience a very real sense of spiritual hunger without having contact with a church ... One of the most frustrating aspects of church life, until recently, has been our ineffectiveness in reaching people with this hunger and getting them within the sound of the gospel. We have longed to find a way of enabling them to discover the liberating life-changing power of God, revealed in His Son Jesus Christ through the Holy Spirit, in a way that allows them to explore in an unthreatening atmosphere of love and acceptance. Until recently they have been hard to interest. (Sandy Millar, previous vicar of Holy Trinity Brompton)[1]

Back in the mid-1970s, so the story goes, a middle-aged male worshipper at a central London Anglican congregation of 'High' church tradition began to pray earnestly that God would do something special at his church. In later years, at a time when the church embraced a more charismatic disposition, prayer coalesced into the prophecy that something special indeed would happen. It seemed unlikely. The church in question was an inconspicuous looking building to be found tucked away behind the far grander Roman Catholic Oratory of St Philip Neri, next to the Victoria and Albert Museum in Kensington. Despite the congregation's early embrace of charismatic renewal, and with all the trappings of Pentecostalism that breathed life into those churches that subscribed to it, many pews remained empty on Sundays and the religious pictures behind the altar stood in need of restoration.

Pentecostal-type prophecies are frequently vague and fleeting; more than often lost in the ether, never to be brought to mind again. Not so with this particular prophecy. Something 'special' did happen at the church. In fact, three things happened. First, the church, Holy Trinity Brompton, grew to become a major base of the renewal movement. Second, it became a centre for the national dissemination of the so-called Toronto Blessing in the mid-1990s. The 'Blessing', as it was more popularly known, was a movement of exoteric and ecstatic phenomena that rapidly spread throughout the global charismatic movement from a church in Toronto, Canada, that was emerging from its own obscurity.[2] There were visions and prophecies, hysterical laughter, shakings, trembling and twitching to be observed at HTB (as the church has become popularly known). The traditionalists among the Anglican establishment were not amused. Professor Arthur Pollard, a biblical conservative, wrote in the *Church of England Newspaper* that such mass emotionalism and exhibitionism was not in keeping with 'Anglican decorum'.

Revivals of the Toronto Blessing kind are as inevitably short-lived as Pentecostal-type prophecy (see R. Warner, 'Ecstatic spirituality and entrepreneurial revivalism'). The laughter died down. The visions and prophecies petered out. However, the Blessing's departure exposed the growing influence of another activity originating at HTB and constituted the third notable development. This was the Alpha course that billed itself as 'a ten week practical introduction to the Christian faith'. It was, in short, a programme purporting to have thoughtfully constructed the simple principles of Christianity to be explored in a relaxed and informal environment for those unchurched who endeavoured to know more.

This was a far more sober enterprise than the Toronto Blessing, but it was not new. The beginnings of Alpha can be traced back to 1969 with the publication of the book *Questions of Life* that was initially conceived as a four-week introduction to the basics of Christianity at HTB. However, Alpha commenced in earnest in 1973 when it was developed as an initiative for HTB's own church members in exploring the fundamental principles of the faith in an informal setting. In 1981 it was extended to its current ten-weeks duration, in addition to a weekend on the theme of the Holy Spirit. Around three dozen people attended.

A decade later Alpha fell under the tutelage of HTB's then curate and now vicar, Nicky Gumbel. In 1996, as the Toronto Blessing was becoming a recent memory, Alpha went public with 2,500 churches in the UK subscribing to the programme. The figure had quadrupled within two years, so that one in four churches took up the initiative. By this time Alpha had also 'gone global'. A further decade on, 10 million people had passed through the programme worldwide, at least according to the Alpha website.[3] In 2007, 31,260 courses were being run in 154 countries and translated into 61 languages.[4]

The structure of Alpha

Part of the enduring attraction behind Alpha is its simplicity: simple in its conception and simple in its application. The course is generally administered in the local church in the evenings (although Day Time Alpha may be run largely to entice young mothers) for some three hours over the duration of eleven weeks (including the beginning or end-of-course meal for those 'just looking'). Ideally it is hoped that the course will be run at the home of a charitable church member, thus creating a more conducive and less threatening environment. A typical evening on the Alpha course, based on HTB's recommendations, includes a collective meal, a short period of worship, a 50-minute talk by Nicky Gumbel on the theme of the week through a video presentation, and a discussion on that theme for 45 minutes.

The overall three-hour weekly programme and its component parts are of interest since they have been set out to create a specific environment and produce calculated effects. Certainly, a great deal of emphasis is placed on the collective meal. It is seen very much in terms of group dynamics, one of the principal means by which the Alpha course leaders and 'guests' can gel, and it is believed to be conducive to creating a relaxed and cordial ambiance. The short period of worship is meant to introduce the non-initiated into church culture and set the tone for the talk that follows. Ideally this is in the form of a video presentation that features Gumbel addressing the theme of the week. Guests are encouraged to make notes in their Alpha 'manuals' for their personal edification and the discussion that follows. The discussion itself usually takes place in small groups of half a dozen to a dozen people, with the recommended ratio of one church member to every two guests. Course leaders, suitably trained at HTB conferences, are recommended to steer clear of argumentation, certainly to refrain from being confrontational or intimidating in the discussion groups. Instead, they are to encourage 'exploration'. They should ideally be unobtrusive and low-key, tolerant of the views of the guest or 'seeker'. If individuals become argumentative or aggressive they are not to be confronted by the course leaders at a personal level.

At this point something should be said regarding the topics, presented as questions, that structure each weekly programme. The 15-topic framework is expected to be rigidly adhered to and constitutes the 'basics' of Christianity. They begin with the question 'Christianity: boring, untrue and irrelevant?' and continue with topics that probably would not be amiss on any comparable course: the person and mission of Christ, faith, reading the Bible, prayer, the Holy Spirit and God's guidance. Others are more selective, such as the nature of evil, healing and evangelism. At the same time, the nature of the questions asked, alongside the substantive content of the answers, which effectively guide the weekly talk and discussion, all embrace a particular dogmatics.

These selected topics obviously also raise a number of further questions in their own right. Who selected them, and why, beyond the more obvious themes, are certain topics highlighted and not others? The more liberal-minded Christian may find himself or herself searching in vain for a glimpse of a social gospel. The non-converted guest may be puzzled as to why this orchestrated agenda that constitutes 'exploring' steers clear of more controversial issues, difficult questions and even doubt. There is nothing on the creation versus evolution debate, gay sexuality, or a discussion of other major religions to be found in this list. Indeed, the erstwhile guest might be puzzled as to why the course is structured with pre-set questions at all and why his or her range of burning issues and objection to Christianity are not likely to be raised.[5]

The significance of some of the discussion themes, as they stand on the Alpha course, should not be underestimated. By no means all churches embracing Alpha are charismatic in orientation, but, to one extent or another, they will find themselves exposed to the teachings and praxis of charismatic Christianity, albeit in diluted form. The distinct dogma of the movement, characterized by speaking in tongues, prophecy, healing, spiritual warfare and baptism in the Spirit, are neo-Pentecostal hallmarks that are stamped all over the 'basic Christianity' of the Alpha programme.

As much may be said of Alpha's two (sometimes merely one) days of 'retreat'. Questions may also be raised, and not only by Alpha guests, as to the nature of the teachings and ministry of what is often perceived as the pinnacle of the programme: the Holy Spirit weekend. Approximately one-third of the way through the course guests will usually be invited away. The weekend is so structured as to fall after the talk on prayer but before the session on healing and for very good reason. The Holy Spirit weekend (which may be held in a variety of settings) is partly an attempt to further enhance an atmosphere that is conducive – creating a casual environment geared to enhancing the relationship between guests and church members.

There is more to the event, however. The discussions, which focus on the three videos on the Holy Spirit, bring aspects of the charismata to the fore. This is especially so in the third video (entitled 'What does the Holy Spirit do?') where Gumbel speaks of the likely occurrence of charismatic phenomena such as speaking in tongues and 'resting in the Spirit' during 'ministry time'. This charismatic aspect is enforced in a fair amount of accompanying

Alpha course literature; for example Gumbel states in his best-selling book, *Challenging Lifestyle*, that,

> We should expect to see the supernatural display of the power of the Holy Spirit as part of his kingdom activity and as an authentication of the good news. (p. 53)

The McDonaldization of Alpha

While earnest questions might be raised regarding the strategy and content of the Alpha course (and we shall return to these matters below), what cannot be doubted is the success of its marketing techniques. Contrasting to the 'soft sell' of the faith, there is an aggressive edge to the marketing. There are Alpha brochures, a poster pack, sweatshirts and car stickers, the Alpha Cookbook and more paraphernalia besides that constitute a thriving industry earning £millions annually. Also reflecting this commercial aspect is the sale of the course's accompanying literature, much of which has been penned by Gumbel. Books such as *Questions of Life* and *Searching Issues* have run off hundreds of thousands of copies with a number of them rarely out of the top list of best-selling Christian books.

The mass production of books and other items, along with the standardized course and its content, more than hints at the Alpha programme's confluence with tendencies in the broader economic and cultural world. Elsewhere I have discussed at length the possibility of describing Alpha as an 'evangelical McDonalds' in the 'spiritual marketplace' (see Stephen Hunt, *The Alpha Enterprise*, pp. 148–54).[6] The term 'McDonaldization' is usually attributed to George Ritzer in *The McDonaldization of Society*. For Ritzer, the term denotes global patterns of production and consumption synonymous with the American fast-food company McDonalds. It represents standardization and a near market monopoly. What McDonalds produces is the same all over the world, the same items and the same image. Yet, what McDonaldization implies is not limited to the fast-food industry. Aspects of education, work, health, dieting, politics, and much more besides throughout social life, are subject to the same processes.

The designation of Alpha as an evangelical McDonalds may seem a rather cruel one. Nevertheless, the major characteristics of McDonaldization, or what Ritzer refers to as 'calculability', 'predictability', 'control' and 'efficiency', are evident to one degree or another. McDonaldization represents the height of rationality: its standardization of procedures, logically calculated ends–means goals, pursuit of monopoly, simplicity, and control over whatever is being 'produced'. It offers the consumer an emotional security that it is the same product the world over, with little deviation. Alpha, whether intended or not, has a near monopoly of this kind of evangelistic programme. Its calculated and standardized means are aimed at refilling the churches, while strict control is placed on what constitutes an Alpha course.

If Alpha is indeed an evangelical McDonalds, this raises further questions as to whether the programme is really geared to an *exploration* of the Christian faith, not to mention satisfying the spiritual hunger that is supposed to prevail among the unchurched, given its built-in inflexibility and undeviating party line. To be sure, innovation is not encouraged as Alpha, resplendent with its own copyright, seeks to be applied to all possible contexts. Like so many other aspects of the course, then, Alpha exemplifies a major trend in the evangelical wing of the church. Over the years there has been a tendency to standardize and 'package' Christian lifestyle and image, as well as mass-marketing God with simplified dimensions of the faith, almost as items of consumption. Certainly such is exemplified by many North American ministries with their mass-produced publications and visual techniques that Alpha would seem to ape.

There are admittedly limits to this McDonalds analogy. Certainly, there is a sense in which Alpha attempts a form of niche marketing that is synonymous with the postmodern economy, although this is arguably more a matter of strategy than orchestrated ploy geared to selling a 'product'. There is Alpha for students, for prisoners, for 'seniors', for the workplace, for the military and for youth.[7] However, only the latter initiative appears to offer a variation on Alpha's major themes, although there is also a further deviation: Alpha for Catholics. This includes supplementary videos and recommended follow-up courses, including 'Touching Jesus Through the Church', which deal with such subjects as 'Who Needs the Catholic Church?', 'What is the Mass?' and 'Mary and the Saints'.[8] Despite these departures, Alpha can be recognized in its shape, structure and image right across the globe.[9]

Designer Christianity?

Arguably Alpha is the first instance of 'mass branding', as its commercial dimension more than suggests. In this regard it perhaps takes contemporary tendencies in the evangelical realm to its furthest conclusion and represents state-of-the-art 'designer Christianity'. How so? First, the working philosophy behind the programme is to ease 'seekers' into the faith at their own pace. This is the 'soft sell'. Endorsing the slogan of the liberal tradition, while carrying a somewhat conservative form of Christianity, Alpha seeks to be 'relevant' to the modern man and woman in the street. Alpha claims to take people how it finds them and repackages Christianity accordingly in the endeavour to bridge the ever-widening gap between secular and church culture. This is perhaps most evident in the structure of the weekly programme, advertising techniques and gentle approach to evangelism.

This endeavour to 'bridge' is not just evident in the design of the course; its consumer ethic and the media used, in turn, indicate what has been learned from social psychology, group dynamics and business enterprise. Part of the softly-softly approach is not to hit the 'seeker' over the head with a weighty Bible. 'Sin' is rarely referred to in the context of Alpha and, to the lament of its more conservative evangelical critics, is inclined to be addressed as analogous to 'getting your life in a mess'. Alpha guests are not to be castigated for their lifestyles, at least until they recognize the error of their ways.[10]

At the same time, and underpinning the concession to niche marketing, is the working philosophy that 'like attracts like' – that people prefer to be in the company of those like themselves and that the contemporary world casts the population in very different social and institutional contexts.[11] Hence, the channelling of Alpha into the world of students, jail inmates and the like.[12] This reflects the trendy idea ingrained in church-growth strategies that potential converts have to be lured out of their former social allegiances and into new (Christian) ones. Gone are the days of Billy Graham crusades and the like as a means of reaching the unconverted by telling them 'how it is'.

Alpha also recognizes that people have numerous commitments and may only be available to take the course at certain times in their busy lives. Alpha, in that sense, thus becomes a variation of the 'liquid' or 'fluid' church.[13] The church adapts to people's lifestyles or, more succinctly, to the time constraints in their personal and working lives, rather than the other way around. This kind of cultural adaptation may in itself be a marker of secularity and recognizes what has been termed the 'new voluntarism' in religious life that accompanies the erosion of religious socialization and firm commitment to one Christian tradition or another over the generations (Wuthnow, 1993). In short, religious belief and participation has increasingly been rendered the subject of convenience and lifestyle choice.

Alpha: is it working?

Given its global spread, Alpha must be doing something right. Its success, I would conjecture, again lies in its simplicity; simplicity as a concept, and simplicity in its application: meal, video, discussion. For some detractors such simplicity is its inherent weakness: it lacks theological sophistication and has been sardonically referred to as so much 'join-the-dots Christianity' (Percy, 1997). This is a criticism that suggests that Alpha does not appeal to all church traditions and theological hues. Despite its charismatic underpinnings and conservative leanings, Alpha attempts to be ecumenical and user friendly. As noted above, it avoids controversial issues that have divided the churches for years, if not centuries. There is no mention of female or gay ordination, or the infant versus adult believer's baptism debate. Yet in finding common ground in the faith Alpha inevitably faces scathing barbs from many quarters. While liberals may search the Alpha horizon for a social gospel, conservative evangelicals are alarmed by the lack of reference to sin. Catholics are concerned with its origins in the Protestant camp, while Protestant traditionalists not uncommonly lament its appeal to Catholics, and all at the same time that Alpha is seemingly locked in its own hermeneutical neo-Pentecostal straitjacket.

Theological quibbles apart, Alpha has found favour in unlikely places. Even critics (including those within the Anglican establishment) of HTB's involvement in the Toronto Blessing could not be more delighted. Alpha has also been applauded by the British media. One of more 'serious' newspapers has declared, 'At a time when our churches are losing worshippers, Alpha is packing them in the aisles.'[14] But is it? Is Alpha all that it is cracked up to be? Is it really working? Of course, much depends on what is meant by 'working'. Its global spread cannot be doubted. Arguably it is the most successful programme-orientated evangelizing tool in the world. The lack of serious rivals is conspicuous. Those that do exist are pale imitations of the real thing and, as the old adage goes, imitation is the highest form of flattery. Yet, has Alpha made a significant dent in church decline? I suspect that in the UK (and I would suggest in North America as well) it has not. In other parts of the world, starved of anything particularly innovating, it may have made inroads. In the UK (and this chapter is limited to appraising the course in this context) the churches are simply not filling up again: the aisles are not 'packed' with new converts or prodigals. The evidence simply is not there. The subsidiary question, then, is why Alpha is not working in the respect of gaining a significant number of converts? We shall return shortly to the whys and wherefores after briefly addressing the proofs that Alpha is not doing the job.

First, we have to look at who is attracted to Alpha courses. Are there limits to the types of people it appeals to as 'guests', despite Alpha's niche marketing? There is evidence that a fair constituent of the UK population know about Alpha. In 2003, according to Mori opinion poll findings, some 20 per cent of the population had heard of the programme. Two years earlier, the same poll found that 15 per cent recognized the logo of a man carrying a large question mark (presumably asking the great questions of life) displayed on church notice boards, advertising hoardings and the back of buses. But the same people were not, in any great number, enlisting on the course, at least the unchurched were not. My nationwide survey (Hunt, 2004, ch. 10), found that nearly 60 per cent of those enlisted were already members of the churches running the course and a further 14 per cent were on the 'fringes' of the church with Alpha seemingly further roping them in. Only 8 per cent designated themselves as non-believers, of whom a third had some experience of church as a child or teenager.

Further evidence points to the limited social composition of Alpha guests. Whatever the attractions of Alpha, its cultural image overwhelmingly appeals to Middle England. The survey found that over 85 per cent were from the professions or clerical and administrative backgrounds. Conspicuously missing were those of a manual background. It follows that such guests were reasonably well educated. Some 20 per cent could claim a degree or professional qualification, a further 32 per cent had been educated to the level of certificate or diploma.

There were other demographic features of those attending Alpha courses. The fact that over 50 per cent were aged between 30 and 50 years old suggests that the programme does not appeal to younger and older people. While we should not be surprised that twice as many women as men were attracted to Alpha (given that the same ratio attend church regularly), it does not appeal to ethnic minorities. Over 85 per cent of those subscribing to Alpha described themselves as 'white'. The picture, then, is that Alpha has an attraction to certain social demographics and not others.

Accepting that there is a limited appeal of Alpha by church and demographic background, how many converts has Alpha recruited? This is, of course, an imponderable given that 'conversion' is a difficult term to grapple with and impossible to quantify. My survey of some three dozen churches, and a handful of prisons and universities, suggests that converts were made but that they were few and far between. Certainly, this does not augur well for mass conversions and churches packed to the rafters. Plausibly, spiritual enlightenment may come further down the road. Alpha presented the basics. There is time to ponder and reflect, then the penny drops at some future date during the spiritual journeying. Yet can we seriously expect a sizeable reversal in those gloomy periodic church attendance statistics that are usually given to indicate the health of Christianity today?

Alpha and 'emerging expressions'

Perhaps not too much should be made of church attendance statistics. Maybe the equation is wrong. It is fashionable to suggest that there is a fair amount of 'believing without belonging'.[15] There is evidence that a good number of people in the UK still believe in God and heaven.[16] Over 70 per cent claim to be 'Christian' (UK National Census, 2001). However, they are far less inclined to subscribe to traditional views of hell and sin in what constitutes a pick 'n' mix Christianity. These are all indications that the foundations of the generationally received faith are being fairly rapidly eroded.

Can anything save the day if Alpha cannot? Much at the moment is made of 'emerging', 'new' or 'fresh expressions' of Christianity, often articulated by a nebulous 'emerging' or 'emergent' church. From its humble beginnings Alpha, despite its difficulties, has been the new expression and success story of the last decade. Now there is a very radical version of the 'new'. It is, however, very difficult to pin down. Scot McKnight nonetheless, in his article 'Five streams in the emerging church', attempts to capture the spirit of the 'emerging' movement ('movement' itself being an unsatisfactory description) as 'the global reshaping of how to "do church" in postmodern culture'. Proponents have alternately referred to themselves as 'postmodern', 'post-conservative', 'post-liberal', 'post-evangelical', and even 'post-Protestant' Christians. What 'emergents' like is the 'fluid church', engaging with postmodern culture, celebrating post-evangelicalism, dialogue, embracing 'authentic' Christianity, the internet and Derrida. What they don't like are metanarratives, foundational theology, 'traditional church mode' nor state-of-the-art, pre-packaged, designer evangelicalism that espouses the self-evidently true. They probably wouldn't like Alpha either.

Those who subscribe to the various expressions of the 'emergent' movement frequently attend local independent churches, 'house churches', or loosely bounded 'meetings'. Others are derived from groupings within the mainline Christian denominations. Collectively, they seek new expressions of evangelism through being relevant to postmodern culture and the localized setting that may or may not include congregational-based initiatives. 'Emerging' Christians, by being 'authentic', wish to reach all and sundry, not just Middle England. They are also doubters, explorers, and critics of their Christian heritage. They are 'in house' 'bloggers' who freely express, forging virtual internet communities with endless fresh ideas.

Is this the way forward if Alpha has, for all intents and purposes, failed? Is it time for a rethink or refit? Are fresh expressions a major way of reaching the unreached? Some siren voices howl at more cultural concessions. But perhaps this is necessary to be 'relevant', to circumvent the 'churched' part of the equation. Yet, there is more to consider. The matter of bridging culture was put to me by an Anglican university chaplain that I interviewed for my book, *The Alpha Enterprise*:

> Twenty years ago the problem for the evangelical enterprise was trying to bridge the gap between God and man. Now there is a cultural gap, a second bridge if you like. There is a lack of any biblical knowledge and Christian basis among students ... they do not know what the questions are. Alpha answers the questions but does not adequately raise them. (p. 214)

With every turn of the cultural wheel the gap between the secular and Christian worlds widens and the secular world is increasingly materialist and consumerist. The new temples are the supermarkets and shopping malls. People want innovation, variety and entertainment. Do they want to ask their own questions? Do they have questions at all? Is the spiritual hunger really out there? It is a negative note to end on, but the seeking may simply not be present. Alpha posters in the 1990s carried such slogans as 'Job, car, girlfriend, season ticket to United. Still not satisfied?' Perhaps the average young British male is happy with his lot. 'You're born. You live. You die. End of story.' Perhaps the average person in the street thinks that it is. '(Alpha) An opportunity to explore the meaning to life.' Perhaps people have no wish to explore.

Of course, the lack of spiritual hunger does not detract from the calling of Christian mission. 'Fresh expressions' may seek a way forward. They 'explore' and ask their own questions, but they are not the same that Alpha asks. The questions fronted by fresh expressions, at least certain elements of them, are forged in 'doubt', and with doubt the foundations crumble and the questions themselves become blurred. The man and woman in the street may not want a foundational Christianity. Equally, they may not want flights of philosophical fancy. Disinterest in either may, in turn, be indicative of quite how far down the secular road we have travelled and how insidious the prevalence of mammon has become.

Part 4

Do we really want to promote a 'mixed economy'?

13

Do we need a mixed economy?

MICHAEL MOYNAGH

The phrase 'mixed economy' church, originally used by Archbishop Rowan Williams, refers to fresh expressions and 'inherited' churches existing alongside each other, within the same denomination, in relationships of mutual respect and support.[1]

Criticisms of the mixed economy

The idea of the mixed economy has been challenged from several angles. From within emerging church circles, inherited church is sometimes seen as the heart of the problem. The institutional church, it is said, is stuck in a Christendom way of doing things – it is hierarchical, often quite formal and has lost touch with contemporary culture.

It is associated with the bygone age of manufacturing, manual work, men's clubs, empire and dogmatic beliefs that many people now find distinctly off-putting. For the sake of mission, if for no other reason, we should leave it behind and start afresh.

A weak version of this argument claims that despite its attempts to do otherwise, inherited church will strangle fresh expressions. New forms of church will be stifled by accountability arrangements, traditional views of ordination ('You can't celebrate Communion, you haven't got a priest') and attempts to institutionalize them ('When are you going to contribute to the parish share?').

The mixed economy has also been criticized from within the institutional church. Some people do not like the distinction between fresh expressions and other forms of church. It risks the implication that fresh expressions are where life and energy exist, whereas inherited churches are little more than 'stale' opposites.

Other people wonder how many fresh expressions are durable. Many seem fragile, flaky and theologically lightweight. Will they stand the test of time or will they be just another fad? Is the inherited church diverting scarce resources into a succession of cul-de-sacs?

Others again fear that fresh expressions are selling out to contemporary culture. They collude with consumerism without offering an effective critique. They reflect a post-institutional culture that distrusts organization, preferring fluid relationships instead. Yet in today's world, if you want to change society you have to be intentional, structured, planned and committed, features that are not always present in fresh expressions.

A response to these criticisms

These challenges contain much truth, but they do not rule out the possibility of a fruitful mixed economy between inherited church and fresh expressions. Several points can be made in response.

First, while much of church may be associated with a past age, this does not mean that church cannot adapt to the very different world that is emerging today. Other organizations have done so. The music industry, for example, has reinvented itself, and one could point to many other business examples. Much of the charity sector has successfully adapted to its changing environment. Fresh expressions represents one (but by no means the only) attempt by some denominations to adapt too.

The jury is still out on how successful these denominations will be. There is, as some critics fear, a real danger that fresh expressions will be institutionalized to death – that in seeking to control new forms of church, the denominations will throttle them. Much will depend on how 'light touch' accountability and other arrangements prove to be.

The Church of England's Dioceses, Pastoral and Mission Measure, due to come into effect in 2008, contains provisions designed to free up existing structures and make it easier to start a fresh expression.[2] The Church of England is also resourcing ordained pioneer ministers who have a specific calling to develop new forms of church. Might these and other initiatives suggest that the institutional church has the capacity to adapt to its changing environment?

The 1960s broadcaster and journalist Malcolm Muggeridge once claimed that ecumenism reminded him of watching the pubs turn out at night. Everyone would be propping each other up lest they all fell down. As declining numbers weaken the mainstream churches in much of Britain, might the sharing of resources in a mixed economy be one of the elements that reverses the decline?

Second, there is a difference between inherited and fresh expressions of church in their approaches to evangelism and mission. Inherited churches tend to have an attractional, come-to-us approach. Activities on the church's fringe are often seen as stepping-stones to the 'main' church on Sunday. Fresh expressions, on the other hand, have an incarnational, we'll-come-to-you mindset. Fringe activities, for example, may be encouraged to grow into distinct forms of church in their own right.

We would do ourselves a disservice if we failed to acknowledge this difference. If we pretended that inherited churches and fresh expressions were the same, as those who resist this distinction seem to imply, it would be almost impossible to describe accurately developments in the church today.

To avoid inherited church being seen as 'stale', it may be more helpful to consider whether inherited and fresh expressions of church have different callings, both equally valid. We return to this in the next section.

Third, while it is true that many fresh expressions are fragile and some have proved temporary, there are plenty of more fruitful and durable examples. A number can be found on the Fresh Expressions website <www.freshexpressions.org.uk>.

We are still at an early stage. The first wave of pioneers flew largely blind, 'making it up as they went along', even though sound principles of church planting existed in the literature and in some of the courses available. The experiences of these pioneers, together with established church planting principles, has made it possible to begin to describe helpful methodologies for developing fresh expressions (see <www.sharetheguide.org>). As these methodologies are more widely understood, might the next generation of fresh expressions prove more durable and soundly based?

Fourth, the critics are again partly right when they say that fresh expressions reflect cultural trends, often around consumption, and appear to be socially conservative. But this is by no means true of all fresh expressions.

One, for example, encourages its members to write letters on behalf of Amnesty International and other NGOs as part of their worship. Other fresh expressions have been started among people on the margins of society. Others still aspire to be countercultural. Only time will tell, however, whether fresh expressions as a whole succeed in being more socially radical than inherited church, by and large, has managed to be.

A theological basis for the mixed economy

A theological case for the mixed economy starts with believers' unity in Christ. All are baptized into the one body. The mixed economy seeks to give expression to this. It wants to avoid the hurt that would be caused to many in established churches if fresh expressions disowned their heritage, and the pain that many pioneers of fresh expressions would feel if existing denominations and traditions said that there was no room for them.

The book of Acts models the mixed economy for us. Ray Anderson in *An Emergent Theology for Emerging Churches* has argued that the Jerusalem church was rather like today's inherited churches, whereas the Antioch church was closer to fresh expressions. He highlights the conflicts between the two and leaves the distinct impression that Antioch was superior. We would want to be more generous to Jerusalem and to emphasize – alongside their disagreements – both churches' mutual respect and interdependence.

The Jerusalem church had parallels with inherited churches today. It had a 'you come to us' mindset. It emerged among Jews who had gathered in Jerusalem from across the known world to celebrate Pentecost (Acts 2.5), and its early growth was based on people coming to Jerusalem from the towns nearby (Acts 5.16). Its first instinct (though not its last) was that Gentile converts should conform to its way of being church. There was strong pressure – largely resisted – for Gentile converts to be circumcised and to observe other ceremonial practices (Acts 15.1–21; Gal. 2.11–16).

The Jerusalem church developed effective mission to its hinterland. In particular, Philip and Peter travelled in Samaria and Judaea preaching the gospel with considerable fruitfulness and encouraging the new believers (Acts 8.1–40; 9.32–10.48; 21.20). Many parts of the inherited church today remain highly fruitful in reaching their 'hinterland' – people who have been brought up within the orbit of church but have ceased to attend. Conventional forms of evangelism and church planting can be effective in drawing them back.

The Jerusalem church even bore some fruit beyond the Jewish and Samaritan populations – think of the Gentile Cornelius. Inherited church can point to similar, if limited, fruitfulness beyond its hinterland.

Jerusalem had a more traditional mindset than Antioch, with a strong emphasis on being true to its Jewish inheritance. Jewish converts were 'zealous for the law' (Acts 21.20). Though causing division at the time, this love of tradition has proved a great blessing to the church, giving Christianity deep Jewish roots.

Acts 6.7 mentions that a large number of priests believed in Christ. Wouldn't these priests have spent hours discussing how their new faith meshed with their Jewish traditions? No doubt Paul learnt much from these discussions, perhaps helping him to make his great synthesis of the Old Testament and Jesus. In a similar vein, the traditions of inherited church can greatly enhance fresh expressions today. Emerging Christians can be rooted in a rich history of faith.

The Antioch church, on the other hand, was more like fresh expressions. It launched a 'we'll come to you' mission. Rather than waiting for potential converts to come to Antioch, it sent out Paul and Barnabas to plant churches across Asia Minor. In doing this, it was faithful to its own origins in incarnational mission.

Converts from Cyprus and Cyrene had gone to Antioch and evangelized the Greeks, reaching people who had been ignored by the original Jewish missionaries (Acts 11.19–20).

It bore much fruit beyond Judaea and Samaria. Antioch reached Gentiles whom the Jerusalem church was unable to connect with, just as fresh expressions – we pray – will increasingly serve people beyond the reach of inherited church. In doing this, the Antioch church developed new patterns of leadership and worship.

For example, it seems that Christians would gather together for a meal, to which everyone was invited and in which there might be a talk about Jesus. Those who were baptized would then go on to a second stage, when they took the leftover bread from the meal and celebrated communion.[3] This was not so different to Liverpool's 'Bread church', where people spend the day making bread together and those who want have a separate time of reflective worship before lunch (see Barbara Glasson, *Mixed-up Blessing*, p. 40).

Antioch created new theology – by Paul notably, as he addressed the pastoral concerns of his new churches. Likewise, some within fresh expressions seek to interpret the gospel afresh for today's culture – not creating theology on a par with scripture, but freshly interpreting scripture for people coming into faith.

Yet both the Jerusalem and Antioch churches were interdependent. They respected each other. The growth of the Antioch church, especially among the Gentiles, provoked a double-edged response from Jerusalem. On the one hand the leaders wanted to see if the growth was from God, and on the other, if it was, they wanted to encourage it. So they sent Barnabas, the encourager (Acts 11.22–23). Here was inherited church, if you like, both holding a fresh expression to account and supporting it.

This pattern was repeated after Paul's first missionary journey. Paul sought the blessing of the Jerusalem leaders for what he had done. In turn, the Jerusalem church had the spiritual insight to recognize God at work, give Paul their support and seek not to burden the new churches with too many requirements (Acts 15.28) – an example that denominations would be wise to follow today.

Whereas Jerusalem had provided Antioch with a spiritual gift by sending Barnabas, later Paul organized a financial gift from his new churches to support the Jerusalem church, which had fallen on hard times (2 Cor. 8.1–9.5). Support had become two-way.

Interaction between Jerusalem and Antioch created fruitful theology. The Jerusalem church strongly affirmed its Jewish inheritance, while entirely new pastoral questions were posed by Paul's Gentile churches. Paul was uniquely placed to bridge the two and create the innovative theology we find in his letters. As pioneers engage both with the traditions of the church and the questions raised by contemporary culture, might not they too develop new understandings that will be true to scripture and enrich future generations?

Finally, the mission of the two churches complemented each other. The apostles recognized that Paul had the task of preaching to the Gentiles, while Peter had been called to the Jews (Gal. 2.7). Might inherited church have the task of attracting people within its orbit, while fresh expressions are to serve people beyond?

This pattern of interdependence is repeated in Acts. Indeed, it is a major theme. The New Testament scholar Loveday Alexander has described a two-fold movement within Acts – a going out in mission and a referring back to centres of the faith (see her article, 'What patterns of church and mission are found in the Acts of the Apostles?'). Peter goes out to Cornelius and then explains his actions to his fellow leaders in Jerusalem. Jerusalem and Antioch have this two-way relationship and so do Antioch and Paul's new churches.

From Acts 11.19 Antioch is more to the centre of Luke's narrative than Jerusalem. Antioch sends out Paul and Barnabas, and they report back first and foremost to the brethren in that church (Acts 14.27–28). Paul subsequently leaves on his second missionary journey, with the aim of visiting the churches he had planted (Acts 15.36). There is a sense in which he is the representative of Antioch, supporting his church plants and holding them to account.

This going out and referring back relationship appears to be repeated again between Paul's new churches in the larger cities and churches in the outlying areas. Ephesus became a centre while Paul preached for two years in the lecture hall of Tyrannus, 'so that all the residents of Asia, both Jews and Greeks, heard the word of the Lord' (Acts 19.10).

One of Paul's converts was Epaphras, a native of Colossae, who returned and evangelized his home city (Col. 1.7, 4.12). When the faith of the new believers was under threat, Epaphras reported back to Paul, who was in prison (possibly in Ephesus) and who responded with his letter to the Colossians.

This back-and-forth dynamic in Acts has been central to the church ever since. New centres of the faith emerge. They go out to people in incarnational mission. But there is a referring back process as these new churches form links with the centres that established them.

Here then, perhaps, is one basis for the mixed economy – a pattern from the very beginning of going out and referring back. In the case of Jerusalem and Antioch, a more traditional church and a fresh expression of church affirmed one another, complemented each other and recognized that they were one in Christ. But at times, as Ray Anderson emphasizes, they also disagreed sharply. Is this combination of mutual support and periodic disagreement likely to characterize the mixed economy today?

Learning to love each other

For the mixed economy to work, inherited and emerging churches need to love each other. There are lessons here for fresh expressions. In making the case for new forms of church, it is inevitable that proponents of fresh expressions should highlight the limitations of existing church. But this can be as easily rejected as heard. The challenge is to make the case in a way that also affirms the contributions inherited church has made in the past and can still make in the years ahead.

Perhaps the bigger challenge is to inherited church. As currently the stronger partner in the mixed economy, it has the opportunity either to help fresh expressions or to do harm. How actively is it seeking out opportunities to provide support?

In my work in the Tomorrow Project, my colleague and I have a 'fun index'. If the index drops markedly, we review what we are doing and ask whether it can be done differently or should be done at all. Imagine that there was a 'love index' to measure the attitude of inherited church to fresh expressions. Where would the index stand?

My sense is that in much of inherited church it hovers somewhere between scepticism and tolerance. Yet for the mixed economy to be really fruitful, shouldn't the index go somewhat higher? Doesn't the institutional church need to be actively *for* fresh expressions, championing their cause? And wouldn't pioneers be likely to champion the inherited church in response?

Making the mixed economy work

What would it mean for leaders of a denomination to champion fresh expressions? The Fresh Expressions Initiative team has suggested the following, based on what is already happening and proving effective:

- Discern what God is doing in different contexts and join in.
- Join up the thinking and leadership across the denomination (or diocese). In particular, bring together the permission givers and the key practitioners. Why not let the strategy unfold from a meeting of the six key movers and shakers in the denomination and the six most fruitful pioneers of fresh expressions?
- Constantly build the mixed economy vision at every opportunity and in all kinds of ways. Use the stories of fruitful fresh expressions.
- Encourage key practitioners of fresh expressions to share their experiences and learn from each other. *Share* (<www.sharethe guide.org>) might help to connect practitioners to national networks so that every piece of wisdom is captured and passed on.
- Set aside some funded posts for fresh expressions and some mission funding. This is already beginning to happen.
- Make sure the training is in place to support fresh expressions. The Fresh Expressions one-year course might be a possibility. (For more details see <www.freshexpressions.org>.)

Conclusion

Fresh expressions owe much to the inherited church. Current pioneers have come to faith within established churches, many have received their Christian training from them and some are financed by them. Equally, many inherited churches desperately need effective fresh expressions. They can't reach large parts of society. Might fresh expressions become an Antioch on behalf of Jerusalem? For this mutuality to flourish, however, existing churches and fresh expressions must learn to love each other.

14

Mixed economy or ecclesial reciprocity:
which does the Church of England really want to promote?

LOUISE NELSTROP

There is no doubt that if fresh expressions are taken at their face value, then they present the Church of England with one of its greatest ecclesiological challenges. Through Bishop's Mission Orders fresh expressions of church can (from 2008) legally operate as churches outside the parish and diocesan structures that have always given the Church of England its ecclesiological frame. Having continuously resisted a more congregationalist model, fresh expressions not only drive in this direction, but advocate that there is no element of the Church's ecclesiological make-up, be it liturgy, hierarchy or authority, that cannot legitimately be challenged. Some within the fresh expressions movement even suggest that traditional church has no long-term future. Little wonder then that many within what is being termed 'inherited church' are feeling defensive and resistant to the proposed new ecclesiology of a 'mixed economy'.

The term 'mixed economy' was coined by Rowan Williams in reference to a model of ecclesiology that sees fresh expressions of church and inherited church functioning alongside each other as equal partners. As he states in the preface to *Mission-shaped Church*,

> we have begun to recognize that there are many ways in which the reality of 'church' can exist. 'Church' as a map of territorial

divisions (parishes and dioceses) is one – one that still has a remarkable vigour in all sorts of contexts and which relates to a central conviction about the vocation of Anglicanism. But there are more and more others, of the kind this report describes and examines. The challenge is not to force every-thing into the familiar mould; but neither is it to tear up the rulebook and start from scratch ... *What makes the situation interesting is that we are going to have to live with variety ...* (p. vii; emphasis added)

However, in suggesting this, Dr Williams advocates an ecclesio-logical position that many academic critics, from within both fresh expressions and inherited church, appear dissatisfied with. On the one hand, Martyn Percy holds that fresh expressions lack the ecclesial density to be fully church (see his chapter in this vol-ume). On the other, the likes of Ian Mobsby (in *Emerging and Fresh Expressions of Church*) and Pete Ward (in *Liquid Church*) suggest that inherited church is structurally incapable of respond-ing to the demands of a postmodern Britain. The question that this chapter sets out to explore then is whether a 'mixed economy' is something that the Church of England really wants to promote.

It does so by exploring this question from the perspective of those within fresh expressions. The reason for this is not because the views of those within inherited church are somehow less valu-able. It is simply that, over the past two years, I have been engaged in a number of detailed ethnographic studies that have sought to explore the views of those who belong to fresh expressions (both members and leaders), comparing their experiences to members of emerging churches in far flung corners of Thailand.[1]

The groups that I have studied are extremely diverse. Within fresh expressions UK there is a youth church, a café church, a network/alternative worship church and an internet church; in Thailand, a base ecclesial community among slum dwellers and a house church for those from high society. I have no desire to gloss over the differences, both taxonomical and cultural, be-tween these groups. Yet all do have at least this much in common, that they see themselves as somewhat 'out of the box', that is on the peripheries of the frame of the main ecclesial establishment. As such, this raises questions. Why attend a church that is on the edge? What kind of relationship do members and leaders of these groups feel they have, and/or want to have, with the established hierarchy? Is the proposed shift to a mixed economy really desirable?

Why have fresh expressions?

Through prolonged periods of participant observation, in which I conducted some 200 interviews, alongside focus groups and data collection through questionnaires, it became clear that certain trends, in the form of themes, emerged across all the groups, despite their many obvious differences. Taking a hermeneutic phenomenological approach, in which I immersed myself in the groups, and then using grounded theory to analyse my data (using Philip Burnard, 'A method of analysing interview transcripts in qualitative research'), one of the main reasons why people attend these out-of-the-box churches is that they give them a sense of belonging. The groups made them feel accepted, as they were. Those interviewed spoke about feeling 'at home', 'safe', of 'friends', 'companions on the way', a sense of 'family', being able to 'relax', and just 'hang out'. This contrasts sharply with their experiences of inherited church, where they had often felt that they were trying to force themselves into a mould, in which they did not fit. As one participant from a high-society church in Thailand commented, 'Pretence takes so much energy. It's like wearing your Halloween costume all year long.' Members associated these feelings of constraint with, what they saw as, the rule-based approach of inherited church. They recalled constantly feeling worried that they would get it (whatever it was) wrong, and so be judged. A member of a UK youth church put the difference like this,

> It's not like all 'sitting down', 'standing up'. It's not like all in a sequence and being told 'your wrong, your wrong' and you should be doing this sort of thing.

The formal structure of traditional church had also meant that many had been afraid to ask for prayer and support. A member of the café church noted a contrast between his experience of café church and traditional church in this respect,

> I think [café church is] an excellent thing to have, because ... [if] you want to talk to someone, who, you know, about a problem, you can come here and talk ... because in church you feel a bit uneasy about talking to people ... because, you're not sure, you know, it's the right time, or but here, it's more open isn't it.

Another dimension of belonging was the move towards a more open approach to rituals, rules and liturgy. Those interviewed raised questions about the necessity/unchangeability of these aspects of church, which if monolithic they felt to be barriers to the gospel. In suggesting this they did not feel they were challenging the authentic Christian message, but cultural norms. They felt that they were cutting away unnecessary 'dead wood'; that which tended to deaden the vibrancy of Christianity, as these rather irreverent comments from a member of a youth church illustrate.

> I like to consider that we're not new, we're even older than the normal Anglican church, and we're kind of like, we're going back to when it was very much alive and, not that I am saying that the Anglican church is dead!!! But, as in, more proactive. Sorry if there are any bishops reading this at the moment!

They also felt that by taking such an approach they were opening themselves up to the possibility of new creativity. One member of a network/alternative worship group spoke of the privilege they felt in being allowed to work with/rework the liturgy,

> I hugely value the planning of the gatherings. I just find it theologically stretching and liturgically creative and really enjoy wrestling with the texts and thinking about the contemplatives who might give us a different perspective on some of the material that we're exploring and I just love that ... and I find it

endlessly fascinating really and very resourcing and just a gift to be able to live with that for a whole month really.

As such, it allowed them to feel that they were realizing their potential as leaders. They felt enabled to explore gifts and talents, and this added to their sense of belonging – for now they felt they had something to contribute, rather than just attending church to sit and listen to an authority figure (which many had found uninspiring anyway). They did not feel that in all this what they were doing was 'new' in the sense of original, and thus stepping outside their Christian heritage. Rather they felt that it was 'fresh' in that it was about deconstructing and then reconstructing the Christian message for the twenty-first century. As another member of the network/alternative worship church put it,

> In [a] sense [there is] nothing new at all, but [it's] fresh because there is something unexpected about its interpretations and its deconstructions and its revelations of what is essential.

What was particularly striking about all the groups I studied was how much members all loved attending church. Their Christian life had become something that they were involved in 24/7. They were excited about it, excited to read the Bible, to become disciples, or just to be there, even when some were unsure about what they believed. This comment from a participant in Thailand really sums up the mood of those interviewed across the groups,

> What a church! What a church! In a good way! Like, oh! This is like what I want, like, that is like, I never know what is it, but this is what I want.

The vast majority of data I collected contains positive comments of this nature about fresh expressions/emerging church, which often contrasts starkly with negative impressions of inherited church. Thus in reflecting on the relative value of an ecclesiology of mixed economy, I was rather struck by the chorus of a recent Kate Nash hit, which talks about how she is holding on to her relationship by her fingertips, unable to let go, even though she knows that it is probably time that she should. Now while Kate Nash probably wasn't intending to make a contribution to the emerging church debate(!), her lyrics seemed to raise the question, if emerging churches are so good, why promote a 'mixed economy'? Perhaps this is just holding on to the cracks in the foundations of traditional church? Is there really a value that means that if one is in the business of defining church for the twenty-first century one still needs to hold on? On the surface, certainly, the themes that arise from my data reinforce readings of church trends by writers such as Mobsby and Ward who, as we noted in the introduction, suggest that there is no point in holding on, at least not in the long term.

Holding on to the cracks in our foundation?

Ian Mobsby argues that the fresh expressions of church currently being promoted by the Fresh Expressions Initiative can be divided into two types – 'inherited' fresh expressions and the 'emerging' fresh expressions (which he studies). Now while there is no claim that the list of 14 types of fresh expression found on the official website is definitive or the types even clearly differentiable from one another, the list proves a useful tool to illustrate what Mobsby means by 'emerging'. For him, only those shown below in bold have structures that can offer a contextualized postmodern theology, and so count as 'emerging'.

1 **Alternative worship communities.**
2 Base ecclesial communities (BECs).
3 **Café church.**
4 Cell church.
5 Churches arising out of community initiatives.
6 Multiple and midweek congregations.
7 **Network-focused churches.**
8 School-based and school-linked congregations and churches.
9 Seeker church.
10 Traditional church plants.

11 Traditional forms of church inspiring new interest.
12 Youth congregations.
13 Fresh expressions for children.
14 Fresh expressions for under fives and their families.

All the others are 'inherited'. As Mobsby states in *Emerging and Fresh Expressions of Church*,

> 'inherited' modes of church ... do not seek to be significantly postmodern in contextual understanding and differ in their model of contextual theology utilising a more 'translation' type approach.[2] This grouping appears to include Cell, Youth and Church Planting new forms ... more 'emerging' modes of church ... do significantly seek to be postmodern in contextual understanding and use a 'synthetic' model of contextual theology.[3] This group appears to include Alternative worship communities, Café churches, and Network churches. (p. 31)

Following what he sees as Caputo's assertion that we are currently faced with a society in which pre-modern, modern and postmodern elements mingle together, Mobsby suggests that the promotion of a 'mixed economy' may have a valid currency in this interim period, prior to society moving into a more fully postmodern phase. He is less certain, however, of the long-term value of 'inherited' models, stressing with scholars such as Brewin that only truly 'emerging' churches are able to offer genuinely authentic expressions of postmodern society. Based on interviews with participants from 'emerging' fresh expressions, Mobsby concludes that the church needs to move away from imperialistic models of church, which link church and society, towards more holistic, relational forms. Thus, according to Mobsby, the long-term future of both traditional churches and these inherited 'fresh expressions' looks bleak.

Mobsby isn't alone in suggesting that traditional church can't survive in its current form. Pete Ward, in his book *Liquid Church*, suggests that the church needs to move towards an essentially relational model of church in which individual Christians are considered nodes in a relationship network of individuals, with church consisting of the relationship groups that these individuals reach. Ward argues that regarding church in terms of networks of individuals dissolves the insider/outsider problem – again providing a kind of belonging-without-believing understanding of church.

> When we start to regard the network itself as church, then the notion of insider and outsider starts to break down. (pp. 47–8)

Ward argues that a relational model of church such as this one, which he terms 'liquid church', takes seriously the image of church as the body of Christ. It is also one that he believes reflects the idea of the Trinity as 'perichoresis' or perhaps the more modern idea coming out of feminist thinking, in which the persons of the Trinity are said 'to dance' around one another. Ward suggests that church so defined also allows products to flow through these networks; thus taking consumer society seriously too. Rather than demonize it, Ward sees in consumer society the potential for spiritual growth. Building also on the idea found in Grace Davie's work, that people in Britain 'believe without belonging', Ward suggests that we need to commodify spiritual products so that they flow through these networks, thus transforming shopping into a spiritually positive activity. In making these suggestions Ward is following Jean Baudrillard, who argues that consumption is always a quest for something more than itself. Thus, for Ward, the emergence of seeker churches and Alpha groups epitomize such a model of church, along with the recognition that the mums and tots group can be church too.

There have been various responses to Ward's general thesis, from the likes of John Hull (*Mission-shaped Church*) and Bradley Onishi ('Grenz's theological method and the commodification of religion'), both of whom criticize a consumer-driven Christianity. Some of the recent *Mission-shaped* publications also seem to take a more counter-consumerist approach.[4] However, regardless of whether Ward is correct in his treatment of consumerism, its importance for this chapter lies in his claim that unless church adapts itself in some way to meet the challenges posed by consumer, postmodern society, it will become either (1) a heritage site – with no practising community and traditions clung to on the grounds of 'cultural worth' alone; or (2) a refuge site – where members cushion themselves against 'real culture' by creating a safe Christian alternative; or (3) a nostalgic community – where members hanker after a golden age that never was, in which all ages, races and classes worshipped side by side. What both these writers therefore agree on is that traditional church needs to change if it is to survive. It is not enough simply to promote a mixed economy.

However, it is also apparent, just by looking at these two examples, that Ward and Mobsby don't agree on the form that the church of the future must take. For Mobsby seeker churches and mums and tots groups aren't 'emerging' fresh expressions, while for Ward they are. In part, this difference lies in the fact that Mobsby follows Stuart Murray in reading postmodernism as characterized by a tendency towards 'belonging without believing', while Ward builds primarily on Davie's idea of 'believing without belonging'. Yet such discrepancies and disagreements also appear illustrative of the nature of 'emerging church' as Pete Rollins reads it in *How (Not) to Speak of God*, where he argues that it is characterized less by concrete beliefs than by collections of highly fragile and diverse conversations.

> While the term 'emerging church' is increasingly being employed to describe a well-defined and well-equipped religious movement, in actual fact it is currently little more than a fragile, embryonic and diverse conversation being held between individuals over the internet and at various gatherings. Not only does the elusive and tentative nature of this conversation initially make it difficult to describe what, if anything, unifies those involved; the sheer breadth of perspectives held by those within the dialogue make terms such as 'movement', 'denomination', and 'church' seem somehow inappropriate. (p. 5)[5]

This idea appears to be echoed by many in the church groups that I studied, who seemed acutely aware of their own fragility and the 'embryonic' nature of their ecclesiology. What is more, none seemed keen to close down any possible permutations of church. Rather they saw themselves as part of an emerging kaleidoscope of church types, that, as such, raise a challenge to any idea of a one-size-fits-all approach – be this a monolithic 'inherited' or a monolithic 'emerging'/'liquid' church. True to the postmodern undercurrents that fuel them, they wanted to be open to other approaches, to new possibilities, and to the closure of closure. The question remains however, as to whether this can be satisfied by a mixed economy, and it is to their reflections on their place within the larger whole that I now turn.

Towards ecclesial reciprocity

The groups that I studied raised a host of ecclesiological and missiological issues too diverse and complex to address in a single chapter. Yet a number of overarching ecclesiological concerns, relevant to the ecclesiology of mixed economy, can be highlighted. Although largely considering their groups to count as authentic churches, there was, in the light of their comments about inherited church, a surprising reticence to be entirely cut off from traditional church or to have to operate outside of the Church of England (or in the case of the Thai churches, their denominations). This final section explores the value that they place on relationship with traditional church and the kind of relationship they were looking for.

As noted above, there was an acute awareness among those within fresh expressions/emerging churches that the forms of church they were involved in were fragile. This fragility had a number of underlying causes. One related to the issue of longevity. There was a sense among the groups that they neither should, nor would be able to become a church type that developed into an institution of its own. The network/alternative worship group were aware that they appealed to a particular demographic. The kind of contemplative spirituality that they espouse tended to attract an older clientele. This meant that they were unlikely to become second generation. Rather, they would be continuously recreated by a generation of new people. As one of those interviewed commented:

> At the moment and of course it is early days, but I don't see it becoming second generation at the moment because there's not many young people that are going to have kids and bring them up in it ... I think because it's contemplative, it's dealing with, and I might say this wrongly, but I think because it's contemplative it keys into a stage in spiritual development that is sort of at a later stage ... it maybe that it's something that people would go to, you know, move more into later.

A similar issue was encountered by those who attended the youth congregation. Age marked a point before which they could not be members and after which they could no longer belong. Equally, other groups felt that it was important that their group should at some point 'die', if it was to remain 'fresh' and 'emerging' – a line of thinking that perhaps sets fresh expression/emerging churches apart from most new religious movements. As such, therefore, they did not feel that in terms of their longevity they were sufficient to form the entirety of the church universal, as it were. In this relation, a significant proportion of participants had retained connections with traditional church on some level. Some had intended to leave but the initial fragility of the fresh expression had meant that they had waited to see what would happen. Once they discovered that they could do both, several of those interviewed (much to their surprise) actually felt more integrated into the parish system. This was facilitated by the fact that their sense of church was no longer limited to it. With that said, for a significant proportion the fresh expression was *their* only church. Yet wasn't *all* that they understood by church.

Tied to this were questions about the role of the sacraments. While those sacraments connected with personal spiritual expression, such as Eucharist, were incorporated into some of the groups, others, especially rites of passage, were not found within the fresh expressions I studied. For these, traditional church was said to be needed. Participants questioned whether it would be appropriate to perform, for example, a marriage ceremony or a funeral in their church. Their church performed its functions, traditional churches performed other roles, and both were needed within their understanding of a mixed economy.

Related to this, the groups also valued the ecclesiological depth that the denomination provided. The youth congregation, for example, valued the support of both the main parent church and being part of the Anglican Communion. As with the other groups, they felt that this provided them with rich theological resources that they could scare do without, guidance in moments of decision-making, and the security of knowing that they were being held accountable. It was this sense of safety and founda-tion, that provided them with a greater sense of freedom for experimentation.

> I think it gives us a safety net ... we can operate within its rules and boundaries ... we operate within the safety net of the church ... in terms of the kind of history that the Anglican Church provides ... we can kind of be held accountable by the structures within the Church of England, to make sure that what we are doing is right and that it's biblical [...] it just provides a whole sense of security.

Leaders in particular commented on the need for boundaries, and the checks and balances that being part of a denomination offered in preventing their group from becoming maverick. Mem-bers also spoke of the rich, often untapped, heritage of their own tradition that meant that they felt no need to look outside. One group (Café Church) commented particularly on how much they valued the formal structures that allowed them to float more freely. This group saw themselves as 'church', but not *a* church. Instead they felt themselves connected to a set of *churches*, each of which had clearly delineated boundaries. Not being totally in-dependent meant that relationships within the group and with other churches didn't have to be formalized on the same level as in these other churches.

> The moment you make it *a* church you have to define leader-ship, accountability, who's in, who's out, more closely, who

makes the decisions, you have to formalize or not formalize relationships with other churches and things like that.

The issue of independence thus raised questions about what those within these groups understand 'church' to mean. While many participants saw themselves as part of church in the sense of being part of a community of believers, this was not *all* that they meant by church. Church was larger than this, filled with rich heritage, traditions and doctrine. Their groups often had a particularly missional focus. Thus some in more seeker style churches noted a lack of theological depth in their group but equally questioned whether their fresh expression was the place for this.

> ... the spiritual formation part is very difficult ... I can person-
> ally see myself possibly going to a different church to get that
> ... [here] it's all about sharing ... from the Bible without any
> sort of either any deep spiritual meditation ... or without any
> more intense theology, or so, there is no forum for those people
> that want something like that.

Some within the groups suggested too that a fresh expression need not be tied to being *a* church in its own right. For them fresh expressions formed part of a spectrum of missional endeavours that moved away from traditional church to varying degrees. What they liked about them was their capacity to be responsive to context, and in some contexts (especially small rural ones) be ecumenical rather than church-planting ventures – which they argued were equally fresh expressions of church since they were enabled by the loosening of the ecclesiological structures that a mixed economy facilitates.

As in emerging churches globally, there was in fact a tendency among the groups towards ecumenism. Although valuing the authority and spiritual heritage of their denomination, this was accompanied by a lack of commitment to the denomination in terms of its specific doctrinal beliefs. While still valuing the security of an authority, these groups all welcomed an element of uncertainty, as emphasized by the fact there was no element of traditional church that they felt should not be touched by de- and reconstruction. This view ties into the sense that many expressed, of taking Christianity back to its basis, stripping down 'church' to its bare essentials, and so offering culturally relevant church.

On many levels therefore, participants expressed something of the fragility of their fresh expressions/emerging churches and the way in which many of these groups related to and depended on traditional and/or other churches – without which they would be unable to fulfil their potential. They saw themselves not as complete expressions of the church universal, but as part of a kaleidoscope of possible expressions within a much larger and more complex whole.

Conclusion

The responses of those within these groups towards traditional church, however, raise questions about what they want from a mixed economy. Do they really want a church in which they operate as equal partners?

The nature of this relationship is one that recent *Mission-shaped* publications have been grappling with. For example, *Mission-shaped Youth* acknowledges that by promoting fresh expressions of church the Church of England and Methodist Council have allowed themselves to become involved in a much larger debate concerning 'What is church?' to which they do not come with ready answers. In attempting a response, contra the feelings of at least one group I studied, Sally Gaze in *Mission-shaped and Rural* suggests a distinction needs to be drawn between 'fresh expressions' and mission initiatives – in that while the former have the potential to grow into churches in their own right, the latter feed existing forms of church, acting as catalysts for change within, and so do not really qualify as fresh expressions. Likewise in *Mission-shaped Youth*, exploring this question of 'What is church?', Charles Russell supposes three non-negotiable characteristics, worship, belonging, and discipline, which, as he defines them, suggest the importance of both liturgy and the sacraments. He wonders, along with Avril Baigent, whether generational churches fulfil the requirement of being the body of Christ. Baigent, for example, likens a youth church to a church full of just one body part. However, it seems unlikely that any of the groups I studied would be happy with such an ascription – seeing themselves as inwardly diverse and such descriptions as ageist – especially given the ageing nature of many parish congregations – who, perhaps, are nothing more than collections of noses or ears?! Yet, while not seeing a one-size-fits-all model as a feasible working model, many of the groups recognized the wisdom and richness that other churches can offer them, and some specifically stressed a need to recognize that while like attracts like, one must strive against McGavran's Homogenous Unit Principle.

On all these counts therefore they wanted to remain within the vine, as it were, not simply as church supplements (since they felt they met the daily requirement of most of their members), but not necessarily as equivalent churches. What members wanted was a much more messy and organic model of church. As two of those interviewed put it, for them it was about creating church niches and a kaleidoscope of church experiences.

> I think it needs to be tailored more, you know, so I don't see anything wrong with lots of niches making a mother church, you know, that's the way it should be really.

> we are trying to express that everybody has a valid view, that nobody is made to feel that they're wrong. That we can all learn from each other. That there is more of a kaleidoscope of experience that makes a whole. And that we are not exclusive but inclusive.

This is a mixed economy of sorts, but not one of competitive equality between 'inherited' and 'emerging' churches. Some within the churches I researched realized that many within traditional church were finding it difficult to understand why fresh expressions were necessary, that they saw them as a form of competition, a sign that they had somehow failed. As one member of a network/alternative worship church put it,

> Inherited church is actually hurting about 'fresh expressions'. They are kind of saying, 'What have we done wrong?' 'Why do we need fresh expressions?' There is this kind of 'Why?' almost feeling.

However, this did not seem to be the relationship that those within the groups I studied were wanting. They were simply challenging the idea of a monolith structure into which all can fit all of the time. For them, fresh expressions suggest that there is something less clear about the edges and that there can be room to support that which floats across the boundaries in a more ill-defined way. It is suggesting, as noted by a participant above, that church needs to become more kaleidoscopic in the twenty-first century. However, this does not mean that the new form will replace the old; rather for them it is that many forms will come to exist within the old (as opposed to alongside it as Rowan Williams seems to suggest).

Thus, rather than those in the emerging church suggesting that traditional church has no future or vice versa, perhaps it's a case of being more aware of the Other, of seeing ourselves as defined in relationship, of being defined by difference. As Nick Waghorn has helpfully pointed out, in such cases we are presented with several choices. One option is that we can pretend that no differences exist.

> Obviously one way of avoiding this problem is to fail to acknowledge that there are alternative ways of doing things, ways pursued by other people. We ignore the other.[6]

Alternatively, feeling threatened by the other, we can try to actively prevent difference, out of the fear that having it will make us doubt ourselves and our way of doing things.[7] (And in suggesting the ultimate demise of a 'mixed economy' perhaps Ward and Mobsby fall into one of these two traps.) Or finally, we can embrace otherness. Rather than prophesying a shift to a church made up of only 'emerging' fresh expressions, it is this latter approach that in fact seems the most fully postmodern. As Michael Horton comments in 'Settlers, pilgrims and wanderers', with a critical eye on some of Brian McLaren's writings, postmodernism demands a respect for otherness.

> One of the key tenets of postmodern theory is to recover respect for 'otherness' – letting those who are different from oneself be who they are without forcing them into playing a role you've scripted for them.

Thus there would seem to be merits in promoting a 'mixed economy'. However, what one means by a mixed economy, how the partners operate, how one promotes ecclesial reciprocity – of listening to and learning from the other, of valuing what is uncertain within a secure frame of tradition – all this still needs to be worked out.

Notes

Chapter 1 What counts as a fresh expression of church and who decides?

1 See Robert Warren's work from the mid-1990s, R. Warren, 1995, *Building Missionary Congregations*, London: Church House Publishing; R. Warren, 1995, *Being Human, Being Church*, Grand Rapids, MI: Zondervan.

2 Pope John Paul II to Bishops of Latin America, Haiti, 1983, quoted on the website of the Catholic Agency to Support Evangelization (CASE): <http://www.caseresources.org.uk/evangelisation/evangelisation_newevangelisation.htm>.

3 Groups consulted at this time included Anglican Church Planting Initiatives (ACPI), The Church Mission Society (CMS), The Sheffield Centre of the Church Army, the Church of England Mission and Public Affairs Division, the Evangelism and Church Planting Department of the Methodist Church, and New Way.

4 See the most recent discussions on Share: the online guide to fresh expressions <http://www.sharetheguide.org/>.

Chapter 2 Mixed economy: nice slogan or working reality?

1 <http://www.archbishopofcanterbury.org/1595>.

Chapter 3 Old tricks for new dogs?

1 For a critique, see John Hull, 2006, *Mission-shaped Church: A Theological Response*, London: SCM Press. Hull argues that he can register his anti-nuclear Christian protest group as a fresh expression of church. In his politicization and radicalization of the term, he is drawing on the liberation theology base communities of South America.

2 See Paul Weston, 2006, *Lesslie Newbigin: Missionary Theologian – A Reader*, New York: Eerdmans. Newbigin contrasts 'associational' (or congregationalist) models of the church with the parish system. While recognizing the power of the associational, Newbigin remains firmly

committed to the parish model (p. 141). See also Avery Dulles, 1974, *Models of the Church*, New York: Doubleday, who develops five models of the church: institution, mystical communion, herald, servant and sacrament. And James Hopewell, 1987, *Congregation: Stories and Structures*, London: SCM Press, who offers four models: mechanistic, organic, contextual and symbolic.

3 As Andrew Walker (1985) pointed out in *Restoring the Kingdom*, London: Hodder & Stoughton, early Restorationist leaders believed that church history had rarely witnessed a 'pure' version of the church. The first four centuries up until Constantine, and the Reformation period (significantly, both anti-establishment eras) were deemed to be times when the Holy Spirit was 'active', and unencumbered by the established nature of an institutional church. Early Pentecostalism (i.e. pre-denominational) was affirmed, as was Restorationism itself, which of course did not regard itself as an expression of denominational identity, but rather a restoring of the kind of Christian fellowship that is allegedly narrated in the New Testament.

4 On this, and for a critique of fulfilment-centred church growth exponents, see Peter Schmiechen, 2005, *Saving Power: Theories of Atonement and Forms of the Church*, Grand Rapids, MI: Eerdmans.

5 Of course, the genius of the deanery system – a legal collation of parishes in the Church of England – is that it consists of a range of extensive and intensive models, and an assortment of hybrids. This ensures that a relatively small area offers different types of parish ministry. The mixed ecclesial economy arguably offers a strong missiological foundation.

6 On this, see Robert Bellah, 1985, *Habits of the Heart: Individualism and Commitment in American Life*, Berkeley: University of California Press (esp. ch. 6) and Robert Putnam, 2000, *Bowling Alone: The Collapse and Revival of American Community*, New York: Simon & Schuster.

7 On this, see Linda Woodhead and Paul Heelas (eds), 2005, *The Spiritual Revolution*, Oxford: Blackwell. The authors argue that formal religious organizations are giving way to individualistic and relational forms of spirituality and sacralized therapeutic insights.

8 mayBe website <www.maybe.org.uk>.

9 This is one of the more puzzling features of the movement. In discussions with some of the advocates of fresh expressions, there is some reluctance to identify metropolitan churches (i.e. where the primary focus is gay and lesbian membership) as fresh expressions. (This suggests that the insights of Bellah and Putnam are illuminating. Fresh expressions do not gather individuals around overt campaigning or left-wing agendas. They are not like the base communities of South and Central America, which are birthed in liberation theology. Rather, fresh expressions are mainly right-of-centre and bourgeois, or individualistic and apolitical – which is, of course, anti-political.) On the other hand, some Christian Unions at colleges or universities, while clearly operating as Christian associations

and *not* churches, appear to be regarded as fresh expressions. So a gathering of a few like-minded and similarly aged persons can apparently register as a fresh expression (of church). Yet many Christians will at least be able to make an innate cultural distinction between 'going to church' (and all that this implies in terms of likely social mix, obligation, diversity, etc.) and 'attending an act of worship' (even one repeated regularly each week) – which may of course have little to do with belonging to a church.

10 See Woodhead and Heelas, 2005. When asked by a lawyer what he had to do to inherit eternal life, Jesus did not reply, 'Well, what works for you?' (Luke 10.25–28).

11 For more about the Methodist Class system see, for example, J. H. Wigger, *Taking Heaven by Storm: Methodism and the Rise of Popular Christianity in America* (New York, 1998: Oxford University Press), p. 85.

12 McGavran argues that differences in economic, social and caste positions (e.g. in India) inhibit church growth. Ergo, by developing 'homogenous units' in which such differences need not be presented or surface, 'like attracts like'. Thus, a church simply for Hispanics, blacks or whites will tend to fare numerically better than attempting one large inter-racial church. There is no deep difference between the missiology that McGavran advocates and that of the fresh expressions movement.

Chapter 4 Formation for ministry in a mixed economy church

1 For more on this see Steven Croft, 1993, *Growing New Christians: Evangelism and Nurture in the Local Church*, London/Grand Rapids, MI: Marshall Pickering/Zondervan; and Stephen Cottrell, Steven Croft, John Finney, Felicity Lawson and Robert Warren, 1996, *Emmaus: The Way of Faith* (6 volumes), London: Church House Publishing, Introduction; 2nd edn, 2002.

2 This is well illustrated by the shifting role of Springboard, the Archbishops' initiative that preceded the Fresh Expressions Initiative. Springboard began its life as an agency to conduct evangelistic missions. It evolved into an agency for renewing and training the whole church in its practice of evangelism.

3 See Robert Warren, 1995, *Building Missionary Congregations*, London: Church House Publishing.

4 The authors have recently published a more detailed study of church leaving: Leslie Francis and Philip Richter, 2008, *Gone for Good? Church Leaving and Returning in the Twenty-first Century*, Norwich: Epworth Press. Francis and Richter's research forms the basis of the segmentation pie-chart in *Mission-shaped Church*, 2004, London: Church House Publishing, p. 37. The segmentation research has been extended and updated in recent years by Tear Fund, who are tracking in detail the shifts by region and age segmentation of the population.

5 See the helpful analysis by John Drane, 2000, *The McDonaldisation of the Church*, London: Darton, Longman & Todd.

6 Both sets of guidelines can be downloaded from the Fresh Expressions Inititative website: <http://www.freshexpressions.org.uk/index.asp?id=1>.

7 The St Paul's Theological Centre attached to Holy Trinity Brompton and now part of the St Mellitus College in London, and the Westminster Theological Centre attached to St Mary's, Bryanston Square.

8 An initial research exercise in 2004 revealed that the majority of training courses running in the country at that time traced their material back in some way to the Hopkins' pioneering work. James Hopewell, 1987, *Congregation: Stories and Structures*, London: SCM Press.

9 For a recent contribution to the literature see S. Croft (ed.), 2008, *Mission-shaped Questions: Defining issues for Today's Church*, London: Church House Publishing, which comprises 14 essays mainly on ecclesiology and mission.

10 The series of short studies, *Encounters on the Edge*, by the Church Army's Sheffield Centre is invaluable here. See for example the recent study of two pioneer ministries and what did not go well: *Encounters* no. 36, George Lings, 2008, *Lessons from Hindsight*, The Sheffield Centre.

11 See particularly E. Boyd MacMillan and S. Savage, 2007, *The Human Face of the Church: A Social Psychological and Pastoral Theology Resource for Pioneer and Traditional Ministry*, London: Canterbury Press.

Chapter 5 Fresh expressions: the psychological gains and risks

1 Cited in Anne Lamott, 2005, *Plan B: Further Thoughts on Faith*, New York: Penguin Books, p. 181.

Chapter 6 Biting that hand that feeds

1 In the Church of England's missionary report entitled *Mission-shaped Church*, 2004, London: Church House Publishing, 12 diverse types of community are encapsulated under the topology of 'fresh expressions'. These range from alternative worship groups and base ecclesial communities through to cell churches and youth congregations.

2 The term 'mixed economy' is used by Rowan Williams to describe the Anglican Church. See interview on <www.freshexpressions.org.uk/section.asp?id=1378> (accessed 15 May 2008).

3 For an interesting exploration of this idea see Jean-Luc Marion, 'Is the ontological argument ontological', in I. Bulthof (ed.), 2000, *Flight of the Gods*, New York: Fordham University Press, pp. 78-99.

Chapter 7 Living in the distance between a 'community of character' and a 'community of the question'

1 Throughout this chapter I will be drawing on the – to varying degrees – complex theological and philosophical ideas of Hauerwas and Derrida, as well as various interpreters and developers of their thought, as they (might) relate to emerging/fresh ecclesiology. I have, however, tried to write in an introductory register that is deliberately 'reader friendly' and assumes no prior knowledge of the work of either Hauerwas or Derrida. As a result of this approach my explanation of aspects of the work of these two important thinkers runs the risk of being too 'simple' and of failing to capture the complexities and nuances of their texts. Nevertheless, this is a risk that I am willing to take in the hope that after reading my application of their work to the emerging/fresh expressions conversation people might feel the need to go to these authors themselves. In addition I also realize that this bringing together of the insights of Hauerwas and Derrida, as well as various interpreters and developers of their thought, might be considered by some to be something of an unholy, or – at the very least – forced, alliance. Yet it is my belief that not only is their respective work of crucial importance for illuminating possible ways forward for the 'emerging/fresh expressions conversation', there are points at which their writing resonates with the same themes. I hope to draw attention to some of these resonances in this chapter. I would however readily concede that their work is radically divergent at other points. At the most obvious level Hauerwas is a Christian and Derrida would not have described himself in that way (although for more on Derrida's 'religion without religion' see John D. Caputo's classic (1997) text *The Prayers and Tears of Jacques Derrida: Religion without Religion*, Bloomington and Indianapolis: Indiana University Press.

2 Jacques Derrida, 1988, *Limited Inc*, Gerald Graff (ed.), Samuel Weber (trans.), Evanston: Northwestern University Press, p. 148.

3 I am aware that not all such expressions are comfortable using the term 'church' to describe themselves.

4 Derrida makes this comment in the context of replying to a question posed by Kearney as to whether he considers one of his books (*Glas*) to be a work of philosophy or of poetry.

5 For well researched, clear and thoughtful articulations of a range of challenges faced by emerging/fresh expressions see the work of Stuart Murray (2004, *Post-Christendom*, Carlisle: Paternoster [especially pp. 253–60]; 2004, *Church After Christendom*, Carlisle: Paternoster); Gerard Mannion, 'Postmodern ecclesiologies', in Gerard Mannion and Lewis S. Mudge (eds), 2008, *The Routledge Companion to the Christian Church*, New York and London: Routledge, pp. 127–52, especially pp. 132–5; and Henk de Roest, 'Ecclesiologies at the Margin', in Gerard

Mannion and Lewis S. Mudge (eds), 2008, *The Routledge Companion to the Christian Church*, New York and London: Routledge, pp. 251–71, especially pp. 261–3.

6 The Church of England's Mission and Public Affairs Council, 2004, *Mission-shaped Church: Church Planting and Fresh Expressions of Church in a Changing Context*, London: Church House Publishing.

7 For example, see Doug Pagitt and the Solomon's Porch Community, 2003, *Reimagining Spiritual Formation: A Week in the Life of an Experimental Church*, Grand Rapids, MI: Zondervan; Myron Bradley Penner and Hunter Barnes (eds), 2006, *A New Kind of Conversation: Blogging Toward a Postmodern Faith*, New York: Fordham University Press; Graham Cray, 2007, *Disciples and Christians: A Vision for Distinctive Living*, Nottingham: Inter-Varsity Press. Particularly brilliant and important is: John Caputo, 2007, *What Would Jesus Deconstruct? The Good News of Postmodernity for the Church*, Ada, MI: Baker Academic.

8 For example, Derrida makes references to 'living between' in *Specters of Marx*: 'If it – learning to live – remains to be done, it can happen only between life and death. Neither in life nor in death *alone*.' The same conditions and caveats Derrida goes on to describe – too complex and lengthy to explore further here – apply to living 'between all the "two's" one likes …' (Jacques Derrida, 1994, *Specters of Marx: The State of the Debt, the Work of Mourning, and the New International*, Peggy Kamuf (trans.), London: Routledge, p. xviii).

9 I am not suggesting that Hauerwas and Wells succumb to this danger, rather that there is a possibility that those in emerging/fresh expressions who are appropriating their thought might do so.

10 Although I am unable to address them here I am aware that there are valid questions as to whether the world is actually watching and, if so, whether some emerging/fresh expressions are sufficiently visible.

11 Interestingly Brian McLaren's recent book seeks to address various economic, environmental, military, political and social dysfunctions through an interpretation of the life and teachings of Jesus. McLaren is an influential figure in the emerging church 'movement' (some resist using that term) and it will be fascinating to gauge the response of those involved to the strong social justice emphasis in this work (see Brian D. McLaren, 2007, *Everything Must Change: Jesus, Global Crises, and a Revolution of Hope*, Nashville, TN: Thomas Nelson).

12 See, for example, Jean-Luc Nancy, 1991, *The Inoperative Community*, Peter Connor (ed.), Minneapolis, MN: University of Minnesota Press, foreword by Christopher Fynsk.

13 See, for example, Geoffrey Bennington, *Interrupting Derrida*, 2000, London and New York: Routledge, pp. 24–5, 30–1, 113–17; Drucilla Cornell, 1992, *The Philosophy of the Limit*, New York and London: Routledge, pp. 39–61.

14 See, for example, Santiago Zabala (ed.), 2007, *Weakening Philosophy: Essays in Honour of Gianni Vattimo*, Montreal: McGill-Queen's University Press.

15 John D. Caputo and Gianni Vattimo, 2007, *After the Death of God*, Jeffrey W. Robbins (ed.), New York: Columbia University Press.

16 Hilary Lawson, in his excellent book *Reflexivity: The Post-modern Predicament*, puts it thus: 'reflexive questions have been given their special force in consequence of the recognition of the central role played by language, theory, sign, and text. Our concepts are no longer regarded as transparent – either in reflecting the world or conveying ideas. As a result all our claims about language and the world – and implicitly all our claims in general – are reflexive in a manner which cannot be avoided' (Hilary Lawson, 1985, *Reflexivity: The Post-modern Predicament*, London: Hutchinson, p. 9).

17 There are further riches contained in the work of both Hauerwas and Derrida relating to the issues under discussion here that I do not have the space to explore. In some places one can find intriguing clues as to how the perspectives of these two, admittedly hugely different, thinkers might be further linked in dialogue. For example, read the following extract from Hauerwas (in *A Community of Character: Toward a Constructive Christian Social Ethic*), that could be connected with the discussion of 'the other' in Derrida:

> From this perspective the church is the organized form of Jesus' story. The church provides the conditions we need to describe what is going on in our lives. That does not mean that all other descriptions are rendered irrelevant, but rather that we learn how to negotiate the limits and possibilities of those descriptions. We test them against the cross. It is in his cross that we learn to live in a world that is based on the presupposition that man, not God, rules.
>
> Jesus is the story that forms the church. This means that the church first serves the world by helping the world to know what it means to be the world. For without a 'contrast model' the world has no way to know or feel the oddness of its dependence on power for survival ... Because of a community formed by the story of Christ the world can know what it means to be a society committed to the growth of individual gifts and differences. In a community that has no fear of the truth, the otherness of the other can be welcomed as a gift rather than a threat. (pp. 50–1)

Chapter 8 Only one way to walk with God

1 All biblical quotations are from the Today's New International Version, unless otherwise stated.

2 I have discussed the concepts of the horizontal and vertical, as images

for relationship with God in the biblical tradition, in my contribution 'Mission shaped and kingdom focused' in Steven Croft (ed.), 2008, *Mission-shaped Questions: Defining Issues for Today's Church*, London: Church House Publishing, pp. 114–32.

3 'The new movement of Jesus' followers saw itself as part of second Temple Judaism and remained very much within that matrix' (Dunn, 2006, p. 156).

4 James Dunn, 2006, *The Parting of the Ways: Between Christianity and Judaism and their Significance for the Character of Christianity*, 2nd edn, London: SCM Press, pp. 185–214, discusses this dispute about the nature of true Judaism. His conclusion is that 'the real issue was, and still is, *which of the two chief strands emerging from second Temple Judaism was being truer to the original and most characteristic impulse of God's call and gifts*' (p. 214, Dunn's italics).

5 Clement of Alexandria, *Stromata*, Book I, chs 21, 25 and 29.

6 This is not to deny that Jesus himself may have interpreted his mission in the light of the Hebrew scriptures. The point is, however, that the pressure of claim and counter-claim encouraged latter development of this tendency.

7 David Bosch, 1991, *Transforming Mission: Paradigm Shifts in Theology of Mission*, Maryknoll, NY: Orbis Books, pp. 56–83. R. Geoffrey Harris, 2004, *Mission in the Gospels*, Peterborough: Epworth, pp. 37–69. Donald Senior and Carroll Stuhlmueller, 1983, *Biblical Foundations for Mission*, Maryknoll, NY: Orbis Books, pp. 233–54.

8 W. Manson agrees that the parable has to do with the failure of the wealthy to heed 'the ethical demands made by the law and the prophets', and that the rich man 'is condemned for his refusal to shew mercy and justice'. He goes on to suggest that the poor man 'is saved by his righteousness' (William Manson, 1930, *The Gospel of Luke*, London: Hodder & Stoughton, pp. 190–2). Manson rightly emphasizes the contrast between the destitute poor and the selfish rich, and that what the rich fail to hear is the ethical teaching of the law and the prophets; but he makes a mistake in thinking that the poor man is saved by his righteousness. Manson suggests that the reference to the resurrection means that 'if the Jews had really listened to Moses and the prophets they would not have denied the resurrection'. The point, however, is that if they had listened to Moses and the prophets they would not have denied the cry of the poor.

9 The contrast between the rich and poor classes is seldom perceived by the commentators, who tend to give the contrast a moral rather than an economic significance. Even Marshall, who sees this, takes it back again very quickly: 'the poor is not specifically stated to be righteous or pious, but this is perhaps to be deduced from his name and from Luke's general equation of poverty and piety' (I. Howard Marshall, 1978, *The Gospel of Luke: A Commentary on the Greek Text*, Exeter: Paternoster

NOTES

Press, p. 632). Nolland is one of the few who realizes that 'the rich man was doing no more than living out the life of his class' (John Nolland, 1993, *Word Biblical Commentary*, vol. 35B: *Luke 9.21–18.34*, Dallas: Word Books, pp. 831–3). Nolland concludes, 'the parable suggests that there is a profound challenge to the social status quo to be found in the law and prophets'.

10 Justin Martyr, *I Apology*, chs 31–53. Kelly describes how Tertullian 'ransacks the Old Testament' for predictions of Jesus Christ. J. N. D. Kelly, 'The Bible and the Latin Fathers', in D. E. Nineham (ed.), 1963, *The Church's Use of the Bible*, London: SPCK, p. 46.

11 'So the Old Testament first comes forth as a type, and the New Testament follows as the true reality' (Robert Fischer (ed.), 1961, *Luther's Works*, vol. 37s, Philadelphia: Fortress Press, p. 254).

12 'To Him, scripture must bear witness, for it is given for His sake' (J. Pelikan (ed.), 1972, *Luther's Works*, vol. 15, St Louis: Concordia, p. 343).

13 The service of nine lessons and carols was created by Edward White Benson (1829–96) for Truro Cathedral for the Christmas of 1880 (Arthur Christopher Benson, *Life of Edward White Benson*, vol. 1, London: Macmillan, pp. 484, 639).

14 Walther Eichrodt, 1961 and 1967, *Theology of the Old Testament*, 2 vols, London: SCM Press. Gerhard Von Rad, 1962 and 1965, *Old Testament Theology*, 2 vols, Edinburgh: Oliver & Boyd. Walter Brueggemann, 1997, *Theology of the Old Testament: Testimony, Dispute, Advocacy*, Minneapolis: Fortress Press.

Chapter 10 Dynamic tradition: fuelling the fire

1 Quoted in S. Hauwerwas, 2004, *Performing the Faith: Bonhoeffer and the Practice of Non-Violence*, Grand Rapids, MI: Brazos Press, p. 83.

2 N. Lash, 1986, 'Performing the Scriptures', in *Theology on the Way to Emmaus*, London: SCM Press; F Young, 1990, *The Art of Performance: Towards a Theology of Holy Scripture*, London: Darton, Longman & Todd; W. Brueggemann, 1993, *Texts under Negotiation: The Bible and Postmodern Imagination*, Minneapolis: Fortress Press.

3 See S. Hauerwas, 2007, *The State of the University: Academic Knowledges and the Knowledge of God*, Oxford: Blackwell, ch. 7.

4 This is the strapline for Oxford's Cutting Edge Ministry <http://www.cuttingedgeministries.org.uk>.

5 <http://selvaratnam.org/2007/05/08/fresh-expressions-hard-question/>.

Chapter 11 Who are fresh expressions really for?

1 For more details of their definition and for more information about the national Fresh Expressions Initiative see <www.freshexpressions.org.uk>.

2 For more information about The Net see <www.netchurch.org.uk> or *Net Gains*, Encounters on the Edge, No. 19, The Sheffield Centre.

3 These figures are from the Church of England Statistics 2005 based on parish returns.

4 The full article can be found in *Rev! Magazine*, May/June 2007 <www.rev.org>.

5 For more information <www.thecrowdedhouse.org>.

Chapter 12 'Packing them in the aisles'?

1 S. Millar, *Alpha Changing Life*, booklet, Holy Trinity Brompton.

2 Namely, the Toronto Airport Christian Fellowship.

3 <http://uk.alpha.org/>. Two million of these were those who had taken the course in the UK.

4 Alpha is also available in Braille.

5 Indeed, course leaders are encouraged to begin the discussion with a number of questions recommended by Nicky Gumbel, 1993, *The Alpha Course: Alpha Leaders' Training Manual*, London: Alpha International Training Resources.

6 Since the publication of the volume I have discovered that the subject of Alpha in relation to processes of McDonaldization was earlier discussed by Pete Ward. See Pete Ward, 1998, 'Alpha: The McDonaldisation of Religion', *Anvil*, 15/4, 279–86.

7 There are also offshoots from Alpha such as the Marriage Course on how to have a successful marriage.

8 This course is presented by Marcellino D'Ambrosio, Assistant Professor of Theology at the University of Dallas, and is recommended as the initial Catholic follow-up to the Alpha course.

9 The reality, however, is that some churches do deviate from the official Alpha programme, especially the Holy Spirit component. See Stephen Hunt, 2004, *The Alpha Enterprise: Evangelism in a Post-Christian Era*, Aldershot: Ashgate, pp. 154–5.

10 Unless, it would seem, they are 'gay' in their sexual orientation and even then it is the sin that is condemned but not the sinner. The issue of gay sexuality has led to a fair amount of acrimony with those of a non-heterosexual orientation. See Hunt, 2004, ch. 13, 'Is Alpha homophobic?'

11 This is by no means a new approach since it was primarily developed at Fuller Seminary's School of Church Growth since the 1970s and is primarily associated with Donald McGavran.

12 Here, Alpha takes its tone from Willow Creek Community Church, South Barrington (near Chicago) – a non-denominational 'mega' church.

13 For the increasing attraction of this form of flexibility see Pete Ward, 2002, *Liquid Church*, Peabody, MA: Hendrickson/Carlisle: Paternoster.

14 Article by Gyles Brandeth, *The Sunday Telegraph*, 14 March 2001.

15 A view usually associated with Grace Davie (1994), see *Religion in Britain Since 1945: Believing Without Belonging*, Oxford: Blackwell.

16 As suggested by the *Tearfund Survey* (2006) and the *European Values Study* (1999).

Chapter 13 Do we need a mixed economy?

1 This chapter assumes the same definition of 'fresh expressions' as that discussed by Steve Croft in Chapter 1.

2 For example, the Measure creates a new Bishops Mission Order, which the bishop can use to authorize a fresh expression that jumps parish boundaries or is non-geographical in nature. Anyone can petition the bishop to grant such an order, which means that an initiative can come from anywhere in the diocese.

3 I am grateful to Dr Alan Garrow for pointing this out.

Chapter 14 Mixed economy or ecclesial reciprocity

1 A short report detailing the research has been produced for Ministry Division at Church House and will shortly be available. A book with a full account of the studies will be published in 2009.

2 By this Mobsby means that such churches seek to retain a handed-down Christian identity rather than immersing themselves more fully within the culture. He relates this to Niebuhr's notion of 'Christ against culture', in which culture is seen as a negative that distracts from Christ.

3 This relates to Niebuhr's idea of 'Christ is above culture', where culture is seen as positive.

4 See, for example, T. Sudworth *et al.*, 2007, *Mission-shaped Youth: Rethinking Young People and the Church*, London: Church House Publishing.

5 Even critics of the emerging church such as Carsons comment on its 'porous borders'. See D. A. Carsons, 2005, *Becoming Conversant with the Emerging Church*, Grand Rapids, MI: Zondervan.

6 Nick Waghorn, 'Construals of the doctrine of the incarnation in Marion and Derrida', unpublished paper given at *Transcendence Incarnate: The Corporeality of the Spiritual and the Spirituality of the Corporeal*, a one day postgraduate conference in continental philosophy of religion, 10 September 2007, Somerville College, Oxford.

7 Nick Waghorn, quoting F. Kerr, 1997, *Immortal Longings: Versions of Transcending Humanity*, London: SPCK, p. 123.

References and further reading

Alexander, L. (2008) 'What patterns of church and mission are found in the Acts of the Apostles?', in S. Croft (ed.), *Mission-shaped Questions: Defining Issues for Today's Church*, London: Church House Publishing, pp. 133–45

Anderson, R. S. (2007) *An Emergent Theology for Emerging Churches*, Oxford: Bible Reading Fellowship

Anselm (1996) *Proslogion*, in *Monologion and Proslogion*, Thomas Williams (trans.), Cambridge: Hackett

Ashworth, J. (2007) *Churchgoing in the UK: A Research Report from Tearfund on Church Attendance in the UK*, Middlesex: Tearfund

Augustine, Saint. (1961) *Confessions*, R. S. Pine-Coffin (trans.) Harmondsworth, Penguin.

Barley, L. (2006) *Time to Listen: Christian Roots, Contemporary Spirituality*, London: Church House Publishing

Barley, L. (2008) 'Can fresh expressions of church make a difference?', in S. Croft (ed.), *Mission-shaped Questions: Defining Issues for Today's Church*, London: Church House Publishing, pp. 161–72

Barr, J. (1981) *Fundamentalism*, 2nd edn, London: SCM Press

Barrett, C. K. (1963) 'The Bible in the New Testament period', in D. E. Nineham (ed.), *The Church's Use of the Bible: Past and Present*, London: SPCK

Barth, K. (1957) *Church Dogmatics*, Vol. II, Part 1: *The Doctrine of God*, Edinburgh: T&T Clark

Bayes, P., and Sledge, T. (2006) *Mission-shaped Parish: Traditional Church in a Changing Context*, London: Church House Publishing

Beatles Bible <www.beatlesbible.com>

Bellah, R. (1985) *Habits of the Heart: Individualism and Commitment in American Life*, Berkeley: University of California Press

Berger, P. L. (1980) *The Heretical Imperative: Contemporary Possibilities of Religious Affirmation*, London: Collins. Original publication 1979.

Blauw, J. (1962) *The Missionary Nature of the Church: A Survey of the Biblical Theology of Mission*, London: Lutterworth Press

Bonhoeffer, D. (1954) *Life Together*, London: SCM Press

Book of Resolutions (2004), London: United Methodist Publishing House

Bosch, D. (1987) 'Evangelism: theological currents and cross-currents today', *International Bulletin of Missionary Research*, 11/3, 98–103

Bosch, D. (1999) *Transforming Mission: Paradigm Shifts in Theology of Mission*, Maryknoll, NY: Orbis Books

Breaking New Ground: Church Planting in the Church of England (2004), London: Church House Publishing

Brueggemann, W. (1997) *Theology of the Old Testament: Testimony, Dispute, Advocacy*, Minneapolis: Fortress Press

Burnard, P. (1991) 'A method of analysing interview transcripts in qualitative research', *Nurse Education Today*, 11/6, 461–6

Caputo, J. D. (1997) *The Prayers and Tears of Jacques Derrida: Religion without Religion*, Bloomington and Indianapolis: Indiana University Press

Caputo J. D., and Vattimo, G. (2007) *After the Death of God*, ed. Jeffrey W. Robbins, New York: Columbia University Press

Carsons, D. A. (2005) *Becoming Conversant with the Emerging Church*, Grand Rapids, MI: Zondervan

Cornell, D. (1992) *The Philosophy of the Limit*, New York and London: Routledge

Croft, S. (ed.) (2006) *The Future of the Parish System: Shaping the Church of England for the 21st Century*, London: Church House Publishing

Croft, S. (2008a) 'Fresh expressions in a mixed economy: a perspective', in S. Croft (ed.), *Mission-shaped Questions: Defining Issues for Today's Church*, London: Church House Publishing, pp. 1–15

Croft, S. (2008b) 'Mapping ecclesiology for a mixed economy church', in S. Croft (ed.), *Mission-shaped Questions: Defining Issues for Today's Church*, London: Church House Publishing, pp. 186–99

Croft, S. (ed.) (2008c), *Mission-shaped Questions: Defining Issues for Today's Church*, London: Church House Publishing

Davie, G. (1994) *Religion in Britain Since 1945: Believing Without Belonging*, Oxford: Blackwell

Davies, E. F. (2005) *Wondrous Depth: Preaching the Old Testament*, Louisville: Westminster John Knox Press

Derrida, J. (1988) *Limited Inc*, Gerald Graff (ed.), Samuel Weber (trans.), Evanston: Northwestern University Press

Derrida, J. (1999) 'Hospitality, justice and responsibility: a dialogue with Jacques Derrida', in Richard Kearney and Mark Dooley (eds), *Questioning Ethics: Contemporary Debates in Philosophy*, London and New York: Routledge

Derrida, J. (2001) 'Violence and metaphysics: an essay on the thought of Emmanuel Levinas', in J. Derrida, *Writing and Difference*, Alan Bass (trans.), London: Routledge (Routledge Classics), pp. 97–192

Derrida, J. (2004) 'Jacques Derrida: deconstruction and the other', in Richard Kearney (ed.), *Debates in Continental Philosophy: Conversations with Contemporary Thinkers*, New York: Fordham University Press

Donovan, V. (2001) *Christianity Rediscovered: An Epistle to the Masai*, London: SCM Press

Drane, J. (2008) 'What does maturity in the emerging church look like?' in S. Croft (ed.), *Mission-shaped Questions: Defining Issues for Today's Church*, London: Church House Publishing, pp. 90–101

Dunn, J. D. G. (2006) *The Parting of the Ways: Between Christianity and Judaism and their Significance for the Character of Christianity*, 2nd edn, London: SCM Press

Epsztein, L. (1986) *Social Justice in the Ancient Near East and the People of the Bible*, London: SCM Press

Finney, J. (1992) *Finding Faith Today*, Swindon: Bible Society

Foucault, M. (1980) *Power/Knowledge: Selected Interviews and Other Writings 1972–1977*, Colin Gordon (ed.), Brighton: Harvester Wheatsheaf

Francis, L., and Richter, P. (1998) *Gone but not Forgotten: Church Leaving and Returning*, London: Darton, Longman & Todd

Fresh Expressions Initiative (2006) *Prospectus: Phase 2* <www.fresh expressions.org.uk/standard.asp?id=1819>

Gaze, S. (2006) *Mission-shaped and Rural: Growing Churches in the Countryside*, London: Church House Publishing

Gibbs, E., and Bolger, R. (2005) *Emerging Churches: Creating Christian Community in Postmodern Cultures*, Grand Rapids, MI: Baker Academic

Glasson, B. (2006a) *I am Somewhere Else: Gospel Reflections for an Emerging Church*, London: Darton, Longman & Todd

Glasson, B. (2006b) *Mixed-up Blessing: A New Encounter with Being Church*, Peterborough: Inspire

Gumbel, N. (2001) *Challenging Lifestyle: Course Manual*, London: Kingsway

Harris, R. G. (2004) *Mission in the Gospels*, Peterborough: Epworth

Hauerwas, S. (1981) *A Community of Character: Toward a Constructive Christian Social Ethic*, Notre Dame, IN: University of Notre Dame Press

Hauerwas, S. (2004) *Performing the Faith: Bonhoeffer and the Practice of Non-Violence*, Grand Rapids, MI: Brazos Press

Hauerwas, S. (2007) *The State of the University: Academic Knowledges and the Knowledge of God*, Oxford: Blackwell

Hauerwas, S., and Wells, S. (2004) *The Blackwell Companion to Christian Ethics*, Oxford: Blackwell

Horton, M. (2005), 'Settlers, pilgrims and wanderers', *Modern Reformation Magazine*, 14/4

Hull, J. M. (2000) 'Religion and Religious Education', in M. Leicester, C. Modgil and S. Modgil (eds), *Education, Culture and Values: Spiritual and Religious Education*, vol. 5 (London: Falmer Press, 2000), pp. 75–85. Available online <www.johnhull.biz/religionism%20and%20religious%20education.htm>

Hull, J. M. (2004) 'Practical Theology and Religious Education in a Pluralist Europe', *British Journal of Religious Education*, 26/1, March, 1–11

Hull, J. M. (2006) *Mission-shaped Church: A Theological Response*, London: SCM Press

Hull, J. M. (2008) 'Mission-shaped and kingdom focused?', in S. Croft (ed.), *Mission-shaped Questions: Defining Issues for Today's Church*, London: Church House Publishing, pp. 114–32

Hunt, M. (1999) *The Stone Carvers: Master Craftsmen of Washington National Cathedral*, Washington and London: Smithsonian Institution Press

Hunt, S. (2004) *The Alpha Enterprise: Evangelism in a Post-Christian Era*, Aldershot: Ashgate

Inglehart, R., and Welzel, C. (2005). *Modernization, Cultural Change, and Democracy: The Human Development Sequence*, Cambridge and New York: Cambridge University Press

Ivision, N. (2006) *Expressions: the dvd-1: Stories of Church for a Changing Culture*, London: Church House Publishing

Ivision, N. (2007) *Expressions: the dvd-2: Changing Church in Every Place*, London: Church House Publishing

Jamieson, A. (2000) *A Churchless Faith: Faith Journeys Beyond Evangelical, Pentecostal and Charismatic Churches*, Wellington, New Zealand: Philip Garside

Jamieson, A. (2002) *A Churchless Faith: Faith Journeys Beyond the Churches*, London SPCK

Jenkins, T. (1999) *Religion in English Everyday Life*, New York: Berghahn Books

Kerr, F. (1997) *Immortal Longings: Versions of Transcending Humanity*, London: SPCK

Lacey, P. A. (1972) *The Inner War: Forms and Themes in Recent American Poetry*, Philadelphia: Fortress Press
Lears, J. (1994) *Fables of Abundance*, New York: Basic Books
Leclercq, J. (1979) 'Contemporary monasticism', *Fairacres Chronicle*, 12/3
Lucy, N. (2004) *A Derrida Dictionary*, Oxford: Blackwell
Luther, M. (1960) 'Preface to the Epistle of St. James', in, E. T. Bachmann (ed.), *Luther's Works*, vol. 35, Philadelphia: Fortress Press

McGavran, D. (1970) *Understanding Church Growth*, Grand Rapids, MI: Eerdmans
McKnight, S. (2007) 'Five streams in the emerging church', *Christianity Today*, February
Mead, L. (1996) *The Once and Future Church: Reinventing the Congregation for a New Mission Frontier*, Washington, DC: Alban Institute
Millar, S. (n.d.) *Alpha Changing Life*, booklet, Holy Trinity Brompton
Mission-shaped Church: Church Planting and Fresh Expressions of Church in a Changing Context (2004), London: Church House Publishing
Mobsby, I. J. (2007) *Emerging and Fresh Expressions of Church: How Are They Authentically Church and Anglican?* Westminster: Moot Community Publishing
Moynagh, M. (2001) *Changing World, Changing Church: New Forms of Church, Out-of-the-Pew Thninking, Initiatives that Work*, London Monarch
Moynagh, M. (2004) *Emergingchurch.intro*, Oxford, Monarch
Muir, J. (1913) in L. M. Wolfe (ed.), *John Muir, John of the Mountains: The Unpublished Journals of John Muir*, 1938, republished 1979, Madison: University of Wisconsin Press

Nelstrop, L., and Magill, K., with Onishi, B. B. (2009) *An Introduction to Christian Mysticism*, Aldershot: Ashgate
Newbigin, L. (1989) *The Gospel in a Pluralist Culture*, London: SPCK
Newbigin, L. (1990) 'Evangelism in the context of secularisation', in E. Jackson (ed.), *A Word in Season: Perspectives on Christian World Missions*, Grand Rapids, MI/Edinburgh: Eerdmans/Saint Andrews Press, 1994, pp. 148–57
Norris, P., and Inglehart, R. (2004) *Sacred and Secular: Religion and Politics Worldwide*, Cambridge and New York: Cambridge University Press

Onishi, B. B. (2006) 'Grenz's theological method and the commodification of religion', *The Princeton Theological Review*, 12/1

Percy, M. (1997) '"Join-the-dots" Christianity: Assessing ALPHA', *Reviews in Religion and Theology*, 4/3, August, 14–18

Percy, M. (2001) *The Salt of the Earth: Religious Resilience in a Secular Age*, London: Sheffield Academic Press

Percy. M. (2005) *Engagements: Essays on Christianity and Contemporary Culture*, Aldershot: Ashgate

Polanyi, M. (1958) *Personal Knowledge: Towards a Post Critical Philosophy*, Chicago: University of Chicago Press

Polanyi, M. (1969) *Knowing and Being: Essays by Micahel Polanyi*, edited by M. Frene, Chicago: University of Chicago Press

Pollard, A. (1994), 'Testing Toronto', *Church of England Newspaper*, 8 July

Pratchett, T. (2003) *The Wee Free Men*, New York: HarperCollins

Putnam, R. (2000) *Bowling Alone: The Collapse and Revival of American Community*, New York: Simon & Schuster

Riewoldt, O. (2002) *Brandscaping: Worlds of Experience in Retail Design*, London/Basel: Momenta Press/Birkauser

Ritzer, G. (1995) *The McDonaldization of Society*, Los Angeles: Pine Forge Press

Roderick, P. (2007) *Beloved: Henri Nouwen in Conversation*, Norwich: Canterbury Press

Rollins, P. (2006) *How (Not) to Speak of God*, London: Paraclete Press

Rollins, P. (2008) *The Fidelity of the Betrayal: Towards a Church Beyond Belief*, Brewster, MA: Paraclete Press

Ronell, A. (2004) (as interviewed by D. Diane Davis) 'Confessions of an anacoluthon: on writing, technology, pedagogy, and politics', in Julian Wolfreys (ed.), *Thinking Difference: Critics in Conversation*, New York: Fordham University Press

Savage, S., and Boyd-Macmillan, E. (2007) *The Human Face of Church: A Social Psychology and Pastoral Theology Resource for Pioneer and Traditional Ministry*, London: SCM-Canterbury Press

Savage, S., and Liht, J. (for 2008) 'Mapping fundamentalisms: the psychology of religion as a sub-discipline in the prevention of religiously motivated violence', in K. Helmut Reich and Peter C. Hill (eds), *Quo Vadis Psychology of Religion? Introduction to the Special Section, The Archive for the Psychology of Religion*, The International Association for the Psychology of Religion

Savage, S., Mayo-Collins, S., and Mayo, B. (2006) *Making Sense of Generation Y: The World View of 15–25 Year Olds*, London: Church House Publishing

Senior, D., and Stuhlmueller, C. (1983) *Biblical Foundations for Mission*, Maryknoll, NY: Orbis Books

Smalley, B. (1963) 'The Bible in the Middle Ages', in D. E. Nineham (ed.), *The Church's Use of the Bible: Past and Present*. London: SPCK

Smith, J. K. A. (2005) *Jacques Derrida: Live Theory*, New York and London: Continuum

Spencer, S. (2007) *Study Guide to Christian Mission*, London: SCM Press

Sudworth, T., with Cray, G., and Russell, C. (2007) *Mission-shaped Youth: Rethinking Young People and the Church*, London, Church House Publishing

UK National Census (2001) <http://www.statistics.gov.uk/census2001/access_results.asp>

Vanier, J. (1979) *Community and Growth: Our Pilgrimage Together*, London: Darton, Longman & Todd

von Rad, G. (1962 and 1965) *Old Testament Theology*, 2 vols, Edinburgh: Oliver & Boyd

Waghorn, N. (unpublished) 'Construals of the doctrine of the incarnation in Marion and Derrida', unpublished paper given at *Transcendence Incarnate: The Corporeality of the Spiritual and the Spirituality of the Corporeal*, a one day postgraduate conference in continental philosophy of religion, 10 September 2007, Somerville College, Oxford

Ward, P. (1998) 'Alpha: The McDonaldisation of Religion', *Anvil*, 15/4, 279–86

Ward, P. (2002) *Liquid Church*, Peabody, MA: Hendrickson / Carlisle: Paternoster Press

Warner, R. (2004), 'Ecstatic spirituality and entrepreneurial revivalism', in A. Walker and K. Aune (eds), *On Revival: A Critical Examination*, Carlisle: Paternoster Press

Warren, R. (1996) *Building Missionary Congregations*, London, Church House Publishing

Watts, F. (2002) 'Interacting Cognitive Subsystems and Religious Meanings', in R. Joseph (ed.), *Neurotheology: Brain, Science, Spirituality, Religious Experience*, San Jose: University of California Press

Watts, F., Nye, R., and Savage, S. (2001) *Psychology for Christian Ministry*, London: Routledge

Wells, S. (2007) *Power and Passion: Six Characters in Search of Resurrection*, Grand Rapids, MI: Zondervan

Williams, E. (2007) *Fresh Expressions in the Urban Context*, Haverhill: YTC Press

Williams, R. (1995) 'Time and transformation: a conversation with Rowan Williams' (interview by Todd Breyfogle), *Cross Currents*, Autumn, 45/3, 293–311

Williams, R. (2004) *Mission-shaped Church: Church Planting and Fresh Expressions of Church in a Changing Context*, London: Church House Publishing, foreword, p. vii

Woodhead, L., and Heelas, P. (eds) (2005) *The Spiritual Revolution*, Oxford: Blackwell

Wuthnow, R. (1993), *Christianity in the Twenty-First Century*, Oxford: Oxford University Press

Yoder, J. H. (1992) *Body Politics: Five Practices of the Christian Community Before the Watching World*, Scottdale, PA: Herald Press

Index

INDEX

INDEX

pathology 56, 62, 63, 64 (see also
mental health problems)

Pawson, David 29

Paul, St 113, 156, 181, 182, 183,
184

Pentecost 23, 109, 129, 181

Pentecostal viii, 58, 62, 66, 161,
162, 205 ch.3 n.3 (see also
neo-Pentecostalism)

Percy, Martyn x, xvi, xix, 27–39,
90, 169, 188

perichoresis (see Trinity) 194

Peter, St 2, 3, 109, 181, 183

2 Peter 138 (1.4)

pioneer ministry ix, 11, 12, 16,17,
43, 46–7, 48, 49, 50, 51, 52,
53, 54, 136, 138, 154, 179, 180,
183, 185 186, 207 ch.4 n.10

Polanyi, Michael 65

Polkinghorn, John 66

Pollard, Arthur 162

politics 33, 37, 74, 80, 90, 91, 93,
96, 100, 101, 112, 117, 118,
166, 204 ch.3 n.1, 206 ch.3 n.9,
209 ch.7 n.11

poor, the 19, 21, 63, 102, 110,
114, 116, 117, 118, 127, 211
ch.8 n.8, n.9 (see marginalized,
oppressed, poverty)

post-modern xvii, 33, 56, 58, 61,
62, 63, 65, 67, 138, 167, 172,
173, 188, 192, 193, 195, 196,
203

poverty 58, 63, 72, 95, 157, 211
ch.8 n.9 (see marginalized, oppressed, poor)

power 34, 90, 91, 92, 98, 99, 102,
113, 116, 117, 130, 138, 147,
158, 161, 166, 205 n.5, 210 ch.7
n.7

Pratchett, Terry 145

prayer x, 16, 18, 20, 32, 33, 34,
37, 39, 43, 45, 73, 76, 84, 103,
115, 119, 124, 138, 130, 132,

133, 134, 137, 142, 143, 144,
159, 161, 164, 165, 182, 190

prophecy 29, 58, 88, 109, 110,
111, 112, 113, 144, 159, 161,
162, 165, 203, 211 ch.8 n.8,
212 ch.9 n.9

Proverbs 107 (2.7b–8, 2.20, 8.20)

Proslogion, the 80–1 (see Anselm)

prosperity movements 34

post-institutionalism xvi, 31, 35,
36, 37, 38, 39, 178

Protestant 34, 117, 127, 134, 170,
172

Psalms 107 (9.16, 33.5, 50.6), 111
(99.4)

psychology vii, ix, xv, xiii, 55–70,
93, 106, 168

Pullinger, Jackie 29

Putnam, Robert 33, 205 ch.3 n.6,
n.9

Quiet Garden Movement, the x,
137

qualitative data 151, 189

radical xvii, 6, 13, 15, 21, 22, 33,
47, 65, 72, 74, 77, 79, 80, 82,
85, 89, 92, 94, 101, 102, 103,
135, 137, 138, 153, 154, 156,
172, 180, 204 ch.3 n.1, 208 ch.7
n.1

Reformation, the 74, 83, 111, 205
ch.3 n.3

resistance 73

Restorationists 28, 205 ch.3 n.3

resurrection, the 17, 91, 92, 109,
110, 211 n.8

revelation 81, 82, 83, 114, 191

Revelation (the book of) 130 (21.5)

revolution 73, 74, 77, 80

Richter, Philip 44, 148, 149, 206
ch.4 n.4

righteousness 107, 116, 117, 118,
211 n.8

Ritzer, George 116, 117

ritual 83, 190
Robbins, Jeffrey W. 101, 210 ch.7
    n.15
'rock and roller' 16
Roderick, Philip D. x, xviii,
    135–47
Rollins, Pete x, xiii, xviii, 71–84,
    195
Roman Catholic 7,127, 161
Roman Empire 113
Romans 156 (12.1–2), 108 (13.10,
    13.13)
Ronnell, Avital 89
rules 57; social 99; facist 100; der-
    rida 126; forum 142; conven-
    sions 190, 198, 210 ch.7 n.17
Russell, Charles 200
Russian Orthodox 135, 137
Ruth 114

sacramental xix, 13, 45, 53, 66,
    140, 144
Samaria 181, 182
Sanctus1 80
Santiago de Compostella 130
Savage, Sara x, xvii, 55–70, 207
    ch.4 n.11
school based and school linked
    congregations and churches 4,
    8, 13, 19, 20, 21, 37, 42, 140,
    192
sect 33
seeker churches xix, 4, 192, 194,
    195, 199
self-expression 59, 62
sex 105, 127, 38; sexism 95;
    sexuality 129, 213; orientation
    (gay) 165
Share (the website) 12, 48, 53–4,
    180, 185, 204 ch.1 n.4
Singapore 126
skateboarder 21
skinhead 16
Smith, James K. A. 100

social action 124, 128
social capital 32–3, 37
social justice 112–13, 115–16, 209
    ch.7 n.11
Somewhere Else (fresh expression
    of church) 156
spiritual capital 37
spiritual direction 56, 128
spirituality ix, xiv, xviii, xx, 32,
    37, 38, 39, 55, 57, 66, 105, 106,
    124; Benedictine 128, 196, 205
    ch.3 n.7
St John's College, Nottingham 153
stories (sharing) xviii, 9, 12–13,
    45, 52, 130, 136, 143
students 21, 153, 167, 169, 173
Stuhlmueller, Carroll 115, 211
    ch.8 n.7
Sudan 126
suffering 106, 117, 119, 142; long-
    suffering 61
Sunday school 42, 153
sustainability 53, 90
symbol 31, 36, 56–7, 60, 65–6,
    120, 138–9, 205 ch.3 n.2

Tearfund 149, 150, 214 ch.12 n.16
teenagers 133, 171
Thailand ix, 126, 188–9, 191
theo-poetics 83
Thomas, Richard, Bishop of
    Dorchester 124–5
Tomorrow Project ix, 184
Toronto blessing 29, 162–3, 170
tradition x, xiii, xv, xvi, xvii,
    xviii, 4, 5, 11–22, 28, 35–6,
    41, 43, 46, 51–2, 54, 55–62,
    64–7, 71, 72, 80–1, 83, 102,
    109, 111–13, 129, 134, 135,
    137–8, 142–3, 147, 151, 153,
    155, 161–2, 168–70, 172, 177,
    180–1, 183–4, 187, 190, 192–3,
    195–6, 197, 198, 199, 200, 202,
    203